NOT THAT BAD

Not That Bad

Dispatches from Rape Culture

EDITED BY
Roxane Gay

HARPER

An Imprint of HarperCollins*Publishers*

HarperCollins books may be purchased for educational, business, or sales promotional use. For information, please email the Special Markets Department at SPsales@harpercollins.com.

FIRST EDITION

Designed by Jamie Lynn Kerner

Library of Congress Cataloging-in-Publication Data has been applied for.

ISBN 978-0-06-241351-2 (paperback)
ISBN 978-0-06-285146-8 (hardcover))

18 19 20 21 22 LSC 10 9 8 7 6 5 4 3 2 1

For every person who has been scarred by rape culture and survives, nonetheless.

Contents

Introduction

WHEN I WAS TWELVE YEARS OLD, I WAS GANG-RAPED IN the woods behind my neighborhood by a group of boys with the dangerous intentions of bad men. It was a terrible, life-changing experience. Before that, I had been naive, sheltered. I believed people were inherently good and that the meek should inherit. I was faithful and believed in God. And then I didn't. I was broken. I was changed. I will never know who I would have been had I not become the girl in the woods.

As I got older, I met countless women who had endured all manner of violence, harassment, sexual assault, and rape. I heard their painful stories and started to think, *What I went through was bad, but it wasn't* that *bad*. Most of my scars have faded. I have learned to live with my trauma. Those boys killed the girl I was, but they didn't kill all of me. They didn't hold a gun to my head or a blade to my throat and threaten my life. I survived. I taught myself to be grateful I survived even if survival didn't look like much.

It was comforting, perhaps, to tell myself that what I went

through "wasn't that bad." Allowing myself to believe that being gang-raped wasn't "that bad" allowed me to break down my trauma into something more manageable, into something I could carry with me instead of allowing the magnitude of it to destroy me.

But, in the long run, diminishing my experience hurt me far more than it helped. I created an unrealistic measure for what was acceptable in how I was treated in relationships, in friendships, in random encounters with strangers. That is to say that if I even had a bar for how I deserved to be treated, that bar was so low it was buried far belowground. If being gang-raped wasn't that bad, then it wasn't at all that bad being shoved or having my arm grabbed so hard it left five bruises in the form of fingerprints or being catcalled for having large breasts or having a hand shoved down my pants or being told I should be grateful for romantic attention because I wasn't good enough and on and on. Everything was terrible but none of it was that bad. The list of ways I allowed myself to be treated badly grew into something I could no longer carry, not at all.

Buying into the notion of *not that bad* made me incredibly hard on myself for not "getting over it" fast enough as the years passed and I was still carrying so much hurt, so many memories. Buying into this notion made me numb to bad experiences that weren't as bad as the worst stories I heard. For years, I fostered wildly unrealistic expectations of the kinds of experiences worthy of suffering until very little was worthy of suffering. The surfaces of my empathy became calloused.

I don't know when this changed, when I began realizing

that all the encounters people have with sexual violence are, indeed, that bad. I didn't have a grand epiphany. I finally reconciled my own past enough to realize that what I had endured was that bad, that what anyone has suffered is that bad. I finally met enough people, mostly women, who also believed that the terrible things they endured weren't that bad when clearly those experiences were indeed that bad. I saw what calloused empathy looked like in people who had every right to wear their wounds openly and hated the sight of it.

When I first came up with the idea for this anthology, I wanted to assemble a collection of essays about rape culture—some reportage, some personal essays, writing that engaged with the idea of rape culture, what it means to live in a world where the phrase "rape culture" exists. I was interested in the discourse around rape culture because the phrase is used often, but rarely do people engage with what it actually means. What is it like to live in a culture where it often seems like it is a question of when, not if, a woman will encounter some kind of sexual violence? What is it like for men to navigate this culture whether they are indifferent to rape culture or working to end it or contributing to it in ways significant or small?

This anthology became something far different from what I originally intended. As I started receiving submissions, I was stunned by how much testimony writers offered. There were hundreds and hundreds of stories from people all along the gender spectrum, giving voice to how they have suffered, in one way or another, from sexual violence, or how they have been affected by intimate relationships with people who have experienced sexual violence. I realized that my original intentions for this anthology had to give way to what the book so clearly needed to be—a place for people to give voice to their experiences, a place for people to share how bad this all is, a place for people to identify the ways they have been marked by rape culture.

As of this writing, something in this deeply fractured culture is, I hope, changing. More people are beginning to realize just how bad things really are. Harvey Weinstein has fallen from grace, named by a number of women, as a perpetrator of sexual violence. His crimes have been laid bare. His victims are, at least to some extent, vindicated. Women and men are coming forward and naming sexual harassers or worse in publishing, journalism, the tech world. Women and men are saying, "This is how bad it actually is." For once, perpetrators of sexual violence are facing consequences. Powerful men are losing their jobs and their access to circumstances where they can exploit the vulnerable.

This is a moment that will, hopefully, become a movement. These essays will, hopefully, contribute to that movement in a meaningful way. The voices shared here are voices that matter and demand to be heard.

NOT THAT BAD

Fragments

AUBREY HIRSCH

He says, "You shouldn't wave those around like that."

You're in the campus dining hall with your friend James. You've just popped a rust-colored birth control pill out of its slot in the rubbery blue envelope.

You say, "I wasn't. I was just taking one."

He says, "You should take them in your room. By yourself. Privately."

"I have to take them with food," you say, "or they make my stomach hurt." It's been that way since you were fifteen and first started taking them. That was years before you actually have sex and, even when you do, you are so afraid of getting pregnant accidentally that you don't let a man come inside you until after you're married.

You take them because your period is a terrifying beast. The hormones gallop through your veins. You wake up in the middle of the night, twisting; your stomach lurches, your intestines heave. The pills help. You don't like taking them every day, though. Even the smell of the blue rubber envelope makes you a little queasy when you, dutifully, pull them out of your purse at the same time every afternoon to sedate the beast inside.

He says, "Still, you shouldn't let everyone see. You don't want some guy to see you taking those and think he can take advantage of you and there will be no consequences."

You put the pill on the back of your tongue and the envelope back in your bag. James watches as you bring your water glass to your lips. You swallow. Hard.

IF RAPE CULTURE HAD A FLAG, IT WOULD BE ONE OF THOSE BOOB INSPECTOR T-shirts.

If rape culture had its own cuisine, it would be all this shit you have to swallow.

If rape culture had a downtown, it would smell like Axe body spray and that perfume they put on tampons to make your vagina smell like laundry detergent.

If rape culture had an official language, it would be locker-room jokes and an awkward laugh track. Rape culture speaks in every tongue.

If rape culture had a national sport, it would be . . . well . . . something with balls, for sure.

YOU DRINK TOO MUCH AT THE PARTY BECAUSE IT'S COLLEGE and you're always drinking too much. The party is terribly generic with beer pong and a bass-heavy sound track. Everyone is drinking foamy beer out of red Solo cups. You think there might even be a black light somewhere.

Daniel knows you don't drink beer, so he has brought you a bottle of cheap vodka, which you drink mixed with even cheaper orange juice.

You flit around for a while, talking to one group of people, then another. A boy in the kitchen—a baseball player—takes his dick out to show everyone how big it is. It is, in fact, very big.

The last thing you remember is lying down on the couch. *Just to close my eyes*, you think, *just for a minute.*

When you wake up, you are in a bed in an upstairs bedroom you have never seen. Daniel is in the bed next to you. Your clothes are on, but your shoes are off.

"Hey," you say, pressing into your temples. Maybe if you press them hard enough the pounding will stop.

"You fell asleep," he says, before you even ask. "I carried you up here."

You say, "You carried me?"

"Yeah. I didn't want to just leave you down there with all those dudes, passed out on the couch like bait or something."

"Did you take my shoes off?"

"Yeah. So you could sleep."

Your mouth feels dry. Everything is blurry. You rub your eyes and take in a breath so you can thank Daniel when he says, "I took your contacts out, too."

You don't know where your gratitude goes, but suddenly it's gone.

THESE STORIES AREN'T WORTH TELLING. THERE'S NO ARC TO them, no dramatic climax. There's nothing at stake, not really. You imagine your listener, leaning in, "And then what happened?" And you have to say, "Nothing. That's the whole story." "Oh," she says, her mouth a firm line.

These are little bits of things that happened, or things you think about. They're light on tension, you know that. There's no real peril. There's no resolution.

Still, they stick with you. You think about them even after they're over, sometimes for a long time. Sometimes for a very long time. That's how you know they're important somehow. It's why you can recall the smell of that party, even many years after the smell of your grandfather's cologne has faded from your memory.

WHEN YOU BECOME A WRITING INSTRUCTOR, EVENTUALLY, you end up with stories about rape stories.

The first story is a rape story on purpose. A student hands it in for a fiction assignment in the composition class you are teaching. In it, the hero finds his petite, brunette English teacher alone in a church. He pulls out a 24k gold–plated gun with a pearl handle, holds it to her head, and rapes her, bending her over the back of a pew. When he's finished, he drives off in a convertible and leaves a bag of money at the police station to avoid arrest.

You are the petite, brunette English teacher. You're only twenty-two, just a few years older than this student who now sits in your office with his hat pulled down over his eyes. You're too timid to call him out on this threatening misogynistic bullshit. What if you're wrong? What if he complains to your boss? What if he gives you a low score on your teaching evaluations? Instead, you critique the story, which isn't hard: It's a horrible story. "The hero is unlikable and the ending is ludicrous." You say all this to your student as he smirks beside you. "And look here," you say, "a slip in verb tense; here, a comma splice."

In the second rape story, the hero meets a girl at a party. She's beautiful, drunk, glassy-eyed, and nearly incoherent. When she's no longer able to walk, the hero, who hasn't had anything to drink, carries her outside, to the beach. He strips off her clothes and has sex with her while she makes soft moaning sounds. Then he dresses her again and lies beside her on the sand.

"The tone is a bit confusing," you tell your student when he comes in for a conference. "It seems romantic, almost. Are we supposed to feel sympathy for this character, even as he's raping her?"

The student looks taken aback, surprised. "He's not raping her. They're having sex."

You point out all of the evidence that he is, in fact, raping her. She's clearly very drunk. She can't even walk by herself. She never takes any agency, just lies there while it's happening.

The student cuts you off. "This is, like, based off me hooking up with my girlfriend for the first time."

It hadn't occurred to you that the student might not have realized he was writing a rape story.

"All I can say," you say, "is that a lot of people are going to read this as rape."

"But it isn't," he says, weakly, sounding more like he's trying to convince himself than you. "It wasn't."

The third story comes to you in a creative nonfiction class. The narrator gets very drunk at a party. She kisses one guy and another kisses her. She runs away and bumps into an acquaintance, who she barely recognizes through a haze of cheap beer. He is aggressive, putting his penis inside of her while she tries to stammer, "wait, wait."

You start the workshop by asking your students to give a quick summary of the piece. Someone offers, "It's about a girl who goes to a party and gets drunk and hooks up with a bunch of dudes."

Interesting. "Does anyone have anything to add or a different read?" The students shake their heads. "Well," you offer, "I think this first part is a hookup, and the second part, maybe a misunderstanding, but I read this last section pretty straightforwardly as being assault."

All of the students look down, rereading the last section. Some of them tilt their heads, as if to say, *Hm.* The essay never uses the word *rape*, but it does say "wrong." It says "wasted" and "sick" and "dizzy" and "vomit." It says "ignore." How is it possible they haven't seen this? How is it possible they are learning about consent from their teacher?

The author of the essay is forbidden to speak by the rules of the workshop, but you study her as she takes notes in silence. *Did she know?* you wonder. *Does she know now?*

YOU RECOGNIZE THE TENSION BETWEEN "I AM A BODY" AND "I have a body," but you are unable to resolve it. "Have" implies that this body is just a possession, that it can be lost or thrown away. That you can do without it. It implies, perhaps, that someone else could have your body and that your body would be not your own. That it would belong to another.

That doesn't feel quite right.

But "am" doesn't seem right either. To "be" a body suggests that you are only a body. You are meat and some blood. You are hard bones and flexing cartilage. You are tangled veins and skin. Is that all, though?

You stand in front of the full-length mirror on your closet door and take inventory. Here are your knees; there are two of them. Two elbows. A chin. A torso with breasts that are heavy with milk. Feet. Hands. Knuckles. Two earlobes. Ten toenails. Several dime-sized bruises. Thousands and thousands of hairs.

There are things you can't see, but you know they're there. Two lungs. A liver. The stacked cups of your backbone. Your heart you saw once on an ultrasound machine. Your womb you've seen four times, but never when it was empty. Nerves. Ball joints. The intricate pleating of your brain.

It is a long list, but also, it is not so long. Looking at it now, you wonder, isn't there more to you than that?

SOMETIMES PEOPLE TELL YOU THAT YOU'RE LUCKY THAT YOU have sons so they won't have to deal with all this crap.

It's true that your kids, by virtue of both being boys, will be in a privileged position, but the idea that they "won't have to deal" with rape culture makes you shudder. You very much want them to "deal with" rape culture the way one "deals with" a cockroach problem.

Sometimes you think about what you'll tell them and come up surprisingly blank. It's the words that fail you, not the ideas. The ideas are there.

Though you aren't sure exactly what you'll say, these are the things you want them to know:

It's not okay to hit the girl you like. And it's not okay to hit the girl you love.

The world around you tells women that they should always nod politely no matter what they're feeling inside. Don't ever take a polite nod for an answer. Wait for her to yell it: "Yes!"

Not everyone gets sex when they want it. Not everyone gets love when they want it. This is true for men and women. A relationship is not your reward for being a nice guy, no matter what the movies tell you.

Birth control is your job, too.

Don't ever use an insult for a woman that you wouldn't use for a man. Say "jerk" or "shithead" or "asshole." Don't say "bitch" or "whore" or "slut." If you say "asshole," you're criticizing her parking skills. If you say "bitch," you're criticizing her gender.

Here are some phrases you will need to know. Practice them in the mirror until they come as easy as songs you know by heart: "Do you want to?" "That's not funny, man." "Does that feel good?" "I like you, but I think we're both a little drunk. Here's my number. Let's get together another time."

Your cousin texts you out of the blue to say, "I just got raped at the bank."

"Oh my God," you respond. "Are you okay?" Your brain goes turbo. You are trying to imagine which hospital she's at, if she's likely to press charges, why she's reaching out to you and what you can possibly do to make this any less devastating.

The flashing ellipsis appears on your phone to signal that she's typing. Then it turns to words that you struggle to focus on: "Yeah. I deposited my check in the wrong account so I've been overspending on my debit card. I got like $175 in fees."

You watch for the ellipsis, but it doesn't appear. After a moment you realize this is the whole story. By "I got raped" she meant "I got charged bank fees for overdrawing my account."

You stare at your keyboard for a while, with its letters and exclamation points and frozen-faced emojis, and then you put your phone away. You can't think of a single thing to say.

Jordana has invented a new kind of rape-prevention underwear. If she orders a batch of five thousand pairs, she can manufacture them for $2.25 per pair and wholesale them for $4.00 per pair. If she orders ten thousand pairs, she can manufacture them for $1.90 per pair and wholesale them for $3.50. Given these figures, and assuming no import taxes, how will she get the rapists to wear them?

Marc leaves work at 6:25 every evening. Moving at a steady 6 miles per hour, he walks eleven blocks north, three blocks west, and one block south to get to his apartment. On his way home, he passes the diner where Gina works. When she works the afternoon swing shift, she leaves work just before Marc passes by. She walks eight blocks north at an average speed of 5.5 miles per hour. Now that it's wintertime and starting to get dark, how far behind Gina should Marc stay so that she won't be afraid that he's coming to attack her?

Carla is editing her online dating profile. When she adds the word *cheerleader*, her message requests go up by 11 percent. When she changes her body type from "average" to "thin," her message requests increase by 42 percent. When she lists "feminism" as an interest, her message requests decrease by 86 percent and the number of rape threats she receives triples. Assuming she goes on an average of three dates per month, how many hours will she need to spend with any given man before she feels comfortable giving him her home address?

A child is raped in Montana. The rapist is thirty-one; the

child is fifteen. The age of consent is sixteen. The punishment for statutory rape in Montana is two to one hundred years in prison and a fine of up to $50,000. If, however, the rapist is only sentenced to thirty days in jail and no fine at all, how much older than her chronological age must the child have been behaving when she seduced him?

THIS IS YOUR NEW THING: WHEN A MAN YELLS AT YOU ON THE street, you yell back. You are tired of pretending you can't hear these men. You are tired of gluing your eyes to the sidewalk in shame. You are tired of taking it, of treating it like a tax you must pay for the privilege of being a woman in public spaces.

You think, perhaps foolishly, that you can explain your feelings to these men and they will listen.

You wear your resolve like armor and it doesn't take long for you to get a chance to put your plan into action. You are leaving the store, a plastic bag of groceries dangling from each hand, when a man walking behind you says, "Hey hey hey! You are beautiful."

You stop walking and he passes you. It's now or never.

You say, "Can I talk to you for a second?"

He stops to face you, about three feet away.

"Why did you say that to me?"

Instead of answering, he just tries his line again: "Hey beautiful girl!"

"Can I tell you something?"

He doesn't answer, but he doesn't move away. He seems confused, like when you push a floor button on an elevator and the doors don't close, so you just keep pressing it. Why aren't you shutting up? This isn't what's supposed to happen.

You say, "When you say that to me, I don't feel flattered. I don't even feel angry, honestly. I feel afraid. Did you know that?"

"Why? Why are you afraid? Afraid of me?"

"Yes," you say. "When men like you yell stuff at me on the street, I am afraid that you will hurt me."

"Oh, I'm scary. Is that what you're saying?" Now, he moves. He takes a big step toward you and, damn it, you flinch.

You say, "Yes," trying to plate the word in steel but it crumbles in your larynx like tinfoil. You start walking to your car.

He follows you the whole way, shouting, "Now I'm scaring you, huh? Now you're afraid of me!"

He's right. He is scaring you. You are afraid. But there's something new, too. Before this, you really thought maybe these guys just didn't know how their comments made people feel. You thought maybe they were trying to be nice. But now you know the truth—they know it makes you feel frightened. They like it.

There's still fear, yes, but now there's anger, too. So much anger that it boxes out some of your fear. The next time you yell back to the man yelling at you, it's easier. And the time after that is easier still.

Now the responses roll off your tongue like perfect round stones. You've worried them in your mind and in your mouth until they are smooth as glass: "Why would you say that to me?" "That is an offensive thing to say." "It's hurtful to talk to women like that." "You should never say that again."

Your prize for all this effort is a small thing, but you cherish it. It is the astonishment on your harasser's face. Sometimes he even mutters a flimsy "Sorry" before he hurries away from you. He doesn't want a conversation. He's not shouting at you as a method of engagement; he's just testing something out. He needs to fumble around for his power in the dark, like a totem he carries in his pocket. He wants to make sure it's still there.

Next time, you tell yourself when it's done, this man won't shout so readily. Next time he will see the woman coming, open his mouth to speak, and for one second, one perfect second, he will be afraid of her.

Slaughterhouse Island

Jill Christman

THE THING ABOUT TELLING THIS STORY EVEN THIRTY years later is that even though I know where the culpability rests—firmly—I have trouble soaking off the most dogged shame. I am scraping away the last of the sticky residue with my thumbnail.

Yes, I did some stupid things. We all do. But now I know we're allowed to be kids who mask our gut-deep insecurities with vanity. We get to wear crop tops and tight jeans with a ribbon of lace for a belt and high-heeled boots. We get to check ourselves ten times in the dorm-room mirror, necks craning to see how fat our skinny little asses look from the back, and we even get to guzzle sweet drinks and swallow harmless-looking tabs we hope might make us feel better or dance faster or look prettier or just forget. We get to want something to come easy for a change. We get to make every choice on that daily life scale from forward-thinking to utter self-sabotage.

And we still don't deserve to be raped. Not ever.

How did we ever get to a place where victim blaming was wedged so far into our brains? *Turn this around*, I think to myself, scraping with my thumbnail. *Turn this around. What would Kurt have had to do for me to feel justified in raping* him?

There's no answer to that question.

I want to fold time. I want to walk into that Italian restaurant in Eugene, Oregon, where my eighteen-year-old self is having her first awkward date with Kurt, take her by the hand, and ask her to join me in the bathroom. Instead of letting her throw up the four bites of creamy pasta she ate for dinner—which I know is all she can really think about as she watches Kurt's pointy teeth flash in the candlelight—I want to pull her around the corner, hurry down the hall in the opposite direction, and make for the exit.

We'll leave together, I'll walk her back to the dorm, and we'll have a talk. I'll save her, somehow, from what's going to happen to us next, even though, sweet girl, I know it's not your fault. None of this was ever your fault. Do you hear me?

Not. Your. Fault.

But from here, back in the future, I can only watch.

"You drive a Porsche"—rhyming with borscht without the final "t"—I'd said, after I'd lowered myself down onto the soft leather of Kurt's sleek silver car, hoping my friends on the second floor of the freshman dorm were peeking from behind the curtains. He'd leaned in toward me, breath too minty, already-thinning dark hair glinting with product in the spring sunshine, and moved his large hand from the gear-shift to my thigh. I think he was trying to look sexy but managed instead to look maniacal.

"Por-shhhhha," he said. "People who don't have Por-shas call them Porsches. People who *drive* Por-shas call them Por-shas."

I moved my knee a fraction, the tiniest of objections, and said, "Well, *I* don't have a Porsche, so I'd better call it a Porsche."

"You're with me now," he said, thin lips curling into a smile. "Now you can call this car a Por-sha."

I hadn't had a date like this before—what I imagined to be a real college date, during which Kurt picked up, moved, or lifted everything that might need picking up, moving, or lifting: the door to the Por-sha, my chair at the table, my body by the arm when another man came too close, and of course, the check. We went to a real sit-down Italian restaurant with white linen tablecloths, candles, and dim lighting, where we talked about the extensive time he and I both spent at the gym on the edge of campus: me in aerobics classes burning away any calories I'd consumed in moments of weakness, and him lifting and slamming giant iron discs in the testosterone soup that was the main gym.

We were both too tan, this being the era of ten tans for twenty dollars in the warm booths on the campus strip. I was in my first year in the Honors College, reading Darwin and Shakespeare and Austen, having my mind blown by Mary

Shelley's *Frankenstein* and theories about sexual selection and how the universe began. Kurt was in business, a supersenior—the first I'd heard such a moniker, though it didn't take me long to figure out that the "super" didn't mean anything good.

Since we had nothing else to discuss, the conversation turned to tanning. I told him how I always fell asleep under the lights, the humming blue womb offering respite from the gray Eugene winter—although I'm sure I wouldn't have said "womb," not that night—and Kurt's teeth glowed in the dim candlelight like something out of a horror movie.

AFTER DINNER, KURT TOOK ME BACK TO AN APARTMENT THAT looked like nobody lived there, gave me something to drink, and led me through the living room with its black leather couch and glass coffee table into his bedroom. Closing the door behind him, he showed me the hand weights he kept in a line by the wall, like shoes, and then pushed me toward a desk. I remember his hands always on my body, and even before he pulled the mirror and the razor blade out of the center drawer, I was thinking, *This isn't good*.

Kurt reached into the pocket of his coat and pulled out a paper packet—druggie origami—tapping two snowy piles onto the glass. I watched him chopping and scraping, wincing a bit at the sound, a fork on china, nails on a chalkboard, a warning alarm I would fail to heed. Down to the roots of my nerve fibers, I knew the thing to do was get out, but this was to be a night of many college firsts: first restaurant date, first ride in a Porsche, first blow. Kurt rolled a crisp green bill from his wallet and showed me what to do.

It burned. And then? Not much. The coke had done nothing more than make my eyes feel really, really wide open. I would be hyperalert for what came next.

Which was also almost nothing. He kissed me, and as he did, he pulled me away from the desk and down onto the bed. He was the world's worst kisser, all probing tongue, like a sea slug trying to move down my throat. I was repulsed, but saved (I know now) by the coke: Kurt couldn't get it up. He rolled against me, and through the thin fabric of his dress khakis, I could feel him against my thigh, soft as a dinner roll.

George Michael sang through the speakers. Rather than pursue what he must have known from experience was a losing game, Kurt sprang from the bed, as if he'd planned it that way, and went to the stereo to turn it up. *I will be your father figure.* Thirty minutes later, when I asked for a ride back to the dorm, he gave me one without much of a fight. In the Por-sha.

The next day, apparently having had more fun than I had, Kurt called to ask if I'd go with him to Shasta Lake, an annual Memorial Day fraternity tradition at the University of Oregon: at least a hundred rented houseboats, each carrying eight or so couples, kegs tapped and flowing, red Solo cups bobbing in the water like buoys.

Imagine the drinking and the drugs. Imagine the sleeplessness and the unfinished brains. Imagine the heat, the dehydration, and the food packed by the boy-men hosting this nightmare. Imagine that nobody on the whole boat had the sense to bring sunscreen. Imagine the depth of seething, un-met need—and then imagine the depth of the water.

Imagine, too, that I'd already made plans to go with a friend from my dorm, a guy named Jeff, who had pledged a fraternity the previous fall. Stretched to his full height, Jeff reached only to my nose, but he was clever and made me laugh, so when he'd quite casually offered to bring me along to Shasta, I'd agreed.

But a real invitation from a real date with a real car and a real apartment with real furniture seemed like just the kick in status I needed to go from full-scholarship hippie kid with Beatles posters and batik bedspreads stapled to the walls of her dorm room to . . . to what?

What did I want to be? Part of the system my liberal artist parents had always rejected? Noticed? Accepted? Desired?

I didn't even like Kurt: he represented everything I'd been taught to distrust in the world, a privileged fuck from the burbs who thought anything could be his for the right price, including me.

So, at first, I did the right thing: I said no to Kurt. But my best girlfriend, D, had *not* gotten a date for the lake trip, and I felt bad leaving her behind. Also, I didn't want to go on this trip as a lone independent—an Honors College student, a veritable freak—in a vast Grecian sea, with Jeff as my sole companion. So when Kurt's frat buddy agreed to take D on the trip with us if I would go with Kurt, I consented.

And then all hell broke loose.

When I told Jeff that I was going with Kurt instead, he flipped out. His room was just below mine, and all night, he played angry music and hung out his window screaming that I was a bitch, a whore, a fucking cunt. Other boys from the dorm joined Jeff in his righteous fury, smashing things against the floor, pounding on my door, and hissing through the crack.

I didn't get mad back. I felt terrible and guilty, cowering in my room while the whole male population of my dorm rose up with a clear message: I had belonged to them and I had strayed from the pack, hooking up with a rogue male and threatening the sanctity of the whole goddamned dormitory gene pool. All night, I took in their anger, crying so hard and so long without the good sense to take out my contact lenses that, in the morning, I had to have an emergency appointment with the ophthalmologist. My corneas were both scratched, one eye so badly I had to wear an eye patch.

I was a sea wench who had survived the shaming, but barely. And there was no turning back now: I would go to Shasta as a pirate, with Kurt.

WE HADN'T EVEN LEFT THE DOCK BEFORE IT WAS OBVIOUS that D's companion wasn't much of a date—they weren't even speaking to each other—but she didn't care. She may as well have been on another boat, lost as she was in drugs, Jack Daniels, and the eyes of a new friend with whom she was swaying near a boom box, hitting rewind on a worn Eagles cassette, "Desperado" locked in as their song. By the time Kurt and his pack of drunken brothers, baked in every way there is to be baked, anchored our boat on Slaughterhouse Island in the middle of Shasta Lake, the deep water was not just a metaphor.

On the roof deck in my magenta bikini, I felt alone and trapped. The fraternity brothers on the boat assigned all the girls nicknames for the weekend, and mine was *Carcass*. Kurt hovered over me.

I knew it was too late to get away, and, somehow, I knew what was coming.

I don't know how many white houseboats docked on our side of the island that night—at least a dozen. After the sun had set, fires sprang up, the music got louder, and voices rose in a discordant roar. I'd refused the coke all day—that night in Kurt's apartment had been enough for me—but when the party was raging, Kurt pulled a baggie out of his pocket and held something out to me in the palm of his big hand. Brown mushrooms like shrunken heads on tiny necks. I took a few and chewed the tough, dry stems, washing them down with a slug from his beer.

When the mushrooms started to kick in, I slipped away from Kurt and the hordes of drunken Greeks, climbing the bare slope where the dark, swaying shapes of human bodies circled the flames, pushing through some thick brush near the top, and finding shelter next to what seemed at the time to be a fantastically magnanimous scrub pine.

From my refuge, I watched the bonfires burning red, a postapocalyptic hellscape, the moored houseboats bobbing like a flotilla of crocodiles. I was well hidden, and far below I could see Kurt moving from boat to boat to boat, up and down the bank, looking for me, screaming my name, yelling,

"Where is she? Where the fuck is she? Who's she with? Who'd you see her with?"

I was with nobody, alone on top of the hill, and I knew when I came down, I would be caught, so I stayed under the tree: two o'clock, three o'clock, four o'clock. The mushrooms wore off, and I was tired—so tired and so cold. When I finally didn't see him anymore, I crept back down to the boat.

This was my thought: *If I am in bed, if I am in bed and sleeping when he finds me, maybe he will let me sleep. I will sleep until tomorrow when the boat will return to the dock and I will be safe.* But when he found me, I was not safe.

They will wake you up to rape you.

The next morning, when the boat docked, Kurt walked up into town and came back with a paper bag of Dunkin' Donuts—cream filled, jelly filled, powdered, and plain, at least two dozen—and he said to me, "Here, Jill. You get first choice."

Six hours before, he'd had a pillow stuffed in my mouth to muffle my screams, and now he had the nerve to give me first choice on a bag of fucking doughnuts.

I wondered then if I could have fought harder—I hadn't bitten off his earlobe and spit it in his face, I hadn't jammed my knee into his testicles with all the force of my starved eighteen-year-old body, I hadn't leaped to my feet and rammed a well-placed heel into his kneecap. I pleaded, I cried, and finally I screamed for help, but I didn't hurt him back because I didn't want to die.

I remember the pillow in my face and, when there wasn't air enough left for screaming, thinking *breathe, breathe, breathe.*

In the bright morning sun, Kurt looked hideous, the bag of doughnuts hanging in the air between us, the smell of hot sugar over stale beer and vomit all around us. His eyes registered nothing, nothing at all, and I imagined clawing them out.

"No, thank you," I said, turning away. "I don't eat doughnuts."

WHEN WE GOT BACK FROM CALIFORNIA, KURT CALLED ME ON the dorm phone in the hall, again and again. Here's what I didn't say: "You fucker. You *raped* me. You think I'm going to *go out* with you?"

Here's what I did say: "I'm busy," and "I can't," and "I have to work/write a paper/do some math."

I didn't call what happened on the boat that weekend *rape*.

And then, a month after Shasta, I agreed to see Kurt.

I had a ticket out of Portland to fly to Savannah, Georgia, and I needed a ride to the airport. Kurt wanted to be that ride. *What harm could come of it?* I thought. Some nice boys from the Honors College—actual friends—got me as far as Portland and offered at least ten times to take me from the bookstore where we were hanging out to the airport. They didn't know what Kurt had done to me, but they knew I didn't like him.

Why did I let Kurt come and pick me up? I still can't answer that question.

"Jill! It's so good to see you," Kurt said when he pulled up to where I was standing by the curb with my suitcase. "I've missed you. Have you missed me?" He tried to kiss me, but I turned my face away. Kurt unlatched the tiny trunk, wedged in my suitcase, and then, putting his hand on the small of my back, guided me to the passenger's side of the growling car.

As soon as I was in, I noticed something hanging from the rearview mirror. Something familiar.

"Hey," I said. "That's mine."

"Yes," Kurt said, touching a finger to the loop of white lace knotted around the base of the mirror. "Your belt. I wanted something to remember you by."

I reached up to snatch down Kurt's trophy, but he stopped my hand and squeezed, leering.

"Finders keepers."

As the Porsche pulled away from the curb, I felt a wave of loathing and fear.

Kurt took the wrong road out of downtown. "Where are you going?" I asked.

"I forgot something at my parents' place," he said. "We're just going to swing by on our way to the airport."

"But it's not *on* the way to the airport." I knew Kurt was living with his parents in the suburbs.

"It's fine," he said, grinning. "You've got plenty of time."

At the house, I wanted to wait in the car, but he said I should come in to meet his parents. They weren't home, of course, and somehow we ended up in Kurt's bedroom. He closed the door.

"What are you doing?" I said. "I have to go!"

Kurt put his face close to my face, the aftershave, the mint, all of him sickening to me. We were in a kind of dance, me backing up until I hit the edge of the bed. Kurt smiled.

He put his hands on my shoulders and pushed me down. I landed flat on my back and he fell over me, pinning me down with his body.

Again. No. Nononono. It was going to happen again.

Then we heard something, someone coming in the door.

Kurt jumped off me and reached down, offering me his hand and pulling me up. I was in shock. I said nothing. There was nothing left for me to say.

Kurt laughed. "What did you think I was going to do, Jill? Rape you?"

In his own terrifying way, Kurt had named his own crime before I could, and yet I never filed a report. I never even said, "You raped me." I did nothing. I got out of that fucking car at the airport and I never saw him again.

IN THE BUNK ON SHASTA LAKE, KURT HAD PUT A PILLOW over my face so no one would hear me scream, but now I wonder: *Who would have heard me?* And if someone had heard, on that boat anchored to an island I didn't know until today was named for an actual meat market and slaughterhouse, who would have acted? Who would have helped me? From the distance of nearly thirty years, my heart made vulnerable by motherhood and my fierce desire to protect my children, I wonder, *How many other women were raped that night on Slaughterhouse Island?*

I feel certain I was not the only one.

In Savannah the summer after the rape, I had sex with more different men in three months than in all the years before and all the years after combined. My unarticulated logic went like this: if I give my body away, over and over, I can prove to myself that sex is my choice—even though, and this seems significant now, I always let the men choose me. Until I was nineteen years old, it never occurred to me that I could do the choosing. *Not you, not you, not you. Yes, okay. You.*

The morning I wrote this essay, I went to my bookshelf and hooked a finger over the red spine of a paperback: *I Never Called It Rape.* The cover is designed to look as if part of the book has been ripped away, and the pages of my copy are browning on the edges. Published in 1988, the very year I went to Shasta with Kurt, reporter Robin Warshaw's book revealed the results of Mary Koss's *Ms.*/NIMH-funded survey. Theirs was the first nationwide study of campus sexual assault ever, and the statistics rattled us all: *Twenty-five percent of women in college have been the victims of rape or attempted rape. Eighty-four percent of these victims were acquainted with their assailants. Only 27 percent of women raped identified themselves as rape victims.*

I bought the book as a senior, when it was a required text for a class called "Self-Defense from the Inside Out." *Holy shit,* I thought then. *Why didn't anybody tell me this before?*

Here, in the pages of *I Never Called It Rape,* I can have a conversation with my college self: she wrote—not a lot—in purple pen, scratching asterisks next to the things that mattered most to her. *One in four female respondents had an experience that met the legal definition of rape or attempted rape and . . . the average age when a rape incident occurred (either as perpetrator or victim) was 18½ years old* and *[Women] were embarrassed about the details of the rape (leaving a bar with a man, taking drugs, etc.) and felt they would be blamed for what occurred, or they simply felt the men involved had too much social status for their stories to be believed* and *In short, many men fail to perceive what has just happened as rape.*

"The question," our self-defense teacher said one afternoon when we were gathered around her cross-legged on mats in the gym, "is not 'What will he think of me?'—if I don't answer his question, if I'm not polite, if I don't want to go—but 'What do I think of *him*?' "

This simple rearrangement of pronouns flipped something in my brain. Forever.

"If a guy on the street approaches you and asks for the time," our teacher said, "you don't have to answer him. Providing the time of day is not your job. If you don't want to talk to him, keep walking."

You don't have to be polite. You don't even have to be nice. Keep walking.

Ask yourself: What do I think of *him*?

Three years after the rape, I began volunteering at a local sexual assault support organization, staffing the crisis line and going with a team to talk to high school students about rape. In 1991, conversations about what constituted true consent were still new, and while the boys sat silently, the girls pushed back. *So you're saying that if I go to a party in a really short skirt, and I'm flirting all over the place—if I get raped, it's not my fault?*

Yes, I'd say. *That's exactly what I'm saying.* Sometimes it seemed to me that the girls just didn't want to hear that rape is never the victim's fault. They wanted to have something to believe in, rules to follow, a formula, reasons other girls got raped and they didn't: short skirt equals rape; too much beer equals rape; unlocked door equals rape. The part I wanted them to understand is that these equations can implode, constricting your whole life, until one day you're sitting in a locked steel box breathing through an airhole with a straw and wondering, *Now? Now am I safe?*

A couple months before the rape, a truck had hit me. It wasn't a big truck—one of those little ones, a Toyota or a Nissan with a canopy on the back. I was riding across the crosswalk on my bike. I knew I was supposed to walk my bike across, but I had the green light and the white walking man, so I had started to zip across when the man driving the truck, not seeing me, made the decision to turn right on red. I went down hard, but I was wearing a helmet, and though the truck didn't stop right away, it did soon enough. My legs and half my twisted bike were under the bumper. When I wriggled free, I felt nothing in particular until I saw the horrified, worried face of the man emerging from the cab, the two women running from the building across the street. "Oh my God, are you okay? Are you okay?" A car stopped behind the truck and more people whose sexes and sizes have been lost to memory got out. Lying on the cold, wet road, I was surrounded by concerned bystanders.

I did feel something: mortification and shame. My arm and leg on the pavement side were both bleeding, but I hadn't been dressed for the weather, or for biking. I was coming back from a class at the gym, so I was wearing a sweatshirt and black Lycra pants. *Ruined now*, I thought. *Shit.*

"Are you okay?" Everybody seemed to be saying the same thing, over and over, and I was worried they were all going to get really wet. It was March in Eugene, with drizzle so thick and gray and constant, I couldn't tell whether the raindrops were moving up or down.

I must have been in shock.

"Are you okay?"

"Yeah," I mumbled, grabbing for the bumper and pulling myself off the ground. Hands all around, but I reached out for none of them. "I'm fine. I'm okay."

Somehow we all got to the sidewalk on the other side. My bike had a twisted rim and was unrideable.

"Are you sure you're okay? Can we help you get somewhere?"

"Oh, no, I'm fine. My dorm's right over there. I'm fine."

And so everybody left, even the little truck that had flattened me, and I thought over and over: *I feel like I've been run over by a truck.* In fact, I *had* been run over by a truck, but I couldn't say that out loud. I couldn't say how much it hurt. Embarrassed by being in the wrong place at the wrong time in the wrong pants, I limped back to my dorm in the rain.

Do you understand yet why we blame ourselves when we are hit, dragging the shame behind us like a twisted rim?

IN 2014, PSYCHOLOGISTS AT THE UNIVERSITY OF OREGON conducted the first comprehensive, university-wide survey of sexual assault and learned that 19 percent of female students are victims of rape or attempted rape during the time they're studying at Oregon.

Nineteen percent. One in five women. Today.

I am still scraping at my story. I can't go back and get the young woman I was from the Italian restaurant before she climbs onto the boat. I can't stop the truck or the rapist, but I can let the girl I was know that I see her. I hear her. I know she is telling the truth.

If nothing changes—and in thirty years, not nearly enough has changed—next year, there will be one hundred thousand more assaults on our campuses.

One is too many. *One hundred thousand.*

In the self-defense class, our teacher taught us that if we couldn't imagine doing something—cracking an assailant in the head with a stapler, opening up a can of pepper spray on an attacker, digging our keys into the eyes of a would-be rapist—we wouldn't be able to act in a real crisis. Wielding the stapler, the pepper spray, and the keys, our teacher taught us the power of visualization, and I learned to imagine in advance what I might be called upon to do in an emergency.

One hundred thousand? This is an emergency.

Together, let's visualize what we need to change the rape culture. I have my keys in my hand and I am holding them like a claw. Let's turn this motherfucking system around.

& the Truth Is, I Have No Story

CLAIRE SCHWARTZ

I too, having lost faith
in language, have placed my faith in language.
                                        —TERRANCE HAYES

1.

This is not about that. This is about everything after.

This is about how, all of a sudden, there was only one *after*. How the infinity of tiny afters—after school and after my most recent birthday and after A. and I ducked behind a couch hiding from nothing and she told me that she was falling in love with me and after my chest opened to a new kind of wanting and after I last had a fever and after the first time

I threw a Frisbee without its careening into the ground—were all swept away into the only after that stretches out endlessly over the unfolding nows. This is about that.

My language is so imprecise. I am thrashing in what I can't tell you.

Like how people north of Pennsylvania say "the city" like there was only ever one and it is, of course, New York. No Newark, no Hoboken, no New Haven, no Boston, no Providence, no Portland. Just New York, dressed in its sparkling lights and beautiful people, its bright red scarves and head wraps and food carts recklessly jettisoning the aroma of gyro and bagels and tacos and pad thai across it all. "I hate New York," I usually say, when the subject comes up, meaning, maybe: *How could any city that flaunts its beauty like that let this happen to me?* Though I know all cities eat their own.

And this is not about the city.

2.

"You're so lucky you weren't killed," the first person I tell tells me. I am a sophomore in high school, and she is an English teacher and my advisor. I have moved to Manhattan from Nashville. I want to go home to my grandparents and my cousins, to the city whose heartbeat and language I know. My teacher is still talking; there is a bug in her hair. I watch the bug slowly climb the mousy blond strands and wonder how I am supposed to respond to her comment. I am silent. The bug inches on.

That evening, in line at the grocery store, I watch the slim, middle-aged white man in front of me calmly hand his Brie to the cashier. I imagine tapping his shoulder and saying, *Oh, what luck! It's wonderful that you're not dead.* When I laugh at my own thought, it sounds like I'm trying to dislodge a stone from my chest. The Brie buyer looks at me. I become engrossed in the gum beside the register.

You're so lucky you weren't killed. The words feel slender and sharp as the blade that was pressed against my neck that night—stroking a border so fine you can touch it and touch me at once with each of its cool metal faces. *You . . . killed.*

3.

At least you weren't killed. At least you have access to medical care. At least you have insurance. At least you have wonderful friends. Because the ones who tell me this are my friends and my teachers and the social worker and the doctor, I hold their words and outstretched hands even though my anger is mounting and I want not to be touched.

These days, I speak few words, and I certainly don't have the vocabulary to dismantle what's been forced on me by people called safe. I don't have breath to say: *No, I will not be grateful for my rights. I will stand with two feet on this earth and I will always say thank you when someone does something kind and sorry when I've done something wrong and never out-side of that. And, yes, I am furious that I am pulled between poles of gratitude and apology—both of which are violent era-sures.*

Thank goodness I wasn't killed.

I'm sorry I'm so inarticulate.

I can't name it then, but I feel the words *at least* eroding my voice. I sense that "at least" marks an end to the story I'm supposed to tell, that I am supposed to say something gracious in response—"thank goodness"—or else nothing more at all. "At least" curbs my telling too much truth. It's a blunt instrument wielded to club a reckless retelling into submission. *The story ends here.* But the truth is, I have no story—nothing I can corral into a coherent narrative.

4.

One wants a teller in a time like this.[1]

5.

That which is not a coherent narrative appears everywhere: in the classrooms where I stop talking; in the school-mandated therapist's office, where we face off in silence for forty-five minutes each week; in food, which I eat too much of or not

---

1 Gwendolyn Brooks, "One Wants a Teller in a Time Like This"

at all. When my best friend comes up behind me and wraps me in a hug, the anger darts up my chest and I instinctively push him away, hard. A few days later, I show up at his house inexplicably shaking after another friend ran up behind me as I was walking home from the library.

"What happened?" he asks.

"Nothing," I tell him. "It was nothing."

6.

You know that moment when you trip and you are poised with equal possibility to fall flat on your face and to take the next step, and your heart shoots up into your throat? Every second feels split—normality and catastrophe equally plausible. The assumptions I once cobbled into a day no longer hold. There is not a man hiding behind that tree. No one will break into my apartment and kill me while I sleep. I will be able to sleep until the morning. I will be here in the morning. The stones that composed the ground on which I've always walked have come loose, swirling unpredictably around my head. (And here, I feel myself saying it: "At least I have ground.")

7.

Eventually, I go to a small liberal arts college in New England. It's beautiful—which is true and also something people say over and over when they don't want to talk about other truths like the relationship between the institution's vast resources and the rampant poverty in the postindustrial towns that surround us, or how the brochures boast that we don't have frats, but the culture of fraternities clings instead to sports teams.

8.

A friend is assaulted by an adjunct professor. The deans tell her to keep it quiet. A sophomore is pressing charges against a student who raped her at a party. The school takes no measures to keep him away from her. Her friends take turns sleeping in her room. Their grades drop. Their relationships become strained. These are the stories we tell each other, quietly.

9.

Sometimes people tell me that something bad happened to me, but I am brave and strong. I don't want to be told that I am brave or strong. I am not right just because he was wrong. I don't want to be made noble. I want someone willing to watch me thrash and crumple because that, too, is the truth, and it needs a witness. "He broke me," I say to a friend. "You're not broken," she whispers back. I turn my palms up, wishing I could show her the pieces.

10.

In college, I write my senior thesis about Audre Lorde, June Jordan, and Pat Parker, three queer African American poets who died of breast cancer. How, I want to know, do they give form to what is happening in their bodies, their minds, as they are dying? How do they make their way in the same language used to write them out of history books? Is it the same language? In so many ways, our contexts are different; but I am beginning to understand that my own white learned unresponsiveness to the shapes of their questions has something to do with the ongoing violence at the heart of this nation.

Jordan wrote: "In the same way that so many Americans feel that 'we have lost our jobs,' we suspect that we have lost our country. We know that we do not speak the language. And I ask you: well, what are we going to do about it?"

We must, she says, make language accountable to the truths of our experience. She advises us to turn away from the commonplace, "I was raped."

When I read these words, I am in a carrel in the basement of the library, my knees pressed to my chest, my elbows tight against my knees. I read the words again, put the book down. I stand up. I stretch my arms toward the ceiling. I trust June Jordan with her scimitar brilliance and truth-telling ethic. The activist and poet, who wrote: "I am black and I am female and I am a mother and I am bisexual and I am a nationalist and I am an antinationalist. And I mean to be fully and freely all that I am!" Jordan, who refused to see contradictions as conflicting. Who insisted that the difficult truth is also the site of her girding question: "Where is the love?"

I take a deep breath and settle back into my chair, poised to receive the new language I know she will give me to speak my experience. "The victim must learn to make language tell her own truth: He raped me."

I am devastated. I don't want to be made the object in my retelling. "I was raped," I whisper.

That, too, feels wrong. I set the book down on the table.

11.

When I was little, I used to curl up in the black-and-white-striped armchair in our living room with a thick book. Sometimes I would read but, often, I just held the book in my lap as a signal to passersby to let me be while my imagination roved. I treasured these moments of quiet. I grew into them, stretching out my girl mind into the implausible and absurd. I love my quiet. I hate how, in the after, my quiet has become silence. The room in my chest that was sky-lit has become a sealed and padded cell.

12.

B.,
Somewhere in this essay is a love letter to you.
Your love brought me back to my quiet. I needed a new

language. I needed a new story—one where I don't have to re-member the beginning and don't know the end. This is a love letter to our love, which was never the kind of durable love that built itself around errands and taxes. It was all our bodies and your brilliance, your language and where our language trailed off together into something dark and shimmering—like the sea, like the mud, like the shape of my imagination when I clutched a book for its world and its heft, like the Nashville summer nights when lightning bugs gifted their tiny glow, unjarred. All halo, all fleeting.

13.

Judith Butler says that we suffer from our condition of ad-dressability. My body feels like my condition, and everything feels like an address.

14.

I look for them everywhere, women like me. And they find me, too. A teacher in my high school tells me, crying: "It hap-pened to me, almost thirty years ago," as I wonder whether three decades will sediment any of this for me. They are in the newspaper where the truth of their testimony is prodded: "The victim claimed . . ." "She believes . . ." They are on the other end of the rape and sexual assault hotline I volunteer with in college. We sit next to each other on the bus. We recognize each other, or we don't. My beautiful friend in graduate school says to me, "I sit down, and I just lose time."

"I know," I say.

15.

In my notebook, I write, *Create: there are parts of you even you can't give away.*

16.

Go to court. Don't go to court. Get a rape kit. Don't get a rape kit. Don't take a class with that teacher. (He's handsy.) Don't take a class with her. (She's unsympathetic.) Don't watch violent movies. Don't watch movies that might be violent. Don't be angry. If you're angry, explain why calmly. If I were you, I wouldn't wear that. I'd rather be dead than be raped. (I'd rather be dead than be you?) Don't talk about rape. Do you have proof? Don't get defensive. Avoid your triggers. Don't eat at restaurants with steak knives. Are you eating? You look thin. You look fat. No one's going to want to go home with you. Don't let people you don't know into your home. Who do you really know anyway? Don't walk alone at night. Don't not walk alone at night. *This* is your life. This is *your* life. This is your *life*.

17.

After college, I move back to Nashville. My girlfriend, M., is a social worker, and she's heard from a colleague of hers of a lesbian therapist who specializes in PTSD. "Do you want to try?" she asks me. "Not really," I tell her, thinking of the mutual stare-down with the therapist I saw in high school, thinking of the doctor who asked if I was "gay before," thinking that I am really, all things considered, finally doing okay. I have a job teaching high school. I can sleep for hours at a time. I can go days, sometimes weeks, without having flashbacks. M. looks at me with exhaustion. "I guess I'll try," I say. A smile pops onto M.'s face like it's been released by my acquiescence.

The therapist's office is attached to her home. She invites me in. I sit on a brown corduroy armchair. She asks me a series of intimate questions as though reading directions for shampoo use. I answer her equally sterilely. To: "Are you religious?" I say: "Jewish."

"Do you have siblings?"

"A younger brother."

"Have you experienced trauma?"

I say, "I was beaten and raped when I was sixteen," as though agreeing, "Yes. Wash, rinse, repeat."

"Oh." She pauses, looking up at me. "At least you weren't killed," she says, writing something down in her notebook.

M. looks hopeful when she picks me up. "How was it?"

"It was fine," I say, and thank her for coming to get me.

In our next session, the therapist says we are beginning Eye Movement Desensitization and Reprocessing. I'd read that the first step involves holding aspects of the traumatic event in mind. I tell her I don't think I'm ready. She tells me, "It will be helpful." I wonder if I can say no. She probably knows what's best.

She tells me to visualize the part of "the scene" I remember most strongly. I throw up in her bathroom. That night, I sleep on the couch.

The next day, I call my friend Anisha and tell her I will never go to therapy again. After a sleepless night fighting to keep the past from consuming my present, I am furious that everything I've worked so hard to rebuild seems to have crumbled. "It feels like I'm right back there, in the week after it happened. The stakes are too high," I say. "I had it all under control. I can deal with this myself."

Anisha tells me, "A good therapist knows you have to live in the house while you remodel."

18.

I lay awake all night thinking about how I am completely exhausted, staving off sleep and trying to stop thinking about what might happen if I allow myself to close my eyes. I watch the sun rise, which tells me it's time to start again.

19.

I find H. on the *Psychology Today* website, a blog that also allows you to search for therapists. According to the site, H. is the only therapist in my area who has noted that he sees transgender clients (and whose description doesn't strike me as completely disingenuous). I am cisgender, but I imagine a therapist who only sees cis clients has little understanding of gender and little recourse for facilitating healing. I call him. We set up an appointment.

At the end of the session, I am amazed at myself for sitting in a room alone with a man for forty-five minutes. I tell H. so, and he nods.

We talk during our sessions, or don't. At the end of each meeting, I promise to come back next week.

A therapist with an office down the hall from H. has a dog. I tell H. I saw the dog, and he is adorable. H. asks me if I'd like the dog to be at one of our sessions. I say, "Yes." I am surprised when, the following week, the dog is in H.'s office waiting for me.

I don't want to thank H. Instead, I say, "I've never really said all of it out loud." H. does not say, "What are you talking about?" He does not say, "Really, eight years later?" Or, "At least you weren't killed." H. says, "I'm here to listen if you want to tell me." And then, "If you don't want to speak, I am still here."

"Will it help?" I ask. I want a definitive answer, even as I suspect that men with definitive answers about my body have something to do with why I'm there in the first place.

"It might," H. says. "Some people find it helpful. Others don't." I say nothing. To make a narrative of what I don't remember feels like a lie. There is no sense here. I stare at a photograph of a huge and knotted tree on H.'s desk but, out of the corner of my eye, I can see him there nodding like my quiet and not knowing is something to affirm. His kindness threatens to loose everything I have wrapped so tightly.

20.

Everything changed that night. I repeat it to myself like a mantra shoving down the question that keeps bubbling up: How can it be that not everything changed? The same dumb sun. The same impossible horizon. Beauty hurts. It enters me even as I have fortified myself to keep everything out.

21.

I realize that I read Jordan wrong. I took her language rather than joining her project. I saw: He raped me. She first said, "The victim must learn to make language tell her own truth."

I made something from it, but I am not better for it.

22.

I am not sorry. And I am not grateful.

23.

> I can do only two things . . . —
> describe this flight
> and not add a last line.[2]

---

2 Wisława Szymborska, "Photograph from September 11"

The Luckiest MILF in Brooklyn

Lynn Melnick

"C'mere MILF tits!"

Sweet tits, hot tits, sugar tits. Oh, hi. Here I am. MILF tits. Still valid, I guess, still viable. MILF-y, but tits all the same. I've been a D-cup since seventh grade, so my breasts have been up for public conversation almost as long as I can remember—along with the rest of me, especially my ass, the way I walk, and how viable a fuck I am to passersby.

Do I want to smoke a joint in your car? No thanks. Why aren't I smiling? I've been having night terrors again, thanks for asking. You'd like to rub your dick all over my ass? Thanks for letting me know.

I'm standing on the corner of my block, my home turf, in front of the public library with my younger daughter, not yet four, who's holding an *Olivia* book and her stuffed cat.

It's quiet. It's one of those days that looks like fall but feels like summer: the leaves whip around as traffic flows but my daughter and I wear open-toed shoes. I'm in a sundress.

Come, listen to me talk about why it doesn't matter what I'm wearing, why it's hot out and I shouldn't have to cover up, why it's not on me, it's on them. I talk a good game, I know the language and the reasoning. I'm tough, I'm badass, I'm right. And I blame myself. The dress could have shown less cleavage.

"C'mere MILF tits!" calls a man out a car window. "I wanna fuck you sideways!"

I look down and away. I have a fearful history. I flinch at loud garbage truck brakes. I've literally been startled by my own kid's shadow. Silly mom. So silly.

"Why did that man yell at you?" my daughter asks.

I'm embarrassed. I'm embarrassed for the objectification and I'm embarrassed by my fear. I've been dealing with this for thirty years and it doesn't change. Wasn't it supposed to have gone away by now? It didn't go away during my pregnancy or when I walked with a baby nestled in a wrap against my chest. It didn't magically evaporate on my fortieth birthday. Shouldn't that be one of the benefits of age? Or am I buying into an ageist way of thinking, that I might one day be seen by strangers as something beyond my sex appeal?

I turn around and make eye contact with a cop standing outside the library. I gesture to him, like *what the hell?* and he gestures back, like *what can you do?* I don't know, you're just a cop and someone made me feel unsafe on the street. Never mind. I was wearing a sundress. I'm a D-cup.

It's not like he touched you.
It's not like he hurt you.
It's not like he raped you.

I'm supposed to be grateful because I wasn't raped. I'm supposed to be grateful because, even though I walk through the world with MILF tits and a sundress, I wasn't raped. And I've been raped, and this is much better. So, thank you. Today I stand outside the library, the luckiest MILF in Brooklyn.

"You still got it!"

It was when I was running late to my daughter's school pickup and a man called "slow down, I love to watch your fine ass move" and, when I ignored him, added "you don't have to be a bitch, you're not *that* fine!" that I finally took to social media to complain. I've been catcalled for decades but I felt unequal to the task of having to switch gears from being in defense mode on the street to smiling at teachers and children. I wanted to know I'm not alone, because I felt humiliated and alone.

My online friends were very nice. Lots of solidarity, lots of "worddd" and "I'm sorry." Some women wondered why they didn't get street harassed, and they felt ambivalent about that. One man wrote "You still got it!"

I'm forty-two. I'll admit forty-two is not what I thought forty-two would be, but, then, I had given very little thought to how middle age might present itself. Objectively, and if I'm lucky, I've likely lived half my life and it's been a good one for longer than I ever thought possible.

I live in a city that I love married to a man that I love. I've published a couple of books, had a couple of kids that I schlep to and from school and activities because I'm fortunate to have a flexible work schedule. I get to the end of the day and I'm so fucking tired I almost can't move my body from the couch to the bed but it's a pleasure, that kind of tired. There was no predicting my life would be this.

A couple of years ago, *Esquire* ran a Tom Junod piece "In Praise of 42-Year-Old Women." Reaction ran the gamut from the *BBC* declaring us "still sexy" and the *NY Daily News* reassuring us we can "still be hot," to the more sensible, feminist media bristling at the premise that "there used to be something tragic about the 42-year-old woman" because the odds that we were fuckable had long since started to tip.

Important lesson, listen: I should be honored to be objectified now that I'm forty-two, I should be grateful. I should have slowed down because I'm not *that* fine, I'm forty-two! I should be glad anyone finds me sexually viable.

I am short, round, wear glasses, didn't get my chipped front teeth fixed until a couple of years ago because I didn't know how to let go of what my life had been, didn't know that I deserved that. I couldn't look in the mirror for years. I have a C-section scar and a few other scars. The skin around my lower midsection is slack from two full-term pregnancies. I can hardly remember to shave in summer and when I do it feels like a statement of some sort. I smoked for two decades and there are lines around my lips. I rarely wear makeup. I'm sure I'm softer than ever, if I could remember what my body was like before. I spent too long defined by how others perceived me, how it felt to others when they touched me. Now I feel so good to myself, but important lesson, listen: my face is falling, it's all falling, isn't it? I'm forty-two.

But wait!! I still got it!! I am not a waste of a body moving through space! I can still bring the titillation wherever I go. If I would just be more amenable, more grateful, you're not hurting me you're complimenting me, smile and say thank you, stop, you're talking to me, you see me and I'm forty-two years old, you want to fuck me and I'm forty-two years old.

Old, old, old, thank you, thank you, thank you.

"Thank you for the nice things you say!"

I had to stop going to the corner bakery one recent summer because a man working there wouldn't stop creeping on me, even when I was with my children. He'd give me my change and slide his hand slowly across mine. He'd tell me I looked sexy. He'd tell me how beautiful I am and then he'd nod to my kids. He'd stare at me so hard that I felt like if I moved I'd stumble. A couple of times he followed just behind me on the sidewalk making grunting noises.

I couldn't get the courage to say: *please stop.*

I know what it feels like to be held down and I know what it feels like to be hit in the face. I know that saying *please stop* made it no more likely that these things would stop.

I quit going to the bakery, even though their coffee is essential to my functioning as a human. So there I was, in my neighborhood, altering my behavior to try to avoid being harassed. Luckily, fall semester came and he went back to study at school.

Here's a partial list, just off the top of my head right now, of all the places I've dreaded, feared, or even stopped going to, because I felt exposed, harassed, creeped on: the bakery, the pizza place, the deli across from work, the deli in my office building, the closer entrance to the subway, the playground with the baby swings, the playground with the frog statue, my daughter's ballet school waiting room, a poetry reading I'd just given, a poetry reading as I was giving it, walking my kids to school, picking my kids up from school, the construction site to the left of my building, the construction site to the right of my building, the airport, the train station, the zoo.

A couple of years ago, I was part of a question-and-answer session involving poetry and photography when an older man in the audience thought a good question to ask was (I'm para-phrasing) why, when I look so nice and respectable and pretty and kinda hot, well,

why do you write all these nasty poems with sex and violence in them?

Are these about you really?

Which parts are true?

The room seemed silent forever but it was probably just a second before I said, "Wow. Okay." I didn't know how to respond.

Ugh, because then I said, "Thank you for the nice things you say" and babbled on about something that included sta-tistics about intimate partner violence, just because I know them, just because my fear of men beating me is not sexy.

But what if I am some kind of Trojan horse of respectability? I was thrown.

This panel was a major deal for me, career-wise. I was being taken seriously in a room of serious artists and I was trying like heck to take myself seriously. And there I was being objectified in front of the entire audience. I blamed myself.

If you wrote poems about the weather.

If you hadn't belted your dress so tight.

If you could talk more intelligently.

So what if I thanked my objectifier? So what if so much of my day involves de-escalation? I'll take my lumps to avoid worse. I should be grateful that I can. I should be grateful that this is what I'm complaining about. I should be grateful that I don't currently fear for my life.

Grateful

Grateful

Grateful

"You'll miss it when it's gone."

I was invisible for years. I was quiet, shell-shocked; I didn't want the attention but maybe would have liked it. In fourth grade, about halfway through the school year, I accidentally went to the wrong classroom and sat there, and no one realized, except me, who burned hot until the end of the day. I didn't even know which would have been better, being found out or not being found out, it was all too much.

This was just before I hit puberty; by sixth grade I was a

B-cup and growing fast. It was confusing but exhilarating, because suddenly I was seen. At home it was something we didn't speak about, and I was afraid to ask for a bra, to admit my burgeoning sexual self, so I just bounced around the school to the delight of the boys who had known me since kindergarten, a good six years before I mattered.

At lunchtime I'd go behind the cafeteria with one boy or another and let them fondle me in exchange for cigarettes, which I didn't smoke (yet) but stored away in a box my grandmother had bought me, but, let's face it, the attention was its own payment. By seventh grade, I learned to give blow jobs in exchange for wine coolers; the semen and the alcohol slid down my throat with such certainty I didn't know how to start saying no. By eighth grade I depended on the alcohol and by ninth grade, when I was kicked out of school for drugs, I had no doubt that the only thing I had to offer the world was my body, and the world pretty much confirmed that for a long time.

Hey, sexy, why you walking away?

Come sit on my lap and tell me why you look so sad.

Looking fine, mama! (I was walking home from a day at the emergency room.)

Eventually—and not long from now, as my oldest is ten—my daughters will be publicly harassed on the street and I will be powerless to stop it. It is very likely that we could be harassed on the same day, that we will find ourselves back in our safe, charmingly untidy apartment, still tender from the words hurled by strangers.

I am incompetent, a failure. For the first time since my oldest was a newborn, I feel unequal to the task of parenting.

My daughters get fed a lot of phony girl power through books and television and clubs at school. And then they go into the schoolyard where they get their real messages, they catch ads in the subway, they overhear conversations at the diner, I take them to *The LEGO Movie*—much admired, roundly praised, critical darling—and they watch as the main female character is objectified throughout the entire thing.

We need a break from all this empowerment.

I'm standing on the corner of Twenty-Second and Sixth in Manhattan. "Miss, Miss!" a man's voice calls to me and I think *it can't be me, I'm no Miss* and I think *what if it's me please leave me alone* and he taps me on the shoulder, I flinch because I flinch, and he says, "I just wanted to say I like your dress!"

Holy crap, he just wants to say he likes my dress! It's a whole new world.

At forty-two (still got it!) (MILF tits!), the harassment has certainly, thankfully slowed, but it doesn't seem to want to go away altogether. And, even though it happens much less frequently than it used to, I flinch and brace myself every time I leave my apartment. I wonder if, when it finally stops for good, if it will be too late to relax, if the muscle memory of the harassment will keep me tense on the sidewalk forever.

I try to understand when people tell me they enjoy it, when women my age say they miss being called names or when they get a kick out of being called to so explicitly:

I wanna fuck your asshole. (I was wearing a down coat.)

I'd like to put my cock between those titties.

Ugly cunt, I'm talking to you!

I know what it's like to feel invisible as a child and I imagine it feels the same as an adult. But it's a pretty sorry situation when the choice is either objectification by intimidating strangers or invisibility.

Once or twice in my life, I swear to you, I've done things other than be a body available for men to enjoy or reject. But I know I have no right to complain. I am lucky. I've been allowed one more day as a woman on this earth, relatively unviolated.

Shouldn't that be enough?

Lucky

Lucky

Lucky

Spectator

My Family, My Rapist, and Mourning Online

BRANDON TAYLOR

ONE OF THE MEN WHO RAPED ME, W., IS DYING FROM cancer, and I'm watching it happen via Facebook. The man who raped me is married to my aunt and is the father of my cousin, who was, at one time, my closest friend in a family in which friends and love were rare. He is not the only man who raped me, but he is the only one who raped me and refused to leave because he was stitched into my life like an ugly scar from a wound healed wrong.

It has been strange to watch him die after wishing for his death for so long, to see it unfold through the lens of my cousin's pain, so at odds with the frustration and fear I felt watching my own mother die. I have watched his face suck in and his enormous gut dwindle at first to a flat surface and then a concave one. There are no pictures of him looking directly into the camera—I don't think I could bear them anyway. He always seems to be looking away or up or down, at the periphery even when at the center of things. There are no direct details about his cancer, his impending death, or his treatment. There are no specifics. It's all hazy and soft, the way things are on the internet with the strangers we imagine we know.

W.'s brother died of cancer. They were twins, their bodies made of the same parts, and so in one way, it doesn't surprise me. There are times when I cough, and I think this is it, this is when my body betrays me and reverts to my mother's body. I imagine that there are ways in which our bodies never really stop being our mothers' bodies. In the bath, I trace my fingers along the lines of myself like a person following a river to its source. When I laugh like her or when I'm mean like her or when I go cold and distant like her, I can feel her lingering, ready to claim what is hers and has always been hers.

If her body could betray her, my body could certainly betray me. There are certain risk factors. I grew up in a family of smokers and breathed secondhand smoke every day for eighteen years. I now have a family history because cancer has slammed into my life like an asteroid striking the earth, leaving behind a crater where my mother once stood. I live in an urban area and breathe the particulate that accumulates in such places. I do not have my mother's chronic cough, but the summer of her diagnosis, we had very similar symptoms: painful swallowing, trouble breathing, sensitivity to acids and cold liquids. There was a moment, fleeting as these moments often are, when I thought the worst, when I feared the absolute worst. But the moment passed—for me.

A MONTH BEFORE MY MOTHER DIED, I GOT ON A PLANE AND went down to Alabama. I had been told that this would bring some measure of peace to her, but in retrospect, I can't help but to think of how cruel a thing it was to do. After all, when she saw me and I saw her, we wouldn't be able to hide from the fact that the whole thing was ending. There is a kind of magic to distance. As long as I stayed away, she could go on thinking that things weren't as bad as they were, and I could go on thinking that I was doing something good for her by doing nothing, by not talking about it or seeing it.

My uncle was having a birthday barbecue in the middle of August, and by some random chance, the party fell on the third day of my five-day trip. My mother was very tired. She found my presence irritating, which was flattering in a way—she wasn't putting on a show of wanting me around. I thought to myself that things might not be so bad after all. At least she wasn't trying to love on me as she had started to do with my brother.

There were a lot of white gnats fluttering in the air like

snowflakes with their own minds, so many of them pouring out of the pecan trees that the food had to be whisked directly from the grill and into the house. I was given the task of standing behind my mother and waving away the bugs from her. She leaned forward in her chair, swaying occasionally if she heard a song that she liked or felt a rhythm that moved her. People kept stopping by her chair to say a kind word to her on their way to grab beers from the cooler. She was loved by them.

I stood behind her for about half an hour, and then I went up the back stairs to use the bathroom in my grandmother's house. I needed to be away from her and done with the impossibly tender act of fanning white gnats from her cropped hair. I stuck my head in the fridge and counted to ten, letting the cool air settle against my face and neck. Two of my young cousins came bounding into the house, laughing. They saw me, waved, and went directly to the back room. I leaned back against the fridge and closed my eyes. The air was so warm, so thick. It was a miserable day for a party. The music was loud—a kind of up-tempo blues—and omnipresent. I looked through the back door down the long stairs and saw my mother surrounded by her sisters and some of our distant cousins. It was familiar to me, this act of looking on from the back stairs. When I was younger, I used to do it all of the time with my cousins when we were banished from the party as the sun went down. "Grown folks only," our mothers said, shooing us into the house. "Go play."

How strange to be back there. How strange to be watching it all unfold from a distance. I was grown now, wasn't I? I was old enough to join them, to be among the adults and to bear their burdens. When I was little, all I ever wanted was to be down there dancing with them, laughing and talking to them as equals, and now that I had permission, which is to say that I had grown past the age of needing to ask permission, all I wanted to do was sit in the house and not have to fan bugs from my mother's hair.

I saw someone pick up the small hand towel I had been using. They looked around in confusion. It was my aunt Arleane, the mean one with the waspy hand and stinging pinches. She'd turn me inside out if she caught me. So I took another breath and pushed open the door and descended the stairs. She met me at the bottom with a firm look.

"Bathroom," I said. She popped my thigh with the towel and pointed me back to my mother.

"Get," she said.

There is a picture of my mother at this party. She's flanked by relatives, peace signs up, smiling. It was the first time I realized that death had brought out in her an almost uncanny resemblance to my brother and my grandfather. Someone uploaded this picture to my mother's Facebook wall, and on the day she died, people streamed in to say how terribly sorry and sad they were that she was gone.

I didn't say anything on social media, though relatives tried to tag me in supportive status updates, which I did my best to untag myself from. I didn't want to be a part of their mourning. I didn't want to be involved in someone else's grief when I knew so little about how to deal with my own.

MY BROTHER'S WIFE RECENTLY POSTED A VIDEO OF MY brother crying at our mother's grave. He was in a low crouch over the plain gray slab, his hand pressed against it for balance. He was wearing glasses that he must have purchased from the drugstore because he's never been to an eye doctor in his life. There was the argyle sweater vest and lilac button-down shirt of some kind, and ugly brown slacks, and huge shoes. Sunday clothes. Crying on a grainy, blurry video taken with a cheap to-go phone down in Alabama, crying like a baby, crying like someone full of softness and heart. The audio crackled, broke open, and his crying turned to a soft wail, and then the video shut off.

I do not know what to do with such mourning or such grief. The world in which my brother is not only moved to emotion but to open tears at the grave of our mother is a world that I don't know how I came to inhabit. Watching the video, I felt as if I had slipped out of my life and into some gray replica tucked behind the real thing, a life glimpsed at the corner of the eye, where anything is possible.

CANCER IS A DISEASE OF PROLIFERATION, A DISEASE OF ABUN-dance. The body consumes itself to make cancer cells, so in one sense, it is a disease of success run wild, turning to ruin. I feel a measure of pain for my cousin as she watches her father, W., die in this way. My cousin and I were brought up together; my father watched her while my aunt worked, and we spent almost every moment of every day in each other's company. Before she was born, I was the baby of the family, and so her mother had doted and loved on me. Sometimes it felt as though we shared a mother and a father, though our parents were brother and sister. In a way, my cousin is my little sister. But she has her own father, and I my own mother, dying and dead, respectively. I check her social media pages frequently for updates on her father, and though I am not sorry he is dying, it hurts to watch her suffer and grieve.

When I moved away from home to go to college, I spoke to my parents once every two months because it was all I could bear. The shape of our conversation was the same every time: hello, yes, how are you, fine, guess who died. It was a never-ending stream of names, some old, some not, but all mostly too young to have died. Second cousins, third cousins, neighbors, friends of my parents, each passing out of this world and into whatever hangs behind this world like a second eyelid.

My mother was placed on a ventilator, and later I was alerted via text message that she had died. I don't mean to imply that I feel angry about this. It was by choice that I refused to speak on the phone to people who thought I needed comfort. The text message was from another cousin, a different cousin, not the daughter of my rapist. I found out my grandfather died by browsing Facebook one morning before a biochemistry exam. I imagine I'll find out that W. died via

Facebook—it must be what I keep looking for, that final update, that final confirmation that he is gone out of the world.

SOMETIMES I WONDER IF MY COUSIN KNOWS THAT I AM HANGing around her Facebook like a ghost, like a fiend. Technology lets us believe we are living parallel lives, both in and out of the world, both here and there. I can skim the facts of other people's lives from their posts like foam from boiled milk.

How many people, when my mother died, came to my page to wish me love and light? How many returned time and again looking for some clue of my pain or anguish or grief? Isn't that what we do? We scent a tragedy in the air and we try to trace it—not to its source, but to those most affected. We try to make sense of it by watching them grapple with it. In this way, we aren't living parallel lives at all. We're leeches, proliferating in a still pool of light. Spectating isn't living, after all; it's consumption. Grist for the mill.

Yet I cannot look away from my cousin's page. There is a point at which the glimpsed becomes the central, becomes the whole of the thing. I turn my head and look, I stare because I know how to watch a person wither from abundance. I know how to read status updates like a person reads the air to discern the chance of rain. There are the upbeat messages, the ones about the fight: At chemo with this guy! He's so strong! He's a fighter! When things are looking grim, there are more vague messages about God and the meaningfulness of His plan: God will always make a way! It's not over until God says it's over!

I find it difficult to imagine how anyone could even feign sadness at W.'s state, though to understand I need only look back at my journals from the time that my mother was sick. It's not that I was mournful or sad exactly, but rather that I didn't want her to die. I wanted her to go on living in the strictest sense of the word; to be standing on this side of death, not even perfectly healed, just not dead. And if I could come to such a place with my own mother, who was in every way poorly suited for the task of motherhood, then I suppose it need not be impossible to imagine that W. could have people in his life, like his daughter, who want him to live.

My brother once called me a hard person. I think he meant that I am a person who does not forgive. This is true. I find it difficult to forgive people who have done harm to me. I am this way out of necessity, because if I do not remember the harm done to me, then no one will, and the boy that I was will have no one to look out for him. If I do not remember and do not hold people accountable for that boy's pain, then no one will remember it, and no one will remember that it was not acceptable for him to be treated that way. If I forgive all of the things done to me, done to the boy that I was, then I will betray everything I promised that boy when we endured those things. The only way through all of it was to promise that I would remember it and that at some point, I would make it known what happened there.

I am a hard person because hardness is what comes from a life lived underground. The hard part of me would like nothing more than to keep refreshing, waiting for the moment when my cousin's grief is obvious and clear, because that will mean that I no longer have to live my life like a clenched fist. At the same time, the fact that my freedom can come only with my cousin's suffering is something nearly unbearable to me. Spectating isn't free. No one gets something for nothing.

The Sun

Emma Smith-Stevens

MY CHILDHOOD HAD BEEN FED TO ME LIKE RANCID MEAT. I was forced to swallow it down, gagging until I vomited. But I was not raped.

There had been a guy in his twenties who scanned my thirteen-year-old body, all Manhattan rooftop-tan and a tiny silver bikini, and said, "How old are you?" And I said "Old enough," and he laughed and said "You're some pretty little jailbait," and he never laid a finger on me. By that point, I had been hurt when men touched me. But this hurt, too, when he turned me down. The truth is I should have been glad—it would have been wrong for him to touch me.

In junior high school, I had been the confidante of the forty-year-old manager of a neighborhood restaurant who said I was the only one who understood his sexual problems with his wife, which he detailed to me explicitly. But to his credit, between his sordid confessions, he taught me a lot about chess.

I had loved a boy, once, and he had dumped me just a week after I went down on him for the first time. But I had felt so fortunate that he had ever wanted me at all.

I gave a blow job to a boy I'd crushed on for a year, in a shed in the alley behind our high school. A few days later, he started hooking up with one of my best friends. But at least, before he ditched me, he smiled dreamily and said, "Wow. Thank you. That is the nicest thing anyone's ever done for me."

That is how I became the patron saint of blow jobs—and isn't that divine?

The previous summer I'd given a blow job to a man in his late thirties, putrid and wearing a wedding ring, in the back of a city bus. He had bought me beer, and I drank it. Later, he pushed my head down into his lap, and I had surrendered to the moment. If what that man did strikes you as wrong, let me reassure you the way I reassured myself: the marriage was only for his wife's citizenship, we were coworkers, and I had acquiesced at every turn—no hesitation or complaint.

I had loved girls to whom I was nothing more than an experiment. But weren't they my experiments, too?

Sophomore year, I had been invited to a birthday party by the hottest guy in my homeroom, and the party had turned out to be five guys watching porn, and me, just me. I quickly downed four or five shots of vodka and thought *Okay, let's cut to the chase, let's not let this be a group activity.* So I took one boy's hand, the one who had invited me, and led him to the bathroom and fucked him so hard on the tile floor, no condom, and later his friends taunted me ("Whore!" "Slut!"). In school the next week, that boy wouldn't speak to me or look me in the eye. But at least I didn't get pregnant or catch anything.

So many times my mind left my body only to return to find it soiled—the foul residue of a grown man, or a boy from my high school, or the grime of a full week without showering. But I had never told anyone no, let alone tried to fight anyone off. I had said, "Yes, give me more," moaned like in a porno.

I could have refused or washed it all away—options not every girl is afforded.

I was hospitalized the fall of my senior year. Maybe it was my third psychiatric hospitalization. Or my fifth or sixth. Whatever the number, it was nothing. There were kids in the adolescent unit with me who had been in and out a dozen times.

My psychiatrist in that hospital, a bearded man in a plaid shirt and khakis, explained my situation to me. "You cut, you burn, you disassociate," he said. "Classic Borderline." And when I told him that I didn't relate to the pamphlet they'd given me about Borderline Personality Disorder, he said: "Listen. This diagnosis is best-case scenario for you. So much better than Bipolar Disorder. Trust me, kid." So I was lucky. Therapy could fix me.

(A few months later, I would be diagnosed with Bipolar I Disorder with psychotic features, be properly medicated, and have my first glimpse of sanity since I was twelve years old. At least I made it to that point. Many people never get properly diagnosed. And people with my illness living just a few decades before me were routinely lobotomized.)

The doctor in that hospital was right about some things. I cut, I burned, my head took me somewhere else—not so much another world as a terrifying version of this one, filled with morbid scenes and demonic voices. Sometimes I lashed out at myself and other people. And who was I to do that? What right did I have?

So the hospital doctor gave me a book about Borderline Personality Disorder to read. He told me to record all my thoughts and feelings in a journal, stop being defensive in group therapy sessions, and I would be okay. But he offered no explanation for my hallucinations and sleeplessness and my sense of unreality, for which I took high doses of antipsychotic medication. Maybe he thought I just liked the drugs, that I enjoyed taking tiny, shuffling steps, and the way my hands shook. If I stood up too quickly, I passed out—a side effect. I slurred. I drooled. My intellect was drowned in the infinite numbness. Thank goodness I wouldn't need to take medication forever, so said my doctor and the pamphlet he had gifted me.

How blessed I was to be in such a good place—a fancy mental hospital. It had grounds with old trees and well-tended shrubbery. A gazebo. The food was edible. All kinds of therapy. Twelve-step meetings. Cigarette breaks whenever. We had a big TV with cable, always tuned to MTV, and this was back when MTV showed music videos. I had been in hospitals before where I hadn't been outside for weeks and all anyone watched was soap operas.

Two guys were always in control of the TV remote. Let's call them A and B. Both were eighteen years old. They weren't psychiatric patients; they were in the hospital for heroin addiction. They loved the band Korn who had a hit song then, "Falling Away from Me." A and B watched the music video for "Falling Away from Me" over and over, turning up the volume whenever it came on.

In the video, a raging father in a stained wifebeater bangs his fist on his young daughter's door late at night, and the terrified girl climbs out her bedroom window and runs away—running, clearly, for her life. Thank God the girl makes it out alive.

The video reminded me of something really upsetting, something I couldn't quite focus on for fear that I would die if I saw it head-on. But I know this for sure: the threatening memory had nothing to do with my own father. Unlike the father in the video, my father was—and is—a kind and gentle man.

One afternoon, the Korn video was playing, the music seeping into the background of my mind, where everything went in those days—the news, the weather, the people who loved me, my physical movements, my emotions, the college application essay I was expected to be writing during my time in that hospital. All the stuff of life—my life—reminded me of the song's title. The video was no more near or far than my own hand, the filthy couch I sat on, the cuts I made on my breasts where the techs never checked, the November leaves I could see out the window, brown and crumbling. The medications made everything that way: here and not-here. But again, I was told I wouldn't need them forever. Borderline, not Bipolar—blessed by my DNA.

I looked at A, skinny and tall with a shaved, narrow head. B was bloated, pale, acned, smelled perpetually of fried food. I floated above myself. The music thrashing from the TV was muffled—the chair I sat in was orbiting space. I appraised my desire to kick my foot through its screen without feeling a thing.

"Wanna fuck?" I whispered to A. A looked at B, and then at the two doorways to the room we were in. There were no techs visible, but they could be listening. "I dunno," he said. He looked nervous. "I don't think so." Then he turned to B. "Do you wanna fuck her?" "Hell yeah," said B. "Let's do this." I had huge pupils, cottonmouth, hairy legs, greasy hair. A and B had called the way I walked "the Thorazine shuffle," laughing. "Living dead girl" was a nickname they'd assigned me, a stolen lyric from some other song.

I followed B up the carpeted stairs, past the meds window, which was closed and locked between meds times, and into a little bathroom. He switched on the lights. I hadn't contemplated the literal meaning of the word *fuck* until he began unzipping his skater-boy jeans. "Fuck" meant his cock—short and thick, already hard—was going to be inside my body.

It wouldn't be at all like the last time I'd fucked, which had been with my boyfriend who was so sweet and always worried about me and had made me a mix CD for the hospital. This time "fuck" meant pain. My pussy was as dry as my mouth. The matter of choice did not occur to me. I was so numb. I was on the ceiling. The Beatles' "Here Comes the Sun," one of the songs on the mix CD my boyfriend had sent with me, played in my head.

B sat down cross-legged on the bathroom floor and I knelt beside him. He took my face in his hands, lowered it down, and I choked. The song's sweet melody filled my mind. I tried not to breathe through my nose. My heartbeat was so slow. Living dead girl.

"Spit on it," said B. "I can't," I said. The meds—I had no saliva. "Okay, get on top," he said. I was looking for a word, but it was so far away, locked in an ancient memory: a health class in junior high school, the aisle of a drugstore, behind the counter of a bodega. "Condom." I remembered it as I said it.

B sighed, pulled a wallet from his pocket, and removed a Trojan. He tore the blue wrapper, which was worn soft around the edges and showed some tears. The latex inside was brittle and split when he tried to roll it on. At least he hadn't refused.

I got on top. I coached myself through every movement: up, down, up, down. "Here Comes the Sun" was building toward the chorus. B moaned, grabbed my hair, pulled my ear to his lips. "I've got AIDS," he said, in a soft, rough voice. And then those reassuring lyrics arrived: my time in the sunlight was almost here. He came inside me, stood and zipped up, left me to clean myself.

I thought: what a trick we had pulled, what a miracle not to have been caught. The chorus's vocals came to an end—and then that pretty riff.

Over the next two days, underneath all the blur of medication, fear piled up in me. It started low in my stomach and gradually stacked up to my throat. I don't remember anything about that period other than the feeling of choking. Then B was discharged from the hospital. As soon as he was gone, I went to the meds nurse, who was young and had a kind voice. "I had sex with him," I said, "and he has AIDS."

She looked horrified. She made me repeat myself. She asked me where I'd done it, and when, and I told her the answers. "Did you use a condom?" she asked. She was wringing her hands. I noticed she was engaged. The diamond on her ring glittered so many colors—too many colors. The brilliance of it stirred panic in me, the first sharp feeling I'd had in weeks. "Sort of," I said. I tried to explain, but she was frustrated. I worried B might get in trouble. "What is *sort of*?" She sounded frantic. I thought: *she hates me*. "I tried to use one," I said. It was the truth—I really had tried.

HIV test, STD test, pregnancy test, calls to my parents, who showed up. We all met with my doctor, who said that the circumstances transcended matters of confidentiality, and he had examined B's medical records. "He is HIV negative," he said. My mother wept with relief, and my father wrapped his arm around her.

All eyes turned to me. I felt required to display an emotion. But all I felt was fuzz filling up my skull, like the filter of a clothes dryer accumulating lint, cycle after cycle. "You are not at risk," said the doctor. "You are HIV negative. But that does not reduce the seriousness of what you've done. Do you understand?" I nodded. "We're going to need you to sign a contract."

I nodded. I'd already signed one promising not to cut myself. Signing my name—I could do that.

"And you will reflect on your behavior and the tremendous danger you put yourself in," he added, "and the suffering you have caused to the people who care about you." I looked at my parents and they looked away. Their faces showed disgust and anger, and fear, most of all. As though looking at me might provoke me, might incite me, like I was a dangerous animal. There were plenty of kids—those less fortunate than I—whose parents wouldn't have cared less.

My parents left the hospital. I was given a pencil, a legal pad, and a list of questions:

Why had I acted out sexually?
What consequences could I have experienced?
What consequences did my actions have for other
    people?
What patterns of promiscuity do I see in my life?
What drives me to be promiscuous?

After answering these questions, I was to write a contract stating that I would no longer engage in sexual behavior at the hospital and sign it. I held the pad and pencil in my hand as a frowning social worker led me to the Quiet Room. It was a tiny, square room where the floors and walls were padded with blue plastic mats. The door locked from the outside. I might have been overwhelmed by claustrophobia in there, but mercifully the door had a small, square window.

The lock to the Quiet Room clicked shut. I sat down and stared at the questions. I put the pad and pencil down on the mat and lay on my back. Above me, two fluorescent lights flickered. I closed my eyes but I could still see the flickering inside my eyelids.

I had no idea how to answer the questions. They seemed to be written in a foreign language. They seemed to pertain to someone else. They seemed like riddles. Fuck that.

The purpose of the Quiet Room, as explained to me by a nurse when I had first been admitted, was to give patients a safe space to calm down if they needed it. I was calm. Most of the patients saw the Quiet Room as punishment. I did feel punished, but that was fine. The mat I lay on smelled like Lysol. I rolled my body up against the door so I couldn't be seen through the window.

I was invisible. I was alone. Nobody could touch me. The room was absolutely silent. Finally, so was I.

Sixty-Three Days

AJ McKenna

It has been sixty-three days since I stopped making excuses for you.

Since I stopped telling this exclusively as a story about my gender dysphoria.

Since I shifted my focus from the fact that you stopped when I screamed, to the fact that you started at all.

Sixty-three days.

What does it say about me that I wish I could go back? Not to before it happened, though of course I wish for that. But I have gotten used to compromise, to settling for less. I would settle for going back to the way I felt sixty-four days ago. I feel weak for saying this, but I would.

I know the strong thing to say is that it is better to admit what it was than to hide from it completely, the way I did for thirteen years. To say that I am facing up to it at last, and that this is a good thing. But I am not strong, and honestly? I resent having to face up to it. I resent having to be a survivor.

"Survivor" is the "special needs" of victimhood. If I say I have survived, I'm fooling nobody. I didn't.

My friends—those who have seen me change over the past five years, seen my body alter from the effects of hormones, and seen me get better at doing my makeup and appearing more confident in how I walk through the world—call me fierce, and I hate the word, partly because it's such a stupid, drag queen cliché, but also because I know just how much it is a lie.

There was nothing fierce about the way I screamed in that room, thirteen years ago, when you refused to listen to me telling you I didn't want your lips around the part of me that I hate to name. There was nothing fierce in my unresponsiveness or in the way I held on to the fact that you did finally stop when I screamed as proof that you hadn't assaulted me.

There was nothing fierce in the way I broke down for the first time sixty-three days ago.

Six days ago on the train, I read an article about men who fetishize women with penises. I closed my eyes against the memory, and when I came to, three-quarters of an hour had passed and, although I had not slept and had not dreamed and had not meditated, I could not tell you what my thoughts had been in all that time besides the one: You made me an object. I was not a person to you, in that moment. I was at best a challenge, an unresponsive organ, a stubborn body.

Twelve years and six months ago, the first girlfriend I had after what you did told me she liked my solid presence in her bed, and this made me feel sad because I never thought of my-self as the strong one. It was always her who had been strong, who had made me feel safe, from the moment at the end of her party when she asked me "May I kiss you inappropriately?"

And I asked her why it would be inappropriate, and she said something about her age and the disparity of social capi-tal between us and how asking it might seem like she'd invited me over just to get off with me and I said that I wouldn't think it inappropriate at all.

And she kissed me, and we slid to the floor of her flat and coiled around each other like the figures in a Francis Bacon triptych for what seemed like hours. I was no more physi-cally responsive to her than I was to you, not the way you demanded. She did not see this as a challenge. She did the things you didn't think of doing. She ran her fingers up and down my back, she touched my hair, she kissed me, bit my nipples, ignored the part of me I hate to name. And when we were done, when we had explored enough and the vodka her Russian friends had brought began to catch up with us, she kissed me good night and went to bed alone. I didn't have to sleep beside her the way I had with you after you stopped, after you told me I could please myself and turned away.

Yes, I slept beside you afterward. Another entry in the case for the defense. Like the fact that I asked you, to start with, made a fool of myself saying how attracted I was to you, how much I liked you, how much it would mean for you to be my first.

Well, I was right about that. It meant a lot. Still does.

How would I explain, in court, that I spent the whole time

terrified of what I'd have to do? That I worked so hard to get you off without the part I hate to name because I didn't want to be reminded what they said my body was, how safe I felt when your skin flushed and you threw your head back from just the touch of my fingers and I thought, *Thank God, I won't have to.*

How could I tell a jury how frightened I was when you said, "Okay. Now you?"

She didn't make me better, the one who came after you. But because I loved her, I found ways around the pain, around the memory. Ways to penetrate that felt, to me, like being entered. I never told her that was what I was doing. I never told her what you did.

I was pretending what you did was not what you had done. That it said more about me than it did about you. That your stopping when I had to scream was kindness.

That was how I described it when I told the woman I would marry, who I would live with for six years. Six years of finding ways around the problem, which I did because I loved her.

How much of the problem is my gender dysphoria and how much of it is the result of the trauma you inflicted? I sometimes wonder if you could ever understand what you did. How your lips and your fingers, the anger in your eyes, made what should have been a pleasure ground a contaminated site? I don't know. I didn't, until sixty-three days ago.

Forty-one days ago I took a transgender man I know to a hotel I was reviewing. We talked, over crab and pork belly, about friends we knew who are poly, about the couples I'm a secondary to and how I feel this suits me. Over cocktails in the bar we talked about relationship anarchy.

Over wine in the hotel room, as we leaned out of our balcony window, I turned to him and asked him, clumsily, if it would be okay if I kissed him? And he told me he had wanted to kiss me for ages. And we kissed, drunk and stoned, clumsily, and found our way to the bed and it didn't solve anything.

In the morning he seemed distant and impatient to get home, and I wondered if this was because I hadn't shared as much as he had in that bed. Because he let me touch the parts of him I would have had a problem naming, while I kept my briefs on the whole time.

Since sixty-three days ago, there is no way around the problem for me. When someone touches it, the part of me I hate to name, I do not see my former wife, I do not recall the way the woman who came after you touched me, I remember how you grabbed me, how you told me that you wouldn't normally do this and opened your mouth, and your anger and incomprehension when I screamed.

Sixty-four days ago I would have found a way around that.

I believe in relationship anarchy because of what you did to me. Because of what Donald Winnicott called *cathexis*. To cathect is to invest, emotionally, libidinally, in hope of reward. Because of what you did, I cannot do this, because it is how you treated me: as someone who would reward you by responding the same way as the men you were used to. When I tell people this, I never know if I am making sense. All I know is that I cannot treat the people that I love as things I take from, that I can see sex only as a process of surrender. But there are parts of me I hoard, parts of me I will not give away, nor sell at any price, because you tried to steal them.

Twenty-eight days ago, at a party at my apartment, I kissed a trans woman I barely knew, and she kissed me better than anyone has in my life, better than the woman who came after you, better than my wife, and this may have been because I was on molly but the way she touched my back was heavenly and she solved nothing. I still fall asleep feeling broken. I still come to with no memory of where the past hour has gone when I read or see something that makes me remember. I still see no way I can live with this.

I still wish it was sixty-four days ago.

Two hours ago, halfway through writing this, I bought a dime bag of weed for the first time since I was a student. I asked my housemate what hours her dealer kept, and she went out to score. I've done a lot of drugs I haven't done before in these sixty-three days—MDMA and speed and laughing gas—and a lot I've done before—poppers, weed, and booze. Oh, so much booze. And that solves nothing either but I don't expect it to. I expect it to help me to sleep. I've been taking codeine, too. I say it's for the headaches.

I have done my research. I have scrolled down the list of porn clips that come up when you type the words *lesbian* and *rape* into Google. I have read about the women in the Congo who collude in, sometimes lead, the rape of captives. I have read the interviews with Justine Chang and Armand Kaye, who made the documentary *She Stole My Voice* about rape in lesbian communities, but haven't managed to bring myself to watch the film. I have read the articles that give the statistics, that explain why even these are inadequate, I have talked to women who've been shouted down for talking about violence in queer women's relationships, with trans women who've been raped by cisgender women at gunpoint. I have listened to one of my best friends tell me she is beginning to think she is "just the kind of person this stuff happens to" and I have told her she is not, that what happened *to* her says nothing *about* her, and I have felt like a hypocrite because I do not believe the same thing about myself.

I screamed and begged for you to stop, but I almost wish that you had hit me, had blackened my eyes or knocked out a few teeth, because it would mean that I fought back instead of begging.

I have looked for counseling and given up on that. Two days ago, I walked into my doctor's surgery to talk about my anemia and I fully intended to tell her about you and ask for some kind of referral, or even just something to help me sleep, some legal drug that I would almost never mix with any of the others, but she said "You don't look your usual self" when I walked through the door and I lost my nerve. I told her about the cough I've had the past few days, how I'm worried that I might have pneumonia again, and when she told me to stand so she could listen to my chest I panicked and asked how much of my clothes I'd have to take off, whether I could stop at my shirt or would have to take off my vest too, felt embarrassed about the suspenders that held up my jeans.

I have been butching up more when I go outside, these last few days. I used to do it for long journeys, but now I feel I need to do it just to go to town. I wouldn't say it makes me feel strong exactly, but it makes good camouflage.

I know this, too, won't solve anything. If writing about you was going to make everything right, then I'd be right by now. In the past sixty-four days I've barely written about anything other than you. I've written blogs and poems, half of a one-woman show, tweets at three in the morning that I deleted when I woke up at seven. You have become my cottage industry and, although I hate the thought of that, I sat at my desk with my mobile phone propped against my aging, web-camless laptop and told you, wherever you are, that:

Sometimes I call you my rapist,
and that feels wrong somehow,
but I cannot keep saying "the woman who raped me"
every time I mention you,
and cannot say your name
because

I only know your first name anyway,
and in saying even that I turn accuser
and am too aware how easily my case could be undone,

an accuser who'd been drinking when it happened;
an accuser who'd consented, at the start;
an accuser who, at the time, was presenting as male:
an accuser who'd be bound to fail, in court.

So I, out of need for variation, name you mine:
My rapist. It feels wrong. Too intimate
somehow, suggests collusion, a joint enterprise
between us. "It takes two,"
they say. "Two, babe: me. You."

It smacks of going steady and those creepy '50s love songs:
Every night, I hope and pray
this fear will go away,

but I cannot say your name, and
the woman who raped me sounds clunky and anyway
is legally someone who can't exist:
English law defines rape as an act
committed only by the male. It's sexual assault
when women do it. As if the two are easily distinguished,
but the woman who sexually assaulted me
is clunkier still than the woman the law calls impossible,

so, sometimes, you are my rapist,
and I wonder if, in some sense, that is true:
was I the only one? You seemed surprised
that I said no. Was it shock that spurred you on
as much as malice? Or instead of it?
And do I want that? Does it make you better,
or me special, if it was only the once?

It doesn't matter if I'm one or one of many.
I may call you my rapist but we know that isn't true.

Whatever law or rumor says, whoever else there was,
you were never mine. You were the rapist I ran into

And I thought *This, this is the one that solves it*, but it didn't. Nothing ever does.

For the past sixty-three days I have tried to solve this, with drugs, with lovers, with words. And nothing has done it yet, and I am beginning to think nothing will.

It's twenty-seven minutes past six as I type this. If I can stay up a little over five hours, I can say it's been sixty-four days.

And I will wish it was sixty-five days ago.

Only the Lonely

LISA MECHAM

THE WOMEN AND I DREW NUMBERS AND TOOK TURNS fetching gifts from under the Christmas tree, opening them one by one, showing all what we'd unwrapped. I was thrilled to be invited to this holiday gathering, joining the PTO president, the head of the Women's Auxiliary, all the movers and shakers on the home front of this rural, sophisticated Connecticut town. My husband, two children, and I had just moved to Weston earlier that summer, so to be included felt good.

I was one of the last to go and when it came to my turn, I chose a small square package, unwrapping it to reveal a silky scarf. Everyone sighed longingly as I held it up between outstretched arms. I feigned excitement as the gift made me anxious; I'd seen others wear scarves like this draped casually, so effortlessly across their shoulders. I wasn't even sure I had anything to wear with it.

The last woman to go grabbed her gift from under the tree and the room exploded with laughter as she unwrapped it and held it high, among the plush-covered chairs and gold-framed art, for all to see. A giant. Purple. Dick.

THE PARTY WAS CALLED A YANKEE SWAP AND IT WAS HELD IN the meticulously decorated living room of a woman whose husband was a Wall Street banker. To participate, we'd each been instructed to bring a wrapped present, a funny "gag" gift or serious luxury item, or anything in between. At this point, we were all three white wineglasses to the wind, but still it surprised me, how much I was drawn to the vibrator. How I felt this overwhelming impulse to rescue it from public shaming.

So before the laughter subsided, I stood up and grabbed the vibrator out of the woman's hand.

I . . . I have a friend who would love this, I said.

The room went dead.

And this would look so much better on you! In a grand comedic gesture, I threw the delicate scarf up in the air so it would flutter down upon the woman's lap. But it missed and slumped to the floor.

Odd glances, weak smiles. Dinner was served.

UP UNTIL THAT MOMENT, I'D NEVER HELD A VIBRATOR IN MY hand and had rarely seen one in action. Once, in college, I'd walked in on some guys in my boyfriend's fraternity communally watching porn. Seven guys in a darkened room, scattered on chairs and couches and the floor, staring at the hot glare of the television screen where an overly hairy guy said, *Come on, baby. You know you love it, baby* while he jammed a dildo as long as his forearm into the asshole of a woman bent over a table. Her moan low, interspersed with piercing cries that did not sound like pleasure.

But at the holiday party, amid all its contained civilization, the vibrator felt like the most powerful object in the room.

After dinner, the women gathered in yet another part of the grand home and poured more wine. I was ready to leave, still embarrassed by my unexpected snatch of this gift. So I excused myself, lamenting the fact that I had no purse, no place to stow the vibrator. Laughter followed me as I left the room.

Hope your friend enjoys that!

I FLIPPED ON THE LIGHT IN THE DARKENED KITCHEN AND SAW one of the husbands standing there, leaning against the counter. I knew him a bit, had talked to him when stuck in the corner at a school function. He was an important man— you could tell this by the way the other men deferred to him. A money guy. A hedge fund guy.

He was drinking—etched glass in hand, filled with an inch of golden liquor. I stopped in my tracks, surprised to see him. There'd been no shout of *Honey, I'm home!*

He didn't say anything; the room was still save for the

motion of his wrist swirling, swirling, swirling the drink around.

A muted shriek of laughter. The women far away on the other side of the house.

Fun party? he asked. He brought the drink to his lips and swallowed it, greedily, in one gulp, eyes on mine.

Oh, yeah, I said. *Look what I picked.* I held up the vibrator.

He walked toward me, blocking my path around the counter. My nose tingled from all that liquor on his breath.

He put the glass down and raised his hand to my collarbone, exposed by the fancy top I'd bought to wear to the party. Dragging his finger from one shoulder, across my throat, to the other.

I want to lick you.

HIS FACE INCHES FROM MINE, CHARGED AIR WHERE OUR mouths might meet. My body's wired response to being wanted by a man so sure of his place in the world.

Like all those boys, watching the woman bent over the table. Her face screwed up in the pain of performance. Tongues darting around their mouths.

I moved past him to the pile of coats on the table, searching for mine as I felt him approach from behind. I wanted to shout, *Get someone else in the room.* But this man, he was power. And me? I was the new girl in town who'd snatched a sex toy out of another woman's hand.

Instead, I turned to face him, placing the packaged device between my thighs, pressing them together, holding it there while I put one arm through my coat, then the other. I pulled the vibrator from between my legs and turned to leave.

Be careful, he hissed, *if you use that too much, your clit will go numb.*

But I was out the back door. Fumbling through the dark, across the expansive property, to the long gravel driveway, to the safety of my car.

At home, I stashed the vibrator way in the back of my underwear drawer.

In Connecticut, I had long stretches of the day to myself. The school bus would come at dawn to pick up my daughters. And my husband always left early for his long commute to work.

It didn't feel right, liberating the vibrator from the drawer in the harsh morning light, but that's what I did, the first Monday after I'd plucked it out of the hands of the woman at the party.

I extricated it from the complicated plastic wrapping. It was bright purple, with sparkles, about six inches long. I had no idea if this was considered a normal-sized vibrator but it was certainly less intimidating than the one I'd seen in the porn long ago. I inserted two batteries and turned it on to the first setting. A slight pulsing. Next setting, more. On the final setting, the vibrator gave off a sound like my neighbor mowing his lawn. I dropped it on the floor and watched it buzz its way under my bed.

What was I doing? All of this, ludicrous. Purple, my younger daughter's favorite color. The drone of it under my bed reminded me of all those women, laughing at me at the party.

I wrestled my way under the bed. Balls of dust and fluff clung to the vibrator's shaft like stubborn pubic hair. I turned it off and thrust it back into my drawer again.

MONTHS LATER. SPRING. BUS CAME. HUSBAND LEFT FOR work. There were school functions and the random dinner party but I couldn't decipher the terms of female friendship in this town. Solitude is one thing but this was a particular kind of lonely, the kind you don't expect when you've checked off the boxes of living a lucky life. All smiles at events, but then, no follow-through. Maybe, I thought, my middle-class midwestern roots were showing—I was an imposter without the financial assets to dilly-dally in elite country clubs and vacation homes.

I was weeding old clothes out of my drawers when I found the vibrator. Still purple, still sparkly. I turned it on. The batteries still worked.

I removed my clothes and lay on the bed. The breeze from the open window was sharp and my nipples grew hard.

Alone in the house, I imagined my husband, how we used to make love. How he'd say, so gently, *You can come again. I know you can.* And he'd give me that gift.

And now, how I couldn't stand to kiss him. He tasted like copper in my mouth. Intimacy replaced by something far more desperate. He'd been staying up late, unable to sleep. His speech, fast and hard, like a train with no destination.

It scared me.

Instead of sex, I'd pull off his pants. How he'd be so hard, which always surprised me because we'd done nothing to get to that point. He was always ready. How he'd put his hand on my head and move me. I contributed nothing but an open cavity.

As I rubbed my nipple lightly with a finger, pleasure rippled through my body, a feeling I'd not had in months. I turned the vibrator on and spread my legs. But it was awkward. I didn't know whether to put it in me or on me.

All I felt was a deadening throb.

your clit will go numb

That hairy man behind. The dildo jamming again and again into the woman's gaping hole.

I turned the vibrator off.

In the wake of its buzz, an aching silence. It was so quiet in Connecticut. Cars rarely passed our house. No sidewalks. Trees competing for open sky.

I closed my eyes and laid the vibrator on my belly, crossing my hands over it.

It's hard to tell people when something is wrong. Hard to whisper, out loud, that your husband might be going crazy. Because maybe it's not him, it's you. The woman married to the bright, young doctor. The woman with two beautiful daughters and two acres of land and two cars.

The woman at the party who grabbed the vibrator.

I came out the front door, wrapped in my bathrobe, vibrator in hand. In front of our house a doe stood, head raised to the branches of a laurel tree, pulling off leathery leaves with her teeth. She skittered off as I made my way into the yard.

It felt good to be outdoors. How desperately I longed for the seasons to turn. Animals, plants, the land—they demanded nothing from me. For once I was glad our house was set back from the road, surrounded by a dense cover of trees. No one could see me out here.

I turned my back on our worn-out house, the stage of my failure, and walked to the far edge of our property marked with a stone wall. On hands and knees I parted the dead leaves, clawed at the soil with the vibrator's purple tip. The surface was harder than I thought, not yet thawed from the harsh winter, so I stabbed it repeatedly against the earth until the ground broke into chunks, triggering the instrument on.

My digging fingers finished the dirty work. When the hole was deep enough, I dropped it in. That implement. For the lonely, unwanted. I mashed dirt, leaves, sticks, whatever I could find until all that was left was the muffled hum of a buried thing.

I sat back against the wall, and my breath turned to gulps. The fresh smell of turned soil in my throat. And my hands, my hands. I wrapped them around my shins and pulled in tight and cried and thought about how when you're hurt, way before you say it, you have to feel it.

How wounded animals in the woods look for a quiet place. How they stay without moving for days.

What I Told Myself

VANESSA MÁRTIR

I DON'T REMEMBER WHO TOLD ME WHAT HAPPENED TO MY mother, but I think part of me has always known. I knew when she beat me until I was a shivering ball in a corner. I knew when she held a knife to me that time I was five, pleading to her partner Millie, "Dare me and I'll kill this little bitch." She stabbed me repeatedly—not hard enough to break skin but hard enough that it hurt. Hard enough to terrify me. Hard enough to make me think that she really wanted to kill me.

Hard enough to let me know that something had happened to her and she never got over it.

I WAS NINETEEN, A STUDENT AT COLUMBIA UNIVERSITY IN love with a drug dealer from Washington Heights. I found out that night that he'd cheated on me for the umpteenth time, and I didn't want him to touch me, but he still did. I told myself it wasn't rape because we were in a relationship. It wasn't rape because I still loved him. It wasn't rape because I didn't fight him off. It wasn't rape because I stayed with him after. It didn't matter that I kept whispering *no, no, no.* It didn't matter that I sobbed the entire time.

At least I wasn't raped like Mom was, I told myself.

THE FIRST TIME IT HAPPENED TO ME, I WAS SIX. HE WAS MILlie's uncle. Val. I was up in the plum tree of the backyard we shared; I had learned how to climb it the summer before and still had the scars on my legs and scuffs on my sneakers to prove it. I'd go up in that tree whenever I wanted to get away from my mother's cruelty. Up there, I could imagine a different life—one where my mother loved me.

I heard him call my name from his window. When I peeked through the leaves, he was dangling a bag, which he pushed into the sunlight so that I could see it. "I got some *turrón* for ju." I recognized the bag: It was the same pistachio and almond nougat that Millie got for me when we visited the carnivals that went up overnight in the abandoned lots that dotted Bushwick in that era. I wanted that nougat bad.

I looked over at our window, where I could make out Mom's bloated belly—we found out later that year that she had cervical cancer—as she cooked in the kitchen. I could smell dinner: fried chicken with tostones and garlic pounded to a sticky pulp in Mom's straight-from-the-island *pilón*. She was too busy cooking to pay attention to what I was doing.

I climbed down and went into Val's apartment, even though I knew I wasn't supposed to. Mom had lectured my sister and me about staying away from men, though she never explained why. I learned why that day, when Val did what he did to my six-year-old body in his living room, which was an altar to all things Puerto Rico.

I LEFT MY MOTHER'S HOUSE AT THIRTEEN AND I NEVER MOVED back; I had to save my own life. I know now that she couldn't mother me—still can't—because of what happened to her. I don't know the details but I do know this: My mother was raped by her mother's husband when she was just sixteen years old. She hadn't been in this country for six months. She still had Honduran soil under her fingernails. My brother was conceived in that rape my mother was blamed for.

No one really ever talked about it.

THAT EVENING AFTER VAL HURT ME, I SAT IN THE TUB THINK-ing about what happened. It was my fault; I'd gone over to him willingly. Now I understood why Mom had lectured us about wearing shorts underneath our skirts and dresses, buttoning our blouses all the way up, sitting with our legs crossed. Now I understood why Mom beat me that time I'd lingered on Tio Damian's lap, ignoring her dagger eyes. She had caught me that night in the shower and lashed me hard with a thick leather belt. "The next time I see you *en la falda de un hombre*, I'm gonna break your face!"

I lay in the tub and let the hot water run until it singed my skin. I wished Mom had saved me the need to learn the why for myself. I wished she'd told me about what some men do. I wished I'd listened. I knew that I was dirty and disobedient and deserved to be punished.

I started scratching my inner thigh and inched up slowly. I clawed until I bled. Then I cried quietly into my bloody hands. Each time I peed, the sting reminded me of my crime.

I mutilated myself for months after, even after Valentín moved back to Puerto Rico. I never got close enough for him to touch me again.

THERE WAS ANOTHER TIME: I WAS ASSAULTED ON A BROOKLYN street when I was visiting my mother, just down the block from where she still lives, I didn't want to tell her what happened. But I couldn't get myself together before I saw her: My shirt was ripped, my hair was a mess, my fists were red and swollen. I had his skin underneath my nails. She heard me sobbing in the hallway and came out running, "*Que te pasó?*" she yelled. I was twenty-four.

This ain't shit compared to what she'd been through.

ON A SUMMER DAY WHEN MY DAUGHTER WAS SIX, I WENT TO the playground with a friend so that my daughter could play while we talked and, as happens often with women, we started talking about the things that girls endure.

When she confessed that she was molested, I nodded and said, "Me too."

I watched as my daughter ran across the jungle gym and started grappling across the monkey bars. She hadn't been able to do it just a few months before; she'd sulked as she watched other kids and gotten mad when I had tried to help. "Lemme do it myself," she'd said, pushing my hands off. She made it a few rungs in and fell. She climbed up, tried again, and fell. I saw her tear up and wipe her eyes roughly. She spent the better part of the afternoon working on getting across those bars. When I asked her about it as we were leaving, she said, "I'm gonna do it, Mommy. Watch."

Sure enough, all these months later, her hands were calloused but she could grapple across all those rungs. She waved at me when she reached the other side. "Look, Mommy! I did it!"

We gave her a thumbs-up and kept talking.

"How old were you when it happened?" my friend asked.

"I was little," I said. "I was six."

"Vasia's age?"

"Yeah." I looked over at my daughter, who had moved on to the swings, and that's when it hit me: I'd been blaming myself for thirty years for what happened to me when I was just six.

WHEN MILLIE WAS ON HER DEATHBED, I TOLD HER WHAT VAL had done to me. I was thirty, then, and my daughter was just a few months old.

Millie looked at me with a solemn expression and said, "You can never tell your mother that."

That was also the day Millie confirmed to me that my mother's suffering was worse than mine. She'd been raped. Me? It wasn't that bad.

"I mutilated," I blurted out to my friend in the park. "I scratched myself until I bled." I immediately regretted it; a long silence followed.

Then she whispered, "I thought I was the only one who did that . . ."

My daughter is now a month shy of thirteen; the age I was when I left my mother's house. I'm well into my forties. My mother is not in our lives. I can't remember the last time I saw her, but her story still haunts me.

I won't lie and say I've completely convinced myself that what Val did to me and what my ex did to me and what that man on the street did to me were as bad as what happened to my mother; and maybe I never will. This I do know: It was bad enough.

Stasis

ALLY SHEEDY

I WAS EIGHTEEN YEARS OLD WHEN I WENT TO HOLLYWOOD to begin my acting career, after growing up in NYC and being raised, in great part, by feminists. My mother, Charlotte, took me to small grassroots meetings that eventually evolved into the women's liberation movement of the 1970s, and I had listened to arguments about the framework of the Equal Rights Amendment, gone on marches, and attended consciousness-raising sessions.

In one session designed for the kids, a woman demonstrated how her walk changed when she put on high heels. What I clearly remember is someone saying, "If I'm wearing those heels I can't run away."

Hollywood was, to put it mildly, a shock.

On one of my first auditions, a director told me he liked me but could not possibly cast me because there was a "beach" scene. Apparently, my thighs and ass were going to get in the way of my fledgling career. I was five seven and weighed about 130 pounds.

It did not matter that I did a good job on auditions, that I was smart, that I had natural ability. My thighs were the "thing."

So I dieted. All. The. Time. I learned that whatever I might contribute to a role through talent would be instantly marginalized by my physical appearance. I learned that my success would be dependent on what the men in charge thought about my face and my body. Everything I had learned back home had to go out the window as I adapted to these new requirements: what I looked like was paramount.

It wasn't even just whether I was pretty or thin; it was that I wasn't sexy. When I managed to land my first part in a big movie, I was given a ThighMaster as a welcome present and told to squeeze it between my legs at least a hundred times a day. A director of photography told me he couldn't shoot me "looking like that" when I walked on set one day. He said it in front of the whole crew. I was too wide, I guess, in the skirt they had given me to wear.

A few years later, I was told point-blank that my career was moving slowly because "nobody wants to fuck you." There was something about me, sexually, that wasn't selling.

It was a challenge for me starting out, but it seems almost impossible for young women now.

I do volunteer work in film and theater with teenage students at a public school in New York. The kids are gifted and, in my junior class, we recently completed a performance of

Shakespeare scenes for the rest of the theater department. I asked four sixteen-year-old actors with real acting chops and courage what they'd experienced trying to make the leap to professional work: Kai, Michelle, Layla, and Jo.

Kai, who played Lady Macbeth, told me she was thirteen when she first got a call from an agent, and they told her father to leave the room: "Then they asked me how tall I was and for my weight and that I should put my weight on my résumé," she said. "They asked me for my cup size. They told me to turn around and then told me 'Work on your sex appeal.'"

At fifteen, she was asked if she would feel comfortable "humping a table" in the audition room and her mother was asked if she would be "comfortable" with Kai working in only a bra and panties.

She explained that she's now sent to auditions in the "slut category" and was told to diet down to a size 4 because her agent would not re-sign her contract if she were above that size. So, Kai said, she understands that "body size comes first": it doesn't matter that she can handle Lady Macbeth at sixteen, because she will be playing thin and overly sexualized characters if she wants to get work.

Layla, who chose to play Iago in a scene from *Othello*, also told me that casting people have been "typing" her: "It's my boob size, butt size, skin tone. I get cast as the hairdresser and not the pretty sorority girl."

Michelle, who played Lady Anne in *Richard III* and also sings, overheard a director saying, "I was so distracted by her boobs I couldn't hear her voice" after an audition. For some roles, she said, "I'm too busty. I'm too curvy."

And it's not just in the acting world: "I was in class and a teacher kept staring at me and staring," Michelle told me. "He kept bringing up his wife to me. Then I left class and my friends told me he said, 'Man, I wish I was still in high school' about me. I reported it and nothing happened. Even teachers will see you in that light."

These are gifted adolescent women who don't get to be judged on their impressive talent: their bodies are already paramount to the work they want to do and it's only going to get worse. At sixteen these students are being judged on their sexual attractiveness. Their talent is a gift, but it is not enough.

As Michelle says: "We are told to 'use what you have to work with . . . boobs, ass.' "

Jo, who played Paulina in *A Winter's Tale*, said, "I don't care how talented you are, it's your 'look.' "

Kai says: "What is 'the look'? What can I be? What should I have?"

Apparently, the look is now a superthin stomach area, big breasts, big butt, gorgeous face, and a freed nipple. When they first told me about the nipple thing, I tried to understand but it was clear that it was not the "burn the bra" mentality with which I was raised. These young women must be comfortable without a bra and with visible nipples under a thin shirt as part of a perfect breast—big enough to be sexual, but not so big that it's "slutty."

Meanwhile, a director recently told Kai: "I don't see the innocence."

"I'm so close to giving up on everything," she said.

These girls say that there is an unattainable image that men have set for them in their professional lives—and that the men subscribing to this image have been raised to think this way.

Layla explained: "Laws can't be changed. It's psychological attitude. It's not being fixed. It gets worse. People think it's being fixed . . . It's not fixed. It can't be fixed."

I realize I am privileged: I am white and work in the film and television industry. I've had great opportunities, worked hard for them, and done the most I could do with them. But I also made the conscious decision to not market myself in a sexual way, and it cost me. It is very, very hard to create a career as an actor without sexualizing oneself; I have been navigating this minefield for over thirty years with varying degrees of success. I've spoken out about the sexism in my industry before and faced backlash. I've been called "bitter" and told my behavior was "cringe worthy." *Whatever.*

There were things I just could not bring myself to do: the film by the (great) director that would require me to shoot a scene in a shirt but no panties, for example. (He was making some kind of statement, I suppose.) I rejected the advice to "date" men that could possibly advance my career. I didn't go on auditions for films that I felt glorified sex work, that depicted women being sexually abused in a gratuitous way, or that required me to leave my sense of self on the doorstep. (All of these films became huge hits.)

But this is the way women are set up in the media. There has been some movement, I suppose, but not much. It's a frustrating and demoralizing struggle with some moments of triumph in spite of itself. And I still love acting. I still love a good role more than just about anything.

Why is the female physical appearance so important in the arts? Sean Penn is the most gifted actor of my generation, and I don't think he's gotten Botox. I don't think Bryan Cranston had butt implants.

What is a woman to do? Turn on the TV and you get a good look at rape culture. I have tried to make a career without contributing to it. I'm still trying.

It used to be, when I was younger, that there was the "bombshell" role and the role of the less attractive friend. At my age, it's a little different: there is one major female role available for every five roles available to men my age. There's the mother role and maybe something a bit more than that. One of my favorite TV roles a couple of years back was that of a rather ruthless lawyer described in the script as "40s," brilliant and . . . thin. Sometimes the characters I play or could play are described as "still attractive," in spite of their age—because women my age aren't usually attractive, or so Hollywood seems to think.

The best characters I get to play are the complicated, dark, kind of crazy ones. I love those characters because I can just do my job and not deal with whether or not some producer finds me "sexy" or reasonably attractive for my age—but I've had to search for those kinds of roles. My kid has asked me why I love playing deranged characters: the quick answer is "no makeup" followed by "no men."

From feminist teach-ins at Columbia and Barnard as a

student, to Hollywood and beyond as an artist, to teaching young actors in a prestigious public school, I can see the fight for women's equality remains. I can look at myself in the mirror without shame (but with endless bills to pay) because I circumvented the exploitation rampant in my industry, somehow. But what do I tell my students? How can I tell them to not accept that their success is dependent on their physicality, but also that they may be contributing to the same stereotypes that hold them back?

The issues women are facing in the film and television industry are not just about fair pay for famous rich white actresses: I find it shameful when my superwealthy peers complain about being paid only $400,000, though it is, indeed, helpful to illustrate the wage gap between men and women in the industry.

It's more important to tackle the absence of a platform for young women who are extremely talented but who are not thin, blond, white, and/or deemed sexually desirable by the powers that be. It's more important to tackle the frustrating status quo where the powers that be are still male and take up disproportional space in the audition room and the boardroom.

We have to end the system where it is only white men who decide when a woman—in any position, "privileged" or not—is deserving of power and agency.

I'm still navigating the sexual appearance standard in professional work. When I am called to consider a role or audition for a role in TV/Hollywood Land, my talent is never in question. The "studio" or the "network" wants me on tape to see what I look like now.

I was never alone in a hotel room with Harvey Weinstein, but I've been at "dinners" that felt like come-ons and I've walked into rooms where I've been sized up and then received phone calls or "date" requests that I've turned down.

Today, if the producer or executive or male director in charge finds me sexually attractive, then I'm on the list. This is how it goes. This is how it IS. If the Harvey Weinstein disaster illustrates anything at all, it illustrates the entirety of the power structure. The lurid details of his rapes are disgusting and yet a shield, in a way, for the greater toxicity of that power structure.

His behavior and his crimes are so . . . what? Undeniable? Shocking? Inexcusable?

Any culpable man in the entertainment industry can pull up some feigned dignity and state publicly (or privately) "Well, I didn't do THAT . . . exactly" as a kind of self-protective blanket of denial. There are some actors that have expressed "support" for the women who have spoken up about Harvey Weinstein who are guilty of the same or similar behavior. It's good PR for them but there are quite a few liars.

There are scores of directors and executives and producers who have not spoken up because they are complicit and behave in just that Weinstein way. They don't want to be called out.

This isn't about naming names. I don't have enough for a lawsuit, but I do have enough for a broken heart/spirit. Nothing will change in Hollywood. Some men will get careful. Some men will pretend they never behaved like predators and wait this out. What's so disheartening is knowing Harvey

Weinstein's sick actions will be addressed (finally) and yet the entire culture and context for his sick shit will remain in place.

I hope I'm wrong.

I hope it changes.

I'm not holding my breath.

The Ways We Are Taught
to Be a Girl

xTx

LATER, YOU WILL TURN IT INTO A POINTS SYSTEM. You won't call it a points system and there won't be any actual points, but regardless, you will keep score. You imagine other girls have their own ways of keeping score; in diaries, in shiny-smooth scars, in how they raise their daughters, in the ways they are lost.

It's an odd tallying; the girls who have the most points are not the winners and the girls who have the lowest points do not win either.

Nobody wins. Ever.

I am a girl with low points.

The ways we are taught to be a girl start when you are very young. When you are being taught, you don't know about the points. When you are being taught to be a girl, the lessons are simply accepted—the price you pay for your curves, your holes. It's only later, when you are older, after you've been taught, that you find out about the score sheet. Prior to that, it's just what happens when you are a girl.

Lesson One

We had a place in the country we'd go each summer, an old place on a half acre on the outskirts of a one-stoplight, white-trash town. Woods, river, and railroad tracks; free-range roaming, sunburn, snakes, tadpoles, crayfish, filth, mosquito bites. I had made a same-age friend who lived with no father, two older brothers, and three sisters in a house too small for its ~~captors~~ inhabitants. It was a six-minute walk from our place, the length of a neighboring horse pasture. The girls' room had pink, spray-painted dots on the walls. The mom kept a giant jar of homemade pickles in the kitchen that my friend and I would eat from, wrapping the dripping, tangy green meat in paper towels and chewing them down to stubs. We walked barefoot a lot. We swam in the river. We climbed trees. We made up adventures. We played dolls sometimes. We were tomboys but we were girls first.

Her oldest brother liked to give me hugs.

One time we were riding a horse together. It spooked and ran and we fell off when it took a sharp turn. Her body fell into a wood post. Mine did not. I remember her crying, taking her shirt off, the pale white side of her scraped and bleeding. I remember thinking, *She has her shirt off and she doesn't care.* I remember bathroom Bactine and bandages and never wanting to ride a horse again.

Adventures.

A fort down by the river. Fiberglass. Aluminum. Boards. Dirt. It had bunk beds. And boys. Her brothers. She brought me there one day. I was maybe seven.

Now I wonder, did she lure me? Was this the plan all along?

Adventures.

They kissed her with tongue to show me how easy it was.

"See? No big deal. Now you try it."

I didn't want to try it. The fort was hot. The door was blocked. I didn't want this.

Seven years old? Eight? Nine? Six? Which age makes it better?

"Just do it!" These weren't the words. These were the words. I was a child. I was scared.

She said them too. Three against one.

I didn't do it. They did it. I did nothing except endure my first lesson on how to be a girl.

I remember not being able to breathe and crying while they felt my perfectly flat chest, their slimy hot tongues pushing into my mouth, alien and gross. I remember pushing and running because I was suffocating, scared, because it all felt like speeding downhill without brakes and if I didn't run I would crash and that crash would cost too many points. I didn't know about the points, but somewhere, deep down, I knew.

I told my parents when I got home. Not everything. We

learn not to tell everything. We know telling everything will make them see the bad in us. How it is our fault. How we contributed. We fear repercussions, albeit lighter than the ones we will administer to ourselves; slut, bad, ugly, weak, whore, trash, shame, hate. We tell just enough, if we tell at all.

I wasn't allowed to play with her after that. I was okay with that.

Summary

Sometimes you will be forced into things you don't want to do. Sometimes you will be made to feel bad you don't want to do the things. After the things are done, you will feel like a bad person. These feelings will never go away. They enter the wet plaster of you and harden into the mold of you. The way you are taught to be a girl will become how you are as a woman—a woman who is, at her core, not good enough, without worth, tarnished.

Points: 2? 3? 1?

Lesson Two

Why was it always friends, friends of? Maybe because the door was already open, less work? Sitting ducks? Easy prey?

That same summer place. The back porch. After swimming. My older brother's friend. My brothers. All of us wrapped in towels, sitting around.

I was an age where there is no pubic hair and you're aware there's none, embarrassed about it. Whichever age that is. My brother's friend overlapping his towel onto mine, his hand snaking in, snaking under, trying to get to the girl of me.

But my brothers are there! Nobody is there. I cement my legs closed. I press so hard and plead so hard with the thighs I will learn to hate for the rest of my life simply because of their roundness.

Why is he doing this?

Why can't anyone see?

Why am I not moving saying yelling screaming?

Why me?

The fingers go as far as he can get them, which isn't as far as he wants to get them, and he gives up. They go play.

I release. My thighs quiver, spent, mostly victorious.

Summary

If they want it, they can take it. What you want or don't want is irrelevant.

Points: One? A half?

Lesson Three

The same summer place. A father's friend, drunk. A master bedroom during a party he sneaks away from. I'm watching cartoons. Still no breasts, no pubes, only a summer tan, shorts, halter top. Risqué? Did my lying on my side, head on my hand, lounge pose siren-seduce him? Or maybe it was my long tan legs? Slut child.

I was watching cartoons. In a room. By myself.

He lay down on the bed, his pose mirroring mine. He begins stroking the mountain-range length of me; head, hair, cheek, shoulder, arm, waist, hip, thigh, calf. An endless petting.

I watch cartoons.

His sour breath, garbled words. His hand. Slow and stroking. Feeling him inch closer, narrowing the valley between us. I want for bedsheets, a night-light, a way to hide, shrink away. Monsters aren't always in closets, under beds.

I watched cartoons, unsure. Uncle ****. He's nice, right? My dad's friend. This is okay, right? Then why does it feel wrong? Why can't I move? Get up? Run? My body betraying me once more.

Once more, a car without brakes.

The door opens and another father's friend rages, rips him off the bed. *What the fuck do you think you're doing?* he asks. And that's when I know, for sure, that was a wrong thing.

I am left alone with the bed, the cartoons, feeling a partner in the wrong thing. If I was a good girl, I would've left. I didn't do anything. I let him. I let him. I let him.

I.

Let.

Him.

My fault.

Summary

If you do nothing, it's your fault. Even if you are a child. Even if you are scared. Even if the man is your dad's good friend who you've known since growing up. Pay attention. Take notes. This is how you are ~~shamed~~ shaped into a woman.

Points: None? One-half?

Lesson Four

Summer again, but this time, a two-week lakeside camp.

The foxiest counselor; dark brown curls, dark brown eyes, summer-tan skin, a cute boy smile. Was I twelve? Thirteen? Eleven?

Yes.

He must've recognized my young girl longing. The look away and smile. The turn, giggle blush. All the puppy love behaviors. I was chubby. Unpretty. Plain. An easy mark. He was a god and he knew it. I was only prey.

He taught sailing and when he asked if I'd like to take the boat out with him—just him and me—of course I said yes. He was beautiful. He was a counselor. An adult. Looking back he was probably only nineteen or twenty but he was a COUNSELOR. To me, that was akin to a teacher. There was no need to worry.

I obviously had forgotten my previous lessons. Bad student.

Bad girl.

He took the boat from the dock out into the lake. Once we were clear, he had me take the rudder and pointing to a spot on the other side of the lake, instructed me to aim for it. He lay on his back, closed his eyes. It occurred to me that maybe this was his clever way of being able to take a short nap.

I was right and also wrong.

As I steered, I stared. His tan body, clad in only swim trunks. His brown, hairless chest, muscled thighs, the smell of him. Not believing my "luck" at being "chosen" by such a cute guy. Me! The chubby, plain girl! The one-piece-swimsuit-with-a-long-T-shirt-over-it girl! So many bikini-cute girls left behind, unpicked. My girl's heart fluttered!

After a while he woke up. Checked how I was doing. Praised me with that smile. Told me I'd done a fine job. Called me a good girl. He lay back down. But he reached up and started caressing my face. He took his thumb and pressed it all over my lips, then into my mouth.

Again, I froze. I did not know what this was. What was this?

In and out of my mouth and I sucked on it. Automatically. I sucked his thumb. I didn't know what to do but I felt that was what was wanted FROM ONE OF MY COUNSELORS so I sucked on it. Like a sleepy baby. Even though it all felt wrong. I was in the middle of a lake, alone. Not alone. I saw the brakeless car then. It was headed toward the crest of a hill. My stomach.

I couldn't see his eyes. He had on sunglasses. But I saw he had a hard-on. I had brothers. I had my dad's *Hustler*s, his *Joy of Sex*. I knew exactly what it was, what it could do.

He began rubbing it over his shorts, while I took his thumb. And then, after a short time, he reached under his shorts and started working himself. Faster and faster until an abrupt groan and stop.

I wasn't sure what happened but I was sure nonetheless.

He jumped in the lake. Swam around for a minute. Then we sailed back. In silence.

He never took me sailing again.

Summary

If a boy treats you like you're special, it's probably because he wants to come and not because you are a treasure he discovered. You are not a treasure. You are a thing a boy can use to make him ejaculate. This makes sense because you already believe this at your core. You have been taught.

Points: Two.

Lesson Five

I loved playing arcade games. My brothers and I would spend our allowances at the mall arcade every week. I was a pro at *Donkey Kong*.

But not on this day. On this day, I had the best game of *Galaga* ever.

Preteen or so, I plugged my quarters in and started killing the insect aliens. As was typical back then, to claim "next game" you'd put your quarter onto the top ledge of the machine, stand behind the current player, wait. So it wasn't alarming at first, having a body behind me.

Not at first.

But shortly after I cleared level one, that body got close.

Really close.

Something hard was pressing into my rear. A constant, noticeable pressure. I thought, maybe the guy—because it was a guy—had bought something at the mall, something long that would stick out of a bag that he might be holding at his side; a roll of wrapping paper or a poster. I wasn't sure, but these were the first things that came to mind.

I kept shooting the alien insects. The hard pressing into my ass continued. My shooting continued. And then he put his arm up onto the top of the machine and suddenly his entire body was curved against mine and I instantly knew what was not pressing into me.

It was not a poster. It was not wrapping paper.

I looked to my right, tried to turn to look at him but his arm had me locked in. He was too close for me to see his face. What I saw instead was an Asian boy standing about ten feet away, staring at us. I thought to myself, *What must this look like? Where are my brothers? Why is nobody seeing I need help?*

I played the game. While he rubbed against me. Level after level. While he rubbed against me. I was having the best game of my life. While he rubbed against me. I couldn't die. While he rubbed against me. I got extra lives. While he rubbed against me. My score went up, up, up. While he rubbed against me. All I wanted was the insect aliens to kill me. While he rubbed against me. All I wanted was for my brothers to see me and know and help. While he rubbed against me. I was frozen, heartbeat ballistic, petrified, body-betrayed once more.

While he rubbed against me I did nothing.

Eventually, my game ended. I remember sort of shoulder rolling him off me, angry, and his face, smiling.

Just to be ultrasure I glanced down. No shopping bag.

I bolted out of the arcade. My brothers were nowhere to be found and I was glad then that they hadn't seen.

Summary
You could've left but you stayed. You wanted it and he knew. The ways we turn the gun to our own temple.

Points: 4

Lesson Six

Up until I was fifteen, I never had a boyfriend. Plain, chubby girls don't get boyfriends.

But my blond, cute, busty best friend had no problem getting boyfriends. She was two years older than me. Not the brightest girl, she'd been held back in school a couple times and that's how we ended up being friends.

Her high school boyfriend Mike drove a Camaro. I'd frequently be the third wheel when we'd drive around to various hidden spots to smoke weed or drink, sometimes drive into San Francisco, drunk walk down Broadway, sneak into the sex shops and peep show and porn booths. It all felt very reckless, and it was. But they were older and cooler and I was just an uncool freshman.

Sometimes Mike would bring one of his friends. They

were usually around his same age, seventeen. Stoners mostly. Long hair, derby jackets, Ronnie James Dio and Black Sabbath lovers. Sometimes when we'd go drive, park, and party, my friend and Mike would go into the car to make out and I would be left with whichever friend had come.

One time Mike brought an older friend. He was dark and fat and had a mustache. Even now I'm not sure how old he was. He could've been twenty-one, thirty-two, forty. All I know is I will never forget that mustache.

This time, Mike and my friend left him and me in the car to go do whatever they were going to do. We were in the backseat and . . .

Summary
Men are strong. Also, see lesson summaries; 1, 2, 3, 4, and 5.
   Points: 8
   TOTAL SCORE: 17?

THE WAYS WE ARE TAUGHT TO BE A GIRL ARE MANY. THESE were my biggest lessons. The smaller ones aren't worth writing about but they add up; the "sit on my lap uncle" who nuzzles your neck and won't let you down, calls his mustache "a caterpillar"—"doesn't it tickle?"—the bouncer who frisks you slow and long and between your legs in a dark hallway when your group has already gone ahead into the club, the "fuck you dumb bitch" when you tell him no, he can't get what he wants, the drunk stranger guy a drunk you is chatting and laughing with who suddenly dives into your mouth with his because being friendly is an invitation, the guy after guy after guy who grinds his dick in your ass when you are dancing with your girlfriends.

What.

He.

Wants.

My score is low compared to some and high compared to others. The harder the lesson, the higher the points. Some girls would kill for my score. This is why I don't talk about my score. I got off easy.

I legitimately think, "I got off easy." I didn't get raped, my dad didn't finger me, my cousin didn't make me suck his dick, nobody ass-fucked me while I was passed out at a frat party. I got fondled, at best. Not that bad, right? Lucky, right? Right. Exactly. This is what I'm saying. I got off easy. Why even write this essay?

Until I became a *seasoned* adult, I thought this was a normal part of growing up as a girl. Weird shit with boys/men happens to you. Look at all the times it happened to me so, obviously, it's just how it is in life, like flat tires, running out of gas, getting a traffic ticket, spraining an ankle, etc. It's fucked up, but it happens and you just deal with it. Move on.

But as I matured and met other women, looked back on my life, I realized it's not normal. It's the exception. It's not "what you get" for being a girl. It's what you get for not having vigilant parents. It's what you get for not knowing how to defend yourself. It's what you get for being young, innocent, and scared. It's what you get when you are unsupervised and stupid. Most of all, it's what you get when men decide to take it from you, regardless of what you want. If all these boys, these men, had chosen to treat me as more than "thing," my scorecard would be empty right now.

None of this was supposed to happen. Didn't have to happen. I wasn't supposed to have a score. None of us were.

Floccinaucinihilipilification

So Mayer

I SURVIVED.

Raped children are supposed to die. What would the culture of the individual white cisgender male straight genius do without us? We are the predicate of their sentences, material for their dispassionate dissections.

We are supposed to die prettily and vacantly so our rage doesn't tear down all their certificates and awards and case files, trash their analysis and ram their face in the privilege that allows them to side with our abusers in silencing and killing us.

"He has sometimes likened his style of writing to that of a medic performing a post-mortem on a raped child—whose job is to analyse the injuries, not to give vent to the rage that is felt."
—Susie Mackenzie on J. G. Ballard,
Guardian, Sept. 6th, 2003

If Ballard's is the model for the experimental, political novel, how is the (un)dead raped child supposed to write, even if she survives?

1. Perform a postmortem on herself.
2. Give vent to the rage that is felt.

They are incompossible, apparently. It's one or the other, science or howling.

It's easier to play dead.

It's a conundrum: if you survive, then it—that, the trauma—can't have been that bad. Being dead is the only way to prove it was. It really was bad. It was terrible. It was so awful there was no way I could survive.

What did this child die of? Shame, mainly. And narrative necessity.

If you survive, you have to prove it was that bad; or else, they think *you* are.

Surviving is some kind of sin, like floating up off the dunking stool like a witch. You have to be permanently *écorchée*, heart-on-sleeve, offering up organs and body parts like a medieval female saint.

What if there's not enough to put on display? If the stories are incoherent, flashes?

As any medic would find, there are parts of me missing.

THERE ARE THE PARTS MANY PEOPLE HAVE MISSING: THE WIS-
dom teeth they had to break my (clenched) jaw to remove; the
ova I (struggle to) shed (despite the cysts); the small scars of
worrying at blemishes and picking at scabs.

There are the more unusual absences, the ones that make
good party stories: feel this bald patch, hard and shiny, the
size of a penny—that's where the obstetrician used a cable
to restart my heart. It stopped while I was in the birth canal.
The cable pulled my hair out by the roots. But I survived.

AND THERE ARE PARTS IT'S HARDER TO TALK ABOUT, OR
harder to see. A litany. Because no medic *did* see, when I
presented at the emergency room and the family doctor's
office with repeated broken toes and fingers, with rashes
and smashed teeth; with anorexia at age six; with what were
called growing pains in my legs (although I never got any
taller) so bad I couldn't walk upstairs to my bedroom; with
a third-degree burn I didn't even feel myself sustaining on
the iron.

That wasn't true; I did feel it. It felt good. It felt ice-cool
on a summer day. It felt like being able to feel.

AFTER THE MEMORIES OF SEXUAL ABUSE RETURNED, WHEN
I was legally (if not emotionally) an adult, I also spent

months in excruciating, sleepless pain as what appeared to be repetitive strain injury in my writing hand—a pain that appeared the first time I tried to write about the abuse: co-incidence or correlate?—was finally traced to fused vertebrae in my neck.

I'd never been in a serious car crash or fallen off a wall. My grandmother—my father's mother—was the first family member to hold me after I was born and after I'd spent a month in an incubator. She dropped me on my head.

It's like a story you tell at parties that seems funny at the time. Or the funny story of how there was so much violence in my childhood that nearly dying at birth and being dropped on my head shortly thereafter seemed worth only a shrug—a matter of course.

VIOLENCE IN A FAMILY COMES DOWN THROUGH GENERATIONS: long before my father (finally) left my mother, her father left her mother, and her father's father left my great-grandmother. I look like her, it's said, this woman I knew as a frail bird, this Jewish woman who fled Nazi-occupied Romania as a married teenager, was deserted, survived the war in England as a registered alien, a single mother with a small son who became the grandfather I never met.

SOMETIMES MY MOTHER TELLS ME STORIES ABOUT HER FATHER, or stories about my father. They are not mine to repeat. "I want you to know," she tells me, as if she feels guilty for explaining our history to me. I am amazed at how much violence we can contain—internalize, suppress, hold on to, narrate. How much we can swallow and still survive.

THERE'S A SCAR ON MY LEG, A SCAR LIKE MANY PEOPLE'S SCARS. It's shiny and pale, even against my Ashkenazi-beige skin. It will never disappear. Like the scar on my scalp, it's marked out by hairlessness, a clear-cut in the forest.

It's evidence of a story like other people's stories. One rainy day I was running to catch the tube home from school. I slipped and fell, sliding under the high step up to the train carriage. Two strangers caught my arms and hauled me on board as the train juddered with motion.

It didn't even surprise me. I have never been in my body: I still, as I did when I was a child, fall over all the time, walk into things, trip and tumble. I am constantly covered with bruises. My body was not my body but a postpubertal amorphous mass of Silly Putty whose shape, position in space, and vector I couldn't control.

On the way home, my friends chattered, hyped by the drama. Pumped full of the adrenaline of the near-miss. Me too. So pumped that I didn't notice, until we got off the tube, that my navy school trousers were soaked with blood, leaking through a small rip in the fabric—a rip that mapped exactly onto a rip in my flesh.

"It's not that bad," said my best friend, but she grudgingly went to the chemist near the tube station and bought some Band-Aids while I waited for the bus, trying not to pass out.

The rip fit neatly under a large Band-Aid. Not that bad.

We had a fight because I felt too faint to hang out. I stormed (limped) off. I don't remember how I got to the doctor's office. I remember that the Band-Aid had swollen with blood, sodden with it, ballooning outward. I remember my sock and shoe were full of blood. I remember that when the doctor cleaned the cut, you could see bone.

THERE ARE LOTS OF PARTS OF MY MEMORY MISSING: THE names of everyone I went to primary school with; family holidays; all the Hebrew (classical and modern) that I learned, five classes a week for seven years. Sometimes it's more subtle and frustrating: the links of causality drop out, as if a vivid memory were a dream I was trying to describe a day later. I get flashes, but not the ligatures that bind the flashes into coherent, narratable memories.

I KNOW WHY I WAS HYSTERICAL AT THE DOCTOR'S OFFICE: IT wasn't the pain of the cut, or the visible bone, or the tetanus jab. It was the thought of having to tell my father why I was late for . . . why I missed . . . I don't know. It doesn't matter. There was something I'd been supposed to do that evening, something he'd yelled at me about that morning, and I was going to miss it.

Whatever it was, it's unimportant. It was unimportant then, and it is now. I survived.

But sitting on the cold ledge of the doctor's table, my

school trousers scissored to bits, I was retching incoherent with tears. Call it shock, call it displacement, call it adolescent hysteria. It was fear.

SOMETIMES I WONDER IF I DID SURVIVE ANY/ALL OF IT, IF I float through a life stolen from ending before it started. I was six weeks premature, tiny as fuck, jaundiced as hell, a wee yellow screamer blessed with a bald patch from birth.

Do you survive if you don't know how you've survived? I remember an elaborate plan to sneak into the kitchen and steal a knife to . . . One of those half-dreamed, half-conscious unraveling thoughts in the dark before dawn. I remember dreaming repeatedly that the walls of the house were made of paper and would crumple. I remember having to pee in a jar because of the anorexia. I remember running and running my fingers over the smooth place on my shin when I'm working, a nervous habit I feel like I've had since I was born.

IN HER MEMOIR *MY FATHER'S HOUSE*, SYLVIA FRASER TALKS about having a photographic memory for details of her childhood, a memory she used to write her early novels. She describes the shock of discovering that the photographic accuracy was a front, a disguise for the sexual abuse she had forgotten until—violently—her body reminded her.

I spent a semester in grad school writing about Fraser's work, and Ann-Marie MacDonald's *Fall on Your Knees*, and

Camilla Gibb's *Mouthing the Words*. I'd moved three thousand miles from my past, from London, UK, to Toronto, Canada, and I was in love with Canadian feminist literature. For months, I studied and framed these, and more—accounts by daughters of sexual abuse by their fathers. Immersed.

It would be another two years before I had any inkling that this immersion was personal.

I survived by reading.

My father taught me to read during the same period of time that he was raping me. He taught me to swim—to breathe without drowning—during the years when he was holding my mouth closed at night.

I write, I think sometimes, because I need to wash words and language clean.

Words were games to my father—crosswords, Scrabble, puns and jokes. Words didn't have meaning, they had value: how much could they be inverted, messed around, fucked with. Used as weapons of control.

What are the only two words in English that feature all five vowels in the correct order?

Abstemious. Facetious.

What are the longest words in the *Oxford English Dictionary*?

antidisestablishmentarianism—*in short, conservatism; getting in the way of change.*

floccinaucinihilipilification—*the action or habit of estimating something as worthless.*

MY FATHER'S FAVORITE COMEBACK IN AN ARGUMENT: "DON'T be facetious."

Nothing I said had meaning. It was always simplistic, flippant, juvenile, unsubstantiable, silly, girlish. The synonyms pile up, evacuating whatever claim I'd made, whatever feeling or fact stood behind the claim, turning my mouth into a black hole.

Now, educated by Rebecca Solnit and Sarah Seltzer, I'd knowingly call what he was doing gaslighting, sealioning, lollipopping. Actually, I'd go one better: I'd call it Cordelia-ing: "Nothing comes from nothing. Speak again." The rendering of a daughter as puppet, scripted, voice too sweet and low to carry meaning.

No. I'd call it floccinaucinihilipilification. All the mansplaining tactics summed up: the action and habit of estimating something as worthless.

It worked.

MY FATHER'S FAVORITE THREAT: "I WILL ANNIHILATE YOU."

annihilate—*to render as nothing, to erase; generally, through violence.*

I survived. I took the language of knives I'd been given and tore down the walls of my home and my body. There are other places where the skin barely meets, places I don't show. Scars only a scan can see. Tattoos that (twelve hours in) reminded me I was not yet ready for a postmortem.

"The creative adult is the child who has survived."
—misattributed by the internet to
Ursula K. Le Guin

In a blog post responding to the meme attributed to her, Ursula K. Le Guin spoke of her:

> *aversion to what the sentence says to me: that only the child is alive and creative—so that to grow up is to die.*
>
> *To respect and cherish the freshness of perception and the vast, polymorphous potentialities of childhood is one thing. But to say that we experience true being only in childhood and that creativity is an infantile function—that's something else.*

Le Guin's post "The Inner Child and the Nude Politician" frees me from the anxiety generated by the meme: that only those who remember their childhoods—to the extent of preferring childhood to adulthood—can be creative adults. To extend creative adulthood to only those who had halcyon days in which the "vast, polymorphous potentialities of childhood" were realized and can be remembered speaks of white middle-class cisgendered privilege.

Acknowledging Le Guin's critique, I can reread the misattributed meme with the emphasis on "survived," rather than "child." I am an adult (and alive) because—however she could—the child I was survived the terrors of childhood.

The child I was is dead, over and over again. It's true. That child is under Ballard's knife, that child is the object of this essay, opened diagrammatically for your consideration.

I am the child who survived—to become the adult who can speak back.

Teach me the word for my own abjection and erasure and you teach me to survive.

JUST AFTER THE MEMORIES CAME BACK, I WENT BACK TO GRAD school. I didn't have much of a choice: I had to stay in classes, keep turning in PhD chapters, or lose my funding and my student visa.

Even if I'd had a choice, I would have stayed. I was where I needed to be.

I was taking a class in indigenous two-spirit poetics, reading Chrystos, Gregory Scofield, and Qwo-Li Driskill write with fire about their scars and survivals, about internalized hatred and intergenerational inheritances of abusive violence.

About how the tenderness of lovers could wound. About the ways in which even the secret hearts and soft parts of bodies were and are colonized.

Their work gave me survival and writing. From them, I learned the blazing insight that rape was not an act between an individual and an individual, hidden in a dark room—that was what my rapist wanted me to think. Rape was and is a cultural and political act: it attempts to remove a person with agency, autonomy, and belonging from their community, to secrete them and separate them, to depoliticize their body by rendering it detachable, violable, nothing.

WHAT HAPPENS BETWEEN AN INDIVIDUAL AND AN INDIVID-ual can be labeled "not that bad." It can be called a "crime of passion." It can be called a misunderstanding, a Freudian slip, a one-time deal, just between you and me, an act meaningless among the vast, insensible crises of genocide. Any measure of comparison feels grotesque when presented as a simile: that rape is "like" colonization—although the metaphor of "rape" is often used to describe the conquest of land.

Flip it around and think of rape *as* colonization: not just a metonym, but a precise synecdoche, part for whole, an action by which genocidal violence, the removal of land rights, and the destruction of coherent culture proceeds.

RAPE AND COLONIALISM ARE NOT COMMENSURATE, BUT they are kin. When we talk about sexual violence as femi-

nists, we are—we have to be—talking about its use to sub-
jugate entire peoples and cultures, the annihilation that is
its empty heart. Rape is *that bad* because it is an ideological
weapon. Rape is *that bad* because it is a structure: not an
excess, not monstrous, but the logical conclusion of heteropatriarchal capitalism. It is what that ugly polysyllabic eu-
phemism for state power does.

R APE WAS WHERE MY REBELLION STARTED. H IS SMALL SENSE
that—small as I was, an infant—I needed to be controlled
was my hint that I had power that had to be curtailed. That
I was alive enough to be annihilated. That my survival was a
threat that needed to be contained.

Rape and sexual abuse made me nothing, and in doing so
made me something.

Something other than the evacuated, erased nobody that
my father hoped to produce. The puppet-daughter, obedient
to the Law. Jephtha's daughter, sent where she's bidden. Lot's
daughter, fixated on patriarchal propagation.

It's the end of the world. It's not. It's not not.

It's what we have. It's what we create from "to survive."
The walls of the suburban conservative religious worldview in which I was raised *were* paper-thin, the surface of a
shadow-play of stick figures (Father, Rabbi, Policeman) performing the same old, same old drama of power.

Rendering something worthless—tearing something
down—is powerful. It's a weapon of power. We know it in
our bodies.

It's time to pull out the scalpel and turn it around. Slash vents in the paper walls of this master's house of heteropatriarchal colonialist mass hallucination that claims to be our reality.

Give vent to our rage. Be bad. Dare to survive.

The Life Ruiner

Nora Salem

I KNOW A GUY I LIKE TO CALL THE LIFE RUINER. HE WAS born in a small Egyptian village with big city ambitions. He moved into my family's then-home in Cairo to make those dreams a reality. He was eighteen; I was eight. And for a period just short of a year, he regularly sexually abused me.

I mostly say "the Life Ruiner" in my own head. It makes him sound kind of like an old-timey criminal, and I try to picture him as such when I do think of him: in a yellow silk shirt, hair slicked back, floppy leather shoes just a little too big for his feet, leaning casually against a beat-up VW bug in which, after his dastardly deed is done, he drives off, cackling maniacally.

Here's a real memory: me in the kitchen of our Cairo apartment, garnishing a very large knife. Eight years old, fed up, and telling him that, if he ever came near me again, I'd stick it in his throat. He laughed.

Still, I didn't tell anyone what he'd done.

IT'S BEEN TWO DECADES SINCE THEN AND ONE DECADE SINCE I managed to tell my parents. Oddly enough, it's especially since I told them that the memories have become more powerful, even occasionally all-consuming. A couple counselors have called it PTSD. It feels more like running my fingers over the rupture between the life I lived then and the one I live now.

I've tried many things to make the memories and their terrible vividness go away: alcohol, drugs, sex, lots of Benadryl-doused sleep to avoid nightmares. And, when that didn't work, a razor to my thigh, a lit cigarette pressed into a palm. All of it made me feel silly and fragile. Sometimes I think it's that feeling—unending weakness, total vulnerability—of which I'm most resentful.

"O my friend searching for an absurdity necessary to train the self to be tolerant . . . do not reconcile with anything except for this obscure reason. Do not regret a war that ripened you just as August ripens pomegranates on the slopes of stolen mountains."
—MAHMOUD DARWISH

The memories come back in bits and pieces; there is no consistent story line. I've learned that telling a story often creates sense where there is none, so I refuse to fill in the blanks.

Those who ask for more details—parents, friends, idiots in a writing workshop—are like dogs nipping at my feet while I try to push the gates of hell closed. Leave me alone. *Leave me alone.*

What he actually did to me is fuzzy, partly because memory plays tricks on me and partly because, in those moments, I did something a psychiatrist would call disassociation, and partly because they were acts that I, as an eight-year-old, didn't understand. I remember bits and pieces: a tongue pressed into my small mouth; a hand in my pants; his weight on top of me, pain; the feeling of my own breath being sucked out of my body.

I am a pomegranate. I am a pomegranate. I am a pomegranate. I can chew on my own sweet ripeness and spit out the seeds.

MY PARENTS HAD PLANNED TO STAY IN EGYPT LONGER, BUT, after a year, my mother and I returned to the California in which I had been raised. We came back, my mom and I, two bodies short. We left my older brother buried in a grave not far from the Mansoura home where my father was raised; my father moved to Kuwait. Even at eight, I knew that my wrecked family couldn't withstand another blow. That, along with my sense of guilt, was the main reason I kept what the Life Ruiner did to myself.

The year we returned was a blur: I cried a lot, but never at home. Mostly, I cried in the bathroom at school.

What is it about secrets that endows them with so much power? More pertinent: Why was I so obsessed with keeping mine? Why for so long?

Perhaps an even better question is: What are the secrets we keep from ourselves? And how do we manage it?

"The idea of a secret that will be revealed always results in one of two scenarios: death and destruction, or self-discovery and recovery beyond our wildest dreams of unification. And in the greatest of sagas, both at the same time."

—Mary Ruefle

When I was in high school, I was obsessed with Mira Nair's *Monsoon Wedding*, a movie about an upper-crust Punjabi family preparing a wedding for their daughter. It wasn't just because I loved Bollywood. It was because I was continually drawn to Shefali Shah's portrayal of Ria Verma, the older, unmarried cousin and good friend of the bride who had been sexually abused as a child. Near the end, in an effort to protect her elementary school–aged cousin, Ria "comes out" as a survivor.

My favorite part of the movie was the moment when the wedding party gets rained on just hours after the confrontational moment and Ria runs out into it, arms wide, face to the sky—the absolute picture of serenity and bliss.

It is hilarious to me now, but I was once absolutely positive that telling my own secret would result in that kind of eternal relief. Once I had the courage to say it, I thought, my life would be solved. Maybe that's why I kept putting off telling anyone: as long as I stayed silent, the possibility of that kind of freedom was just around the corner.

The day that I finally told my parents was nearly the worst day of my life, second only to the day I lost my brother.

Was I destroyed or unified by the revelation? Neither. Both. I guess the jury's still out. Ruefle is right about sagas, but applying the same logic to a lifetime—in which destruction and self-discovery occur over and over again like the wheels that keep the whole lopsided contraption clattering along—is more complicated.

I wonder what the Life Ruiner thinks about his secret. I wonder if he's chosen to forget or if he's rewritten history in a way that allows him to escape guilt. I wonder if he's told anyone. I wonder if, when he did, he cried tears of relief, if he felt renewed. I wonder if a woman let him cry on her shoulder and if that woman had already promised to love him eternally or if she had just done so in her head.

I know one thing about Life Ruiners: they know when they've got you.

I LIKE TO THINK THAT I'M A GOOD PERSON: MOST ANIMALS really like me and I've helped a couple friends move out of their apartments. Does God (or whatever force moves this universe) not agree? If so, I'd like to offer it up that I really feel like I've exhausted myself proving that I didn't deserve what he did to me or that, at the very least, I deserve some serious cosmic retribution for it.

Nonetheless, he did what he did and I have the nightmares to prove it. Sometimes, they're just parsed memories—slide shows of horror, replays of some of the worst moments I've lived. More often than not, they're more metaphorical: I dream of saving girls—around the same age that I was the first time—from burning buildings or sinking boats, but I never succeed. The dream always ends with me watching them succumb to the waves or turn into ashes.

In another dream-mare, I'm in an ocean myself: miles and miles of bright, jewel-toned turquoise, but nothing lives here. There are no fish, no coral, no sharks, not even plankton. It's just me, lost, and water as far as the eye can see.

I don't want to write of myself this way as though I'll be like this forever. But won't I? What proof do I have to the contrary?

"No matter what happens to our bodies in our lifetimes . . . , they remain ours."

—MAGGIE NELSON

When I first read that, it comforted me. I underlined it. I was reminded that, regardless of the fact that someone once took my body and made use of it, it was I who still possessed it fully. But once, I thought of it as a reminder that I take this body (I get this one, and only this one) with me everywhere, and so I take everything that happened to it along with me. We are chained to each other—this body and me. The body holds on; the mind remembers.

Am I ruined, after all? Answering that would require me to imagine a universe in which this never happened to me. What would I look like? Act like? How would I love?

It is very hard to imagine; the pain of envisioning myself and my life without this sort of trauma is nearly physical. I can't sit with it for long.

When I do anyway, the first thing I see is the happy absence of the emotional pain I've lived with for two decades. But it's when I get to what would fill the empty spaces that the pain would leave behind that it gets impossible. I have a sense that there might be endless lives I haven't and couldn't live: the girl without my fears or nightmares, the girl for whom trust is not an impressive feat, the girl who can stand to live in her own skin without ever knowing that the ability to do so is a blessing.

The thing is, I can picture the world in which I never met the Life Ruiner or, at least, one in which he never got an opportunity to ruin my life. But the universe in which something like that could never happen to me—or in which, even if I were never hurt in that way, I could be that girl of my own dreams—I'm not sure that place exists.

This is partly because it happened again: different steps, but the same tune. It was my junior year of college; I was at a house party. I told him, *No, I don't want to have sex with you.* But when he was inside me, I didn't scream. I didn't yell for help or push him off me, even though I had done just that a couple weeks prior, when at yet another party, yet another man had whipped out an unwelcome dick.

Maybe I was just wearied.

Having lived two drastically different stories of sexual assault, I've learned some interesting things about responses. When someone hears a story of child abuse, they usually respond in one of two ways: (1) a look of absolute horror and sympathy with what seems to be an almost overwhelming impulse to comfort you (regardless of your actual emotional state at the time) or (2) a look of absolute horror and with what seems to be an almost overwhelming impulse to flee from you.

On the other hand, when someone hears of an adult woman being raped at a house party, the reactions are much more varied. Were you drunk? Had you hooked up before? Could there have been some misunderstanding?

People will always respond differently to the story of a sexually abused third grader than they will that of a young woman who is violated by a friend at a booze-soaked house party. There is a kind of fairness in that, since they are very different stories. Yet, in many ways, they are so intimately intertwined: they both rely on the belief in ownership of the vulnerable body, whether female or child or both. The idea that one violation is vastly worse than the other is probably not so different a rationalization than what goes through a date rapist's mind.

Those who are disgusted at the idea of touching a child may be the exact same that would grope an adult woman in an alleyway or on a crowded subway train—or worse.

IN THE FIRST OF ELENA FERRANTE'S NEAPOLITAN NOVELS, Gigliola, the childhood friend of the eponymous narrator, is raped by the two wealthy brothers who terrorize the neighborhood. In the third, *Those Who Leave and Those Who Stay*, Gigliola, having been seduced by promises of riches and prestige, is married to one of those rapists. Her husband, Michele, treats her poorly, beating her and cheating on her with many other women. The narrator, Elena, comes to visit Gigliola, who was once proud and boastful, and hears about the latter's misfortune:

"And she suddenly asked me, as if she really wanted an opinion: 'Do you think I exist? Look at me, in your view do I exist?' She hit her full breasts with her open hand, but she did it as if to demonstrate physically that the hand went right through her, that her body, because of Michele, wasn't there. He had taken everything of her, immediately, when she was almost a child. He had consumed her, crumpled her."

I immediately recognized this scene. My biggest fear is that I'm not actually real. Of all my nightmares, the absolute worst are the ones that wake me in a panic and force me to pace my bedroom in search of some undeniable proof of my existence. I riffle through drawers and shelves, pull out pieces of jewelry that my mother passed down to me, look at books in whose margins I've written. *Yes, there you are*, I tell myself.

Perhaps the most horrifying thing about nonconsensual sex is that, in an instant, it erases you. Your own desires, your safety and well-being, your ownership of the body that may very well have been the only thing you ever felt sure you owned—all of it becomes irrelevant, even nonexistent. You don't need to be a helpless, innocent child to be changed by that.

WHEN I WAS STUDYING ABROAD IN SALVADOR DA BAHIA, BRA-zil, I came home to my host family's apartment late one night. It was in a fancy building near the coast, guarded by an attractive, young doorman. The doorman often complimented me or made a gross joke in passing. Knowing what often happens to women who don't, I played along, said thank you, laughed. That night, however, the doorman wanted proof of my affection. He followed me into the lobby and started groping me. He tried to kiss me and I pushed him off. Finally, I got into the elevator and pushed the button to close the doors. That's when he gave up. I distinctly remember the image of his arm retreating from the door right before it would've been crushed between the two slabs of metal.

When I recounted the story to a friend, she shook her head. "You shouldn't have encouraged him," she said. "You really only have yourself to blame."

I was angry at the time but, in retrospect, I see that my friend believed in the woman who was untouchable, the woman who could do the right things, the woman who could just "be careful" and thereby escape the horrors that await so many of us. Or maybe she believed that the things that happen to lots of other women don't have anything to do with what can or will happen to her. She's wrong, of course. But her willingness to believe it laid bare a hopefulness that still breaks my heart.

Why tell this story at all? Why contribute to the compendium of stories about girls being used? Why ask all these questions that don't have answers?

It's hard to admit, but part of it has to do with the need for an audience. We don't exist without other people; therefore, our pain isn't real until somebody else looks at it and goes: "Damn, that looks like it hurt." When you're lost in the terror of your own memories, or when your actions occasionally prove their loathsome hold on you, the antidote to losing your mind is to have a handful of people around who know your wound and will verify its existence.

But why spend hours diving into the deep well of it, knowing that it'll only reignite the struggle? Why share it with strangers?

In Toni Morrison's *Beloved*, she recounts the horrors of a dehumanization that I can still barely comprehend, even after multiple reads. With the end of the three hundred pages of *Beloved*, she responds to similar questions with the sort of elegant and complex clarity that only she is capable of: "It was not a story to pass on. This is not a story to pass on."

I'm writing this for the other girls, some of whom may be in my family. The boys, too. I'm writing this for my friend who told me to blame myself. I'm writing this so it can be a part of the compendium of other sad and bad stories like these, because maybe the compendium will say something in totality that we cannot say alone.

Like all the writers I read, I'm writing to prove that I exist.

THE LIFE RUINER ALONE DIDN'T RUIN ME. THE WORLD THAT made him did—the place that continues to manufacture replicas of him and continues to create the circumstances in which he and his replicas thrive.

What is there to do about that?

I THINK OF EGYPT AS A KIND OF HOME, EVEN THOUGH I ONLY spent one continuous year there and nearly all of it was excruciating. I know a lot of people who could make strong arguments as to why I can't claim it—arguments with which I wouldn't disagree.

Still, my stubborn mind continues its attachment. And when I think of Egypt as home, there's one memory that always comes back up: I'm in the third grade and it's a warm night in Mit Garah, the farming village where the majority of my family lives. We cross the dirt road in front of the four-story building where everyone—aunts, uncles, cousins, grandparents, nieces, nephews—lives together and we enter the cane and cotton fields and make a beeline for the small river that runs through it. The sun is about to set and the sky is bathed in orange and pink and the minaret just two blocks away is preparing to sound the adhan for the maghrib prayer. We (the kids, just the kids) are looking for frogs. They are tiny and precious, about the size of a thumbnail and very, very jumpy. We catch bunches of them but they never stay put. So, in the end, we don't really catch them after all.

On good days, I think of my heart like one of those frogs. My trauma, my PTSD, my ongoing battles with memories, all the surprising ways the damage rears its head—all of these are the cups we put the little frogs in or the small hands we tried to use to cover the lip. Still, the frogs escape: not despite their smallness or vulnerability, but precisely because of it.

And then maghrib is called, and as we gather to pray, the frogs go back home to the waters they were meant for.

All the Angry Women

Lyz Lenz

Every Tuesday night, I meet with angry women.

They don't look angry, at least initially. They look like you would expect midwestern mothers to look—midwaist and heavy sighs. And they don't technically come to this Victorian house in Iowa because they are angry. They are here for what is marketed as a Bible study, but it is really so much more.

I choose to think of it as group therapy.

I signed up for this class I now lead when I was twenty-five and angry. In the year prior, my father-in-law had died, my sisters Becky and Cathy had been in a devastating car accident, and Cathy had temporarily lost her ability to walk. (When she learned how again, she discovered she wouldn't be able to have children.) During her long hospital stay, in those hazy days when we didn't know whether Cathy would live or die, which no one ever discussed openly, I had to fight my family to keep the man who had sexually abused her for three years in her teens out of her room in the ICU. He was married to another sister and told everyone he wanted to support Cathy.

When I saw him walk into the hospital waiting room, I went to the bathroom and vomited. Then I drove home and told a friend, who was at my house delivering frozen lasagna. She drove me right back to the hospital and made me tell a social worker, who told the doctors, who barred the man from the hospital room.

Across the hospital, far away from Cathy in the ICU, Becky screamed at me from her hospital bed. Even at twenty, even while injured, she felt caught between the divisions in her family. Her whole body was in a brace and each word made her body tense with pain, but she still yelled at me.

"How could you tell everyone our business? How could you do that to Mom and Dad? How could you? You never know when to shut up!" My mother stood in the corner of the room, looking at me as Becky yelled. Maybe another sister was in the room, too. All I remember is their silence as Becky screamed, her voice strong despite her pain.

I walked out of the room and shut the door. I could hear her still as I backed into the hallway. No one ever spoke of it again.

Two months later, I found myself on the floor of my living room, facedown and crying. I heaved and felt my ribs push into the oak floors. I was angry beyond belief, but I had nowhere to put that anger. The shelves of my heart were full.

I walked down the block to a women's shelter in my neighborhood and signed up for a class. I had met the director once at a church I attended. The class advertised itself to women in the church as life-changing—that phrase was written on the cover of all the materials and used by women who'd taken the class. The class itself was almost silly, forcing us to write letters to our past selves, repeating affirmations to each other, holding a baby doll and pretending it was us. But the mantra of the class is "feelings are for feeling," which was exactly what I needed.

Because I needed to find a place to feel angry.

Now, I facilitate that class on Tuesday nights, listening as women bring their own anger. It follows them in through the door. *Where can I put this?* they want to know. *Where can I set it down?* I pat the cushions next to me. *Put it here.*

The Proverbs in the Old Testament advise that it is better to live in a desert or on a roof than in the same home with an angry and contentious woman. My mother recited this verse to my sisters and me when we would yell and scream against injustices—our shorts were too short, our voices too loud, slips must be worn under dresses, dishes must be done while our brothers played. The words were used to silence us.

The hot angry bile of our anger was swallowed back down. It made us uncouth and unlivable.

"No one will want you with all that anger," my mother told me as I angrily packed for college. They hadn't wanted me to go, not to a Lutheran college. They wanted me to go somewhere more "Christian." Or to just stay at home. It had taken everything I had to apply for school, find a way to pay for it, and then leave; I had been fueled only by anger. Anger was the only thing that made me strong enough to leave the only home I knew. I held on to it and nurtured it every night, reciting my parents' litany of offenses over and over into the dark of my room. I needed to leave. I needed my anger to help me.

My mom stood in the doorway the night before I left. I had sewn my own pajama pants when she refused to buy me some. I had cobbled together scholarships and grants, when she refused to pay for my tuition. Now, as I loaded up a suitcase with towels stolen from her linen closet and an alarm clock from the guest room, she watched me, saying nothing as she saw me steal from her.

Instead, she said, "Stop being so angry. You will drive everyone away."

Her voice was calm and quiet. I didn't look at her, instead focusing on my heavy bag. Her words were meant as a kindness, a gentle warning; it was one she must have learned herself, packing away her own anger, somehow making it all fit into her heart.

Every woman in my class walks into the room with a heavy load. They have learned the same lessons as my mother and I. If you are angry, men will run to the roof, they will flee to the desert; your anger will make you alone. Your anger will render you unlovable. They heft their bag of contraband emotion into their lap. *Where can I put this?*

Our society has a place for actual abusers: jail. There are systems and processes in place to handle them and rehabilitate them. The faith I grew up with demands forgiveness for abusers, but angry women? They must be silent.

Abusers have a pathology. They have a system. They have

restraining orders and court-mandated anger management classes. Once, I heard a news story about sex offenders who had been driven out of their homes by laws mandating that they stay away from schools. A hotel had opened its doors to them so that they wouldn't be homeless. Even they had a place to lay their heads.

My anger was still homeless.

Jesus is allowed table-flipping rage. We speak of men and their rage as if it is laudable. "Men just get mad and punch each other and it's over," we say. "Women are just bitches; they never let it go."

That's because we never can let it go. Because where would we put it? What system? What faith? What institution has room? Has patience? Has understanding for an angry woman?

Sandy, a woman in one of my Tuesday night groups, speaks softly, but carries years of abuse and pain inside her. She told me a story of a group of men at her church critiquing her appearance. "That," she said, in a voice that I had to lean forward to hear, "makes me angry and, well, that's just not nice, is it?"

I pat the cushion next to me. *What does nice have fuck all to do with anything? Put your anger here, my friend. Put it on this couch next to mine.*

I can feel their anger in me. It pulls at my skin and swells my heart. Their anger prickles my skin, like so many armies rising to fight. I am angry too. I am angry for them. Angry for me. Angry for all those women in homes with men on the roof, avoiding them.

I can only facilitate this course once a year. I'm afraid the anger will break me.

MY MOTHER TOLD ME I WAS ANGRY SINCE BIRTH; FAMILY lore, though, holds I was a happy child, up until the moment I wasn't. I would suddenly start screaming inconsolably. "You would just have these freak-outs," my mom likes to say, smiling. "Like you just needed to get it all out of you."

I have never known if the stories were apocryphal or self-fulfilling prophecies.

The day my mother fully condemned my anger, we were in her SUV. We were sitting in front of my parents' house in Florida, which was green stucco, eating Sonic burgers. The lawn thick and coarse was studded with my father's plastic light-up flamingos. We had been running errands and talking about my wedding.

My mother was angry at me. Angry because I hadn't taken her suggestion of using silk flowers. Angry because I wanted to buy real ones, even if that meant more work. She was mad about the money too: I was taking some money from my in-laws to help with the wedding and I was dipping into my own savings to pay for it. This made her mad, but time has erased from my mind the precise reasons why.

I said, "I abhor fake ones." The taste of mayonnaise and meat still sat in my mouth. Even before I said those words, I knew they would make my mother snap.

She turned off the car and gripped the wheel. The air was still between us. The clicking of the cooling engine seemed like a warning. I held my Coke in my hands. The Styrofoam was cold and pliable. I was sweating. I thought, *I should grab the door. I should leave.* I knew something was coming for me. Instead, I turned to face my mother.

"You have always been angry," she said. "You have always been angry at me. Hated me. Even when you were little. You've always been mad."

"This is ridiculous," I said. "How can a baby be mad? It's just a baby and this is all just about flowers."

Even as I said it, I knew it wasn't just about flowers. This was about something else. Something that at twenty-two, I could feel moving underneath me, but I couldn't see. I could feel it shaking the places where I stood, where I sat, and where I lay down. But I could not name it. My words made her eyelids twitch. She wasn't looking at me. Her jaw clenched and released. Clenched and released. I opened the door and got out. For the rest of the day, I vibrated with my mother's rage, which hung over us until I left to go back to Minneapolis and finish planning my wedding.

We had real flowers—hydrangeas and roses.

I now know that the moment in the SUV, between the smell of our greasy burgers and the swish of the watery Coke left in our Styrofoam cups, was the world of my mother's anger. A vast world that involved many small pains and even more large ones, grief, anxiety, and the secrets tucked in between. Her mother was there too, looming somewhere underneath the stack of white napkins or the straw wrappers on the floor. I can only guess at what else was there—her own marriage, her own fears and private losses. She had nowhere else for them to go, so here they came, tumbling out in a conversation about fake and real, hydrangeas and roses.

"WHY ARE YOU SO ANGRY?" A BOYFRIEND DEMANDED OF ME once. He listened to Korn and Metallica, raging with his music as it blared in his dorm room; I loved to blast out Green Day's "Minority" screaming out, "I don't need your authority / down with the moral majority!"

He had thought it was funny and quaint even: my rage on a playlist was cute. My rage in his face when he made fun of the *Vagina Monologues* was not.

"Whatever happened to you, it's not enough for you to be this pissy," he said. We broke up the next week.

Years later, someone would email me after reading an article I wrote. "Whatever you are mad at," the emailer explained, "someone else has it worse. Why are you so mad? You don't get to be mad."

Anger is always reserved for someone else. And yet, I've been in a room with a woman who escaped a war, who lost her father in ethnic cleansing, whose mother burned her hair, whose cousin raped her. "What right do I have to be angry, when I am alive?" she said.

Anger is the privilege of the truly broken, and yet, I've never met a woman who was broken enough that she allowed herself to be angry.

An angry woman must answer for herself. The reasons for her anger must be picked over, examined, and debated.

My anger must stand the scrutiny of the court of law, of evidentiary procedures. I must prove it comes from somewhere justified and not just because one time some man touched my sister. Or because at one time some man touched some woman and he will continue on and on. Or because my pay is unequal and the pay of women of color is less equal than mine. Or because I had to have my husband tell my parents to stop forcing me to meet my sister's abuser for a reconciliation meeting, because they wouldn't listen to me, because my angry vagina rendered me mute.

I used to imagine I killed that man. I imagined it in different ways every night before I went to sleep. My anger soothed me. But in my dreams it was his turn to kill me.

ANGRY WOMEN ARE ALWAYS THE VILLAINS.

A betrayed Medea sacrificing her children, the product of her womb the only avenue of her control. Glenn Close in *Fatal Attraction* boiling bunnies and lashing out with a knife. Brontë's woman in the attic, burning everyone and everything with her rage.

In *Domestic Tranquility*, F. Carolyn Graglia asserts that when she was a feminist she was angry and unhappy, and submitting to gender roles made her tranquil and at peace. At Baptist summer camp when I was twelve, a counselor dismissed Virginia Woolf as "just another angry woman."

Our anger undermines us. Why else would we try so hard to get it in check? Hiding tears in an office bathroom, clenching our jaws in SUVs with our mother, smiling tight, white, desperate smiles at the men whose words and hands crawl up our legs.

My own family stopped speaking to me for a year because I was too angry about my sister's abuse.

"We can't talk to you when you are like this," one of my sisters told me over the phone.

"Why aren't you like this?" I asked.

"Anger is never the answer," she said.

A few weeks after my family stopped talking to me, my parents celebrated Christmas with the man who abused my sister. In the NFL, men who are accused of rape and domestic violence soon make their way back to the field—if they are ever required to leave. But angry women are never allowed to be anything more than the shrill cries from the sidelines.

Forgive the abuser. The only solution for female anger is for her to stop being angry.

And yet, when Jesus flipped tables in the temple, his rage was lauded. King David railing to the heavens to rain fire on his enemies is lauded as a man after God's own heart. An angry man in cinema is Batman. An angry male musician is a member of Metallica. An angry male writer is Chekhov. An angry male politician is passionate, a revolutionary. He is a Donald Trump or a Bernie Sanders. The anger of men is a powerful enough tide to swing an election. But the anger of women? That has no place in government, so it has to flood the streets.

SO EVERY TUESDAY I SIT WITH A CHORUS OF ANGRY WOMEN. Together we learn our brash harmonies. Angry women fight.

Angry women care. Angry women speak and yell and sob their truths.

In the class, we hold baby dolls and talk to them, learning how to talk to ourselves again. We write letters to past versions of ourselves, giving those little girls a chance to yell and rage.

Sometimes I have to hand out a list of feelings.

"Use this list to help identify what you feel," I say. In my six years of helping with this class, I have found that, despite the advice for men on the internet, women are actually very good with the facts of their lives and not with the feelings.

"You have to name your feelings," I tell them. We all wince a little even as I say it, but I make no apologies—not anymore, anyway. My words may sound like New Age bullshit, but whatever else belongs to us, whatever else we own, we should be allowed to name it. That gift was given to Adam in the garden. It's the gift I try to give to the women in this cold drafty room in the century-old mansion that now houses those of us who are tired and broken and angry.

So far no one who has come to the house has retreated to the roof or the desert. I asked the woman who founded the house if she knew she'd just be opening the doors for a bunch of angry women. She laughed, "I needed a place to put my anger too. I did it for me."

So here is a type of Eden, where the creations we name were made in us long ago, before we were even born, anger sliding on down through the double helix, handed down from our mothers. We put our anger down, the tidy packages, the stolen suitcases, too tired to care if we are chasing anyone up to a roof or a desert.

Sometimes I wonder if the Proverbs weren't an admonishment of an angry woman, but a warning about the depth and breadth and scope of her wrath. A woman's anger needs the whole house; go somewhere else. Anywhere else. Her anger is not going away.

Good Girls

AMY JO BURNS

THE TRUTH NO ONE TOLD YOU IS THAT, IN ORDER FOR A good girl to survive, she must make some things disappear. You know because you used to be one of the good girls; you used to know how to forget.

But the truth you're trying to tell yourself now is that you don't need to be "good," not anymore. You need to be seen, and in order to be seen, you need to let yourself remember.

You were walking alone in the woods on the afternoon that you remembered the name of a man you'd sworn to forget. Twelve years had passed since you took that vow as a ten-year-old, and this name belonged to a man whose secrets you'd once known well, though he'd only ever known one of yours. He'd been the only piano teacher you'd had, and you just one of his many pupils. Back then, you'd been one of his good girls. Back then, he'd been teaching you how to make some truths disappear.

In the fall of 1991, seven of your fellow students in western Pennsylvania defied their good girl graces when they came forward to admit your teacher had put his hands on them during their lessons, touching them softly to the beat of the metronome.

You, though, feared the consequences of telling the truth more than the burden of staying silent. Your indoctrination into the sorority of good girls had begun long before your piano teacher ever put his hands on you. Good girls knew how to keep a smile at the ready (lest you be called conceited), how to turn their homework in on time (lest you be called lazy), and how to keep their mouth shut (lest you be called a troublemaker). Those of us who chose to stay silent didn't need to be told to do so.

There was an ungainly rhythm to the response to the accusations, the way his denials drowned out their honesty, and the way an entire town was outraged, but not on behalf of the victims. Parents, teachers, and even fellow students called this man a casualty of a conspiracy plotted by girls—good girls like you—whose backpacks were filled with permission slips and retainer lids, whose heads were full of spelling words and state capitals. Much of the furor spread not because a crime occurred, but because these girls had the nerve to *say* that it had.

A good girl is a quick study, and this is what you, always a good girl, learned: It doesn't matter how good you are, because a man will always be better.

The people of your hometown—small in size and big in illusion—prided themselves on being a virtuous community with righteous men at the helm. Your piano teacher was a member of the town's most potent clique of leaders—men who taught science and math to elementary school children, coached a varsity sport, and played the church organ every Sunday. To attack or question one of those men was to criticize the town itself, and you didn't dare blaspheme the only place you'd been taught would protect you from the rest of the world. You were just a girl, after all. Maybe you were, in fact, predisposed to fantasy, just as these men who fought in wars beside each other and hunted deer back-to-back assured themselves that you were. You knew that a girl, even a good one, was at best an unreliable source, and, at worst, a liar.

After word spread about who had snitched, those girls who weren't you sat alone at lunch tables, were cornered by other students after school, and had to sit in the classrooms of teachers who'd donated money to the piano teacher's legal fund. One young woman's family eventually left town because the environment had grown so hostile. Another was your best friend; she didn't know that you had lied when you said he hadn't touched you. You didn't dare tell anyone—not her, not even yourself. You knew a good girl has to forget in order to survive.

Another lie you were told is that the passage of time will blunt a wound. But by the time you turned eighteen, the weight of being one of the good girls made you buckle at the knees. Too many smiles, too many secrets, too many rules. As an adolescent you trusted no one. No matter how straight your As or unscathed your heart, the secret bled you from the inside out—even after you'd all but forgotten what the secret was. There is no path lonelier than the one a good girl forges for herself.

Still, you felt claustrophobic in the town that bred crop after crop of good girls only to surrender their innocence as payment for its fantasies. You didn't want to be named in anyone's ransom note. So, instead, you ransomed yourself to higher education in Upstate New York, six hours from home.

Then on a crisp, fall afternoon during your senior year in college, your piano teacher's name flashed in your mind. The good girl in you could no longer contain it; your memory paid your virtue no mind. The leaves scattering the path that day were bright and fragile, not unlike the ones that folks back home used to rake into piles and burn on the weekends. Your piano teacher's house—and the dark basement where he'd taught his lessons as he let his hands wander all over you— had been hidden among a crowd of trees. Leaves had always cloaked the path leading to his door on the first days of lessons every autumn.

He'd taught students in your town for decades until he finally pleaded guilty and went to jail for a year, the leaves aging from emerald to ruby to goldenrod to ash and then starting again, welcoming close to a hundred students to his basement for half-hour stints at a time. When you began taking lessons, you would have paid a good girl's fortune to be his protégée, to stand next to him beneath his spotlight. By the time you finished taking lessons, you had.

As you stood in the forest, you felt the snarl of his name

on your lips, and you jolted at the memory of the day his hands discovered your body.

It was hot that summer afternoon, and you'd just gone swimming before heading to his house. You'd signed up for summer lessons with him, hoping to improve for next year's recital. That session began just like every other—you warmed up your fingers by playing music scales and then traveled the keys, unsure and timid. Then you felt his hand creep under your armpit toward your breast, a silken, gossamer motion. You arched your back in alarm, but you kept on playing, just like good girls should. The song ended, and he took his hand away. When the lesson finished, you ran out to your mother's waiting car, and you drove home with the windows down. You ran your fingers through your hair, still damp with pool water. You kept taking lessons, and you never said a word.

Before that day in the woods in Upstate New York, when you couldn't not remember, you hadn't thought much about your old piano teacher, even if you still felt his influence. But soon you discovered that, when you first try to be honest about what happened, telling the truth feels like rebreaking a crooked bone. Over the years you'd grown so accustomed to the weight of concealing this man's iniquities that it unmoors you to wriggle out from under it. But you did it anyway, clumsily at first, blurting the truth out to your roommates, a few friends, and even a stranger or two. It was like discovering your own dubious treasure; you needed someone else to see it in order to verify its existence. But no one knew what to say.

I always knew something was wrong with you, one friend admits.

God has forgiven you for lying, now that you've confessed it, claims another.

Is this why you don't eat? asks someone else. *Why is it that women are always blaming all their problems on men?*

Blaming your problems on him? It took you twelve years to assign him any blame at all. As one of the good girls, you'd convinced yourself that concealing your piano teacher's "indiscretions" was the selfless thing to do, the feminine thing to do. That kind of allegation could ruin a man's career, for Christ's sake, but we girls will bounce back. We've found a buoyancy in the thrall of a man's world, the pointlessness of it.

It took you twelve years to see that being "good" had gotten your piano teacher everywhere and you nowhere at all. So you decide, for the first time in your life, that you aren't going to be one of the good girls anymore. You decide that "good" is not an adjective that ought to be applied to a person, as it only rendered you inanimate and inhuman, like a piece of cheese or a watercolor painting.

The good girl is nothing more than a myth. We long for her for the same reason we long for utopia: Neither exists.

So you sit down to write about it, and you write and write and write. Writing about it feels like falling through the sky; the day when someone wants to publish it, you land with a hard thump. Yes, you're elated, but you also realize that you can't hide anymore. Everyone is going to know your secret; everyone will know that your piano teacher put his hands on you and you lied about it.

The funny thing is that soon you realize that you actually don't mind strangers knowing. You don't even mind friends and acquaintances knowing. What you're worried about is everyone who still lives in that town knowing, everyone who is about to find out you're not one of the good girls anymore.

Still, when you're asked what your book is about, the same, tired awkwardness ensues when you use words like *sexual* and *assault*—words that, when paired together, are dirtier in the mouth than any cuss. You get used to it. That discomfort is why you wrote the book, after all.

You spend the summer trying to prepare for something for which you cannot prepare. A voice in your gut tells you that publishing your story will come at the cost of everything you hold precious. The voice sounds a lot like loneliness.

You try to combat your fears by reminding yourself why you wrote the book: because silence was not the cure everyone swore it would be. You repeat the mantra over and over, even in the middle of the night while your husband sleeps soundlessly next to you. Part of you hopes once folks from home read the book, they'll understand the importance of speaking the truth, even over twenty years later.

But then a few days before the book comes out, word spreads about the crass and selfish thing you've done.

You brace yourself; you planned on this kind of backlash. You expected your piano teacher's cronies to come out of their retirement homes to defend their old pal. *Who do you think you are?* you wait for some of them to ask. *You ain't lived here in years.* You think you wouldn't mind taking them to task, no matter how public it is.

They, however, aren't the ones who come after you. The ones who come after you aren't men at all: They are girls a lot like you, some of whom are the daughters of your piano teacher's staunchest supporters. You didn't expect the backlash to come from women you'd imagined would find relief in your words; you hadn't planned on good girls turning against one of their own.

A few days before your book's release, you receive a message from an old member of your cheerleading squad. *You better not have written about me,* it says in so many words. *I have people to protect.*

You have cashed in on a terrible memory for your own gain, says someone else. *I hope you enjoy the money.*

She's a liar, swears someone else on social media. *The truth shall be revealed.*

Another calls you a coward. Yet another invites you out for a meal only to tell you you've become the abuser by bringing all this up again.

You used to be one of the good girls, they all seem to say. *When did you go astray?*

You go for a walk on the autumn day of the book's debut, and the white sky reminds you of the day you first remembered your piano teacher's hands on you. Now it feels like a new kind of remembering, a reckoning. You tell yourself: *I am not afraid. I am not afraid. I am not afraid.*

But you are.

You choose to accept that you cannot legislate anyone's reactions. Instead, you recognize something familiar in the voices hurling condemnation: They are afraid, just like you. You remember how vicious the mood turned back in 1991, how unsafe it was to feel how you felt. You choose to hear the criticisms, even those that liken you to the piano teacher himself; you also choose not to respond. You still aren't sure if this is the right decision because it only makes people angrier.

You give book readings and answer questions. You learn to look people in the eye. Your heart aches for the young women who stay after the events to confide in you, for how effortlessly they understand why you kept your secret for so long. You start to understand why it isn't safe for some women and men to ever share their secrets: Their families will implode, their livelihoods are at stake, their marriages may end. This you know: The truth may set you free, but the truth will also cost you.

You'll be called brave over and over, which you will hate. No one means for it to sound reductive, but it does. You worry that they don't mean superhero-brave, but cancer-brave, walk-the-plank-brave.

People will also shoot compliments at your husband like Cupid shoots an arrow. *Wow,* they'll say. *That's some guy you got, supporting you like this. Most men wouldn't.* And you'll agree and mean it. Your husband is the best human you know. And yet, you'll wonder why the bar for his support is so low. Why shouldn't he be proud to stand next to you? Why should he be ashamed about something done to his wife, long before you met?

After a year, you'll marvel that the book gave your voice back to you. Friends you thought you'd lose because you aren't that good girl they used to know, but you learn that was never why they loved you anyway. You'll receive a few messages from your piano teacher's fellow victims—some who spoke up and some who did not—and you'll read those letters aloud to yourself until you've memorized them. One woman will travel over three hours to hear you read. Another will come out of hiding to stand up for you. Another one will write to say that she thinks the book might be the start of redeeming what happened. You'll think: *I didn't believe in that kind of redemption, but these women changed my mind.*

And after the noise dies down and you return to your desk and your quiet life, you'll see that you are changed. Not changed by the book itself or its acceptance or its censure, but by the importance of speaking the truth first to yourself. The invariability of it, the solidity of it, the company of it. You'll write a letter to that good girl who is still stowed away inside you. When you grow older, you'll tell her, you will not get over what happened, but you will reach the other side of it. You will keep it in your back pocket rather than live with it roped around your neck. Soon, you'll no longer miss the girl that you were before that afternoon. There are better things to be than good.

Utmost Resistance

Law and the Queer Woman or How I Sat in a Classroom and Listened to My Male Classmates Debate How to Define Force and Consent[1]

V. L. Seek[2]

1. In law school, you are taught how to write academic articles for publication in law reviews, which is the art of crafting the perfect title, of making your student analysis of strict scrutiny and constitutional law sexy, of disguising your theory-heavy piece as something that is not too political and therefore not too divisive. You are taught the art of the paragraph-long footnotes that cite obscure case law or define a seemingly obvious word with thirty-something synonyms. This is not that. Its edges are not dull and its words arguably divisive (though I struggle to think of any article about rape, legal or otherwise, that is not cause for debate). But we have wasted too much time softening the corners of our speech and blunting our legal arguments to nudge legal reformation to our desired outcome when it comes to rape. We have wasted too much.

2. Many legal academic papers criticize the law, but to criticize academia is a different kind of purpose and a different kind of risk, especially when one is housed in its ivory tower. I think of these things when I write under my name, and when

I.

My life at twenty-one was all short skirts and red wine and big talk about life after college.

Twenty-two was a move out west and a first year of law school, going out but not staying out, annotating case law, and settling into the comfort of a long-distance girlfriend and thousands of miles and a computer screen separating our bodies. My mother never taught me to knit but somehow I taught myself and managed to deeply and expertly weave delusion and denial into the threads of the blanket I buried my feet under to keep warm in the new Colorado nights. Yes, it was cold out here, I told my friends, but not as cold as you would think.

II.

"There must be the utmost resistance by the woman by all means within her power."
    State v. McClain, 149 N.W. 771, 771 (Wis. 1914)

That summer I was twenty-one, just before my senior year in college, I worked as an intern at a prep school in a small town in the Northeast. I took the train up from Baltimore to get there. I was the only person to get off at the stop. The train

---

I instead choose to write under my pen name, I wonder if I am contributing to the problem or still fighting for a solution.

had emptied in New York and never filled back up, so I'd spent much of the ride staring out the window and romanticizing the upcoming months. My bags were spread across several seats, and I found a safety in the isolation that did not surprise me. My stop had no train station, no platform. I dragged my bags down the steps and found myself facing a one-room train depot and a gazebo draped in patriotic flags. I waited for my cab for two hours, thinking that everyone who passed me must know that I wasn't from around these parts. In the cab, the driver offered a knowing sigh when I told him where to take me. We drove up the hill.

There were parts of the job that were exactly as I imagined: taking residents of my dorm to visit the family-owned candy shop in town, teaching writing to eighth graders already primed to write their college admissions essays, supervising the Fourth of July lawn games and cookouts (that summer was too dry for fireworks), beholding the steps and rooms boasting plaques and the names of presidential alumni.

But there were other parts I hadn't imagined. The twenty-minute walk to the single town bar that we made every night in heels. The spot under the tree where people would go to smoke, steps away from the campus perimeter. Daily breakfast with other interns who would show up with a bruised eye and smile ("I couldn't feel my face") and talk about the drugs they took last night.

Drinking on the campus was not allowed, and so those of us with IDs and nights off would make that nightly pilgrimage to the one bar. Some nights we came back early, others we returned with our heels in our hands, and a few nights we took a cab (it was the same driver every time). The drinks were cheap and I was newly twenty-one.

Our last night of work was the first night we could drink on campus: The students had left for the summer and the halls and dorm rooms were empty for the first time in six weeks. A night was planned, starting at a colleague's dorm and stopping by six others that housed us before ending up at the town bar. The crawl was themed, so we spent the day at the Goodwill crafting our costumes. We spent our last paychecks on the alcohol and I remember that liquor store and that bottle of wine so well. I remember holding it by its neck as I walked from my friend's room to the first party of the night. I remember holding it by my side for group photos. And I remember vomiting it back up the next morning.

We got to the first party at eight. By 8:30 my night was over; I never made it to the bar.

The next morning I lay on the floor of a shower stall of that first dorm under a stream of water. The hot water was turned all the way up, but it felt like ice on my skin. I didn't know how many hours I had been on that floor. I was shaking. My underwear was on the other side of the room. I was so concerned with cleaning up where I had been sick. I took off my soaking wet clothes and tried to stop shaking. I wrapped a towel around myself. It was barely the size of my torso. In the mirror I saw scratch marks on my back and bruises on my chest (I wouldn't notice the bruises on my thighs until later). I pulled my shirt back on to cover them. It was heavy and made me shake harder than before. I walked back to my building and called a security guard to let me in because I couldn't find my key in that bathroom. (My friend would return my purse later that day. "You left this behind when you left with. . . ." She trailed off with a teasing knowingness suggesting she did not know at all.) I didn't meet the security guard's eyes. I knew he was thinking that I had too much to drink last night—that I had let this happen.

For years, that night was my fault. I knew what rape was. I knew what consent was. I knew about first- and second-wave feminism. I knew queer theory. But I swallowed the blame like that bottle of red wine and repeated to myself the lies that would run on loop for years to come. *You have only yourself to blame. It was not that bad. You're okay. You're alive. At least you don't remember it all. The bruises are gone. You can forget about it. No one ever has to know.* Even now, these lies taste familiar, comfortable, in a way that the words *survivor* and *victim* never have.

III.

"In a civil case, the court may admit evidence offered to prove a victim's sexual behavior or sexual predisposition if its probative value substantially outweighs the danger of harm to any victim and of unfair prejudice to any party. The court may admit evidence of a victim's reputation only if the victim has placed it in controversy."
FEDERAL RULES OF EVIDENCE 412(A)(B)(2)

In the beginning of law school, you have a pervasive idealism about the law. Fresh off writing an essay about justice for all and changing the world using the rule of law for the admissions committee, you are thrown into classrooms with peers who ostensibly want the same—teachers and debaters, Peace Corps members and journalists. It doesn't take more than a week with the Socratic classes and the formulaic writing and the memorizing of case law for that initial unbridled idealism and passion to slip away.[3] I, however, clung to the ideal of law school despite my bad grades and the professors asking why I wasn't in law review or mock trial or moot court, despite the classes that I walked out of and in which I couldn't will my hands to stop shaking.

In Criminal Law, there was an entire chapter devoted to rape. It was my second semester, almost two years after I'd been raped. Around that time, the debate on the merit of trigger warnings was becoming mainstream, and it was present in our classrooms. My fellow law students were more than happy to chime in with a First Amendment or "slippery slope" defense; I didn't engage and I didn't care. I didn't reflect on my past experience as it interacted with my present: Trigger warnings were an academic debate, not a practical one. Distilling two pages of facts into a pithy "issue is how to define force"

---

3. This is not to imply that all social-justice-minded people who go to law school become corporate-defending drones. Nor should you infer that all lawyers have subscribed to the "ask questions but only so many" mind-set with which I am familiar. But there is a reason that these are the moments I remember and the people I can't forget. It was harder to think of examples to exclude than to find ones to mention.

note was how I was going to be a lawyer, not how I was going to finally come to terms with my own rape.

We barely got to the second case in class, before the questions—repetitive and probing—began to chip away at the protective dissociation I used to stay disengaged. How do we define force? What does it mean to "resist to the utmost"? How do we define consent? From an evidentiary perspective, can we ask what she was wearing? When can we ask about previous sexual partners, experiences, and proclivities?

With each question, each case, and each eagerly volunteered comment, I got colder and colder. I could not stop shaking. The room was eighty degrees and I was wearing a winter coat. I told myself I was just angry. There was so much to be angry about: the patriarchy, the precedent of rape law, the slow strides of legal reform. I had so many reasons that were not "I was raped." I had so many reasons that were not remembered trauma. That night, I cried while talking to my girlfriend and I wasn't able to explain why.

In Evidence, we learned how to discredit a witness on the stand. We learned the exceptions that would allow you to introduce a witness's sexual history to undermine the idea that she was raped. How much did you have to drink that night? Would you say it was your usual custom to dress in this way when going out? And you gave him your phone number? Do you normally accept a drink from any man who buys you one? Did you have sexual relations with him in the past? How many, would you say? And all of those times were consensual? Did you ever say no? You didn't scream?

And you continued to be in a relationship with him? But it's hard to remember now what happened on that day, isn't it? In Ethics, I learned that an attorney who collected money from his friends for a football game was disbarred because he kept the money for himself. I also learned that a senior attorney who repeatedly sexually harassed a female attorney was not disbarred because the court did not consider his daily groping to be conduct involving "moral turpitude." In seminars, I wrote papers with facts that would not fade from my mind[4] and that made me pick fights with my girlfriend because it was easier to accuse than admit. In clinical classes, I talked with my public defender friends who told me how to make a witness seem like a "lying bitch" on the stand. In the hallways, we debriefed from classes and criticized our classmates. "I've woken up after a lot of drunk sex and regretted it, but *I* didn't say it was rape," a girl told me. She was my closest friend.

It was isolating. Maybe it was retraumatizing, but I didn't let myself use that word. Trauma was for other people, I thought. And so I did not speak often in class. I had no interest in debating the law, in briefing a case, or commenting on the intersection of trigger warnings and the First Amendment. But law school—the law as it was taught, as it was received, as my classmates minimally questioned it, and as I understood it—was a trigger warning. That night when I was twenty-one

---

4. These facts included: Most rapists are repeat offenders. Trauma resolution is never final. In 1825, a rape conviction required the testimony from two male witnesses. In rural America, rapes increase during hunting season.

had shifted a bullet into the chamber. And I spent three years trying to move away from the line of fire.

IV.

"She must follow the natural instinct of every proud female to resist, by more than mere words, the violation of her person by a stranger or an unwelcomed friend. She must make it plain that she regards such sexual acts as abhorrent and repugnant to her natural sense of pride."
State v. Rusk, 424 A.2d 720 (1981) (Cole J., dissenting)

There is an art in deceiving oneself and I have always liked to be the best at everything. For me, coming out as a queer woman and a rape survivor have been inextricably linked. The way I relied on easy lies to avoid my own trauma was the same way I justified staying closeted. It was always "later" or "someday" or "no one's business at all."

But that summer when I was twenty-one, I thought that maybe "someday" was sooner than I'd initially believed, because there was a girl. I practiced saying the words in front of myself, hoping to see a more honest version staring back at me. *Queer. Lesbian. Dyke.* The words were foreign but they came from a mouth that understood them all the same. They felt wrong to say aloud but my tongue knew the shape to make and I heard my own truth pouring from a body that had spent years convincing herself otherwise. I wanted to come out. I wanted to speak my truth. I wanted to tell that girl I loved that there was a reason I named every woman in my writing after her. I was in love with her name and the way she laughed at me.

I had planned to come out my last year of college but those plans changed after the summer. What had felt so close to the surface, I once again forced back under. What I had romanticized as speaking my truth became so entrenched in doubt. Doubt about my identity, about that night, about whether it was all worth it. I was committed to shame because it was familiar. I was terrified about the questions of the men I had slept with and dated. And what about all of them? I was terrified that someone would somehow know I was raped and tell me that was why I was gay. I was terrified that it was true.

The shame and doubt that I struggled with about my sexuality was easily transferred to my trauma. I am not surprised by the statistics that show an increased rate of violence against queer people. Nor am I surprised that 46 percent of bisexual women face such violence, as compared with 14 percent and 13 percent of straight and lesbian women respectively.[5] The culture of shame and silence shrouds survivors of sexual violence, but also queer people who are so often considered other. "How did you know you were gay?" is another version of "Can I believe you?"

When your truth is so inherently questioned, it is easier to say nothing than anything at all. I know this because I live

5. Centers for Disease Control, "The National Intimate Partner and Sexual Violence Survey: An Overview of 2010 Findings on Victimization by Sexual Orientation" (2010).

in a bastion of liberalism, I have aligned myself with open-minded people, I have spent my life devouring queer feminist theory, I have spent years in therapy, decades in yoga, and months in meditation to grow and heal and understand and yet, despite everything, when I write about that night I still worry if my story is believable.

V.

If I were trying to convince you of a legal position, this is where I would conclude. I would summarize my arguments, allude to the case law, and propose a workable solution. But a conclusion seems out of reach when we are still stuck debating the facts, deciding whom to trust and what is true. We are trapped in a legal system that has never favored women and has never believed survivors. And we are mired in a circuitous and damning dialogue, so powerful that it invalidates our experiences, our traumas, our truths—a dialogue so powerful that we begin to doubt whether our experience was ever there at all.

Bodies Against Borders

Michelle Chen

SEXUAL VIOLENCE IS A GLOBAL EPIDEMIC THAT IS ALL around us, yet it is nowhere, precisely because it permeates every facet of our presence in the world, echoing throughout our political and popular cultures, ricocheting off the cement walls that define our boundaries.

My exposure to the concept of rape as a global mass phenomenon, and the violation of women's bodies at the borders of nation-states, came the way it does, sadly, for many Americans: through news articles, the antiseptic analyses of humanitarian field reports, sociological studies. And while my journalistic work often takes a critical look at issues of sexual- and gender-based violence, it's often from a distance—perhaps the price media workers have to pay to get "close" to a story learning how to emotionally detach from the subject.

The subject is what I wanted to revisit in this essay. The flip side of treating "victims" or "survivors" as subjects of a narrative is that the process of intellectualizing the issue also requires neatly transmuting the subject into the object. And objectifying people who have lived through sexual violence is not a good place to begin, or end, any story—not our own, and not theirs. I know I can never "restore the dignity" of victims I've never really known, I don't seek to "give voice" to (or ventriloquize on behalf of) people rendered silent by politics and projections of our collective social anxieties. When exploring the experience of sexual violation at the border, I do bring my own experiences with gender oppression to my lens, but I don't dare claim the telling of their stories as an exclusive right, when, in many cases, the stories are all they're able to carry with them. I'm just trying to explore the territories that are supposed to be fixed, hard, official—and to peer beyond the wall. Maybe then as storytellers we can reveal real people behind those "enemy lines," reveal our families in the gaze of the "alien," and witness the wars being waged within, as nations trade bodies for political power and rob people of the right to own themselves.

Unmoored and in flight, the refugee is vulnerable to every kind of harm—from homelessness to fraud—but sexual violence is the most intimate and most public act of brutalization, and it erupts wherever laws and social norms are unraveled. As transient bodies drift in search of sanctuary, gendered violence can buttress a social taxonomy of dominance and oppression, demarcating the rapeable and those with the power to rape, siphoning spheres of male and female, captors and prisoners.

Or it can create new hierarchies between the "host nation" and uninvited "asylum seeker," the occupier and occupied.

National borders are the floodgates of the body politic. Once one boundary has been crossed, all other thresholds get a little thinner—the flesh is pricked, the periphery easier to penetrate. The currents of mass migration have both pierced and hardened social divisions, in ways both unnervingly familiar and unimaginably violent.

But some form of patriarchy persists across and between every border, even in a space of lawlessness, whether it originates from the actors in a military conflict, aid agencies and religious institutions, or the corrosive poverty exposing migrant communities to the most savage form of theft.

The place where sexual violence is most readily weaponized is the one where other social instruments have become unhinged: the interface between two societies. Sexual domination, a familiar pillar of every nation-state's culture, fills the liminal spaces opened by mass displacement.

The world is covered in 65 million official recognized forcibly displaced people—an unprecedented population flow since World War II—ranging from schoolchildren fleeing alone as "unaccompanied minors" to wearied exiles who have waited indefinitely, sometimes for years, to return to war-torn homelands. Tens of millions are considered "internally displaced," within their own countries. Another 150 million are considered migrant workers, who are, in a sense, refugees of poverty. To call this exodus a "crisis" is actually a misnomer, since migration is a constant state of being for a considerable portion of the population. But geopolitical flash points have

flared around particular fault lines between Global North and
Global South.

One is the United States–Mexico border, where tens of
thousands of Central American refugees, many of them mothers and children seeking asylum, have entered since 2014.
The other major north-south crossing is along the borders of
southern Europe, from the Mediterranean coast of Italy to the
Balkans, where hundreds of thousands of Syrian and Afghan
refugees have thronged by land and sea. The shores of Australia
have also drawn a refugee influx in recent years, washing up on
boats from troubled areas around the Indian Ocean.

Patterns of sexual violence perpetrated against these migrants are virtually impossible to measure in strictly numeri-
cal terms. Overall, aid agencies and researchers report that, on
typical routes of "irregular" migration, gender-based violence
is endemic. Sexual violations—primarily experienced by tran-
sitory women and girls who make up a large minority of the
global migrant population—thread through a prism of structural violence, with roots on either side of the border.

The borders migrants traverse are sites of immense suffering. Yet each body on the borderline is a contested space
where refugees negotiate security or dispossession, depending
on who is doing the crossing, and who gets crossed.

Calculated Risk

When asked, many migrants say the journey itself is no more
dangerous than staying still. People do not move out of ig-

norance or sheer panic; they respond rationally to irrational events. Why remain in a place when oppression or calamity has destroyed every reason to stay? War, genocide, ethnic persecution, and ecological disaster present migrants with an impossible choice between familiar violence and unknown danger.

Though women are a minority within the overall migrant population, in countries stricken by war and poverty, the cultural and structural constraints of gender oppression may be all the more reason to want to leave. A rural pregnant teenager orphaned by civil war can either migrate internally to seek factory work in the city, or try her luck on a smuggling boat; she might be misled about the relative risks of the overseas journey, but knows she faces tragic stakes whether and wherever she stays or goes.

Jumping on a dilapidated boat bound for the Italian coastline, where about one in eighty-eight migrants died last year (in 2016), or crossing the Arizona desert where thousands have vanished over the past decade is a calculated risk.

And the risk of sexual abuse is seen as an inevitable cost of political trespass. On the vast, heavily patrolled corridor along the US-Mexico border, aid organizations estimated in 2014 that 80 percent of women and girls had been raped in transit—an apparent increase from a 2010 Amnesty International study showing that 60 percent were raped. The pattern coincided with a recent spike in the number of young girls traveling alone from Central America to the United States.

Victimization in transit is, however, just one extremity of a phalanx of gender-based violence engulfing Honduras, El

Salvador, and Guatemala. The three small Central American countries at the core of the regional exodus have among the world's highest rates of female homicide—an outgrowth of transnational drug war policies and decades of political and economic crisis. Girls are regularly coerced into gangs or threatened with rape. Mothers have stopped sending their daughters to school to keep them safe. And when hiding indoors gets too dangerous, youth go north, joining thousands of "unaccompanied" children and teens, marching alone to the border, violable at every turn.

As human rights lawyer Elvira Gordillo explained in an interview with *Splinter*, typically, migrants "know the price to pay for getting to the United States . . . is being sexually violated."

On the other side of the Atlantic, migrants from the Middle East and Africa have washed up on the Italian and Greek coastlines and thronged to the rim of Eastern and Central Europe. While thousands have died en route to "Fortress Europe," many of those who reach the borders of the world's wealthiest economic bloc end up languishing indefinitely in detention centers as they plow through the asylum bureaucracy. A churning shadow population of "irregular" migrants floating through European cities is filtered into a professionalized humanitarian aid regime, or they fall into the underground economy's smuggling and human trafficking industries.

European Union ministers, meanwhile, remain continually deadlocked in negotiating a continent-wide humanitarian resettlement policy, reducing refugee bodies to political talking points in Brussels while rape survivors may be left to camp outdoors along border fences.

Survival Rape

The worst violations often happen before migrants reach Europe. On the route through Africa to the tip of Libya, which is the main hub for smuggling boats across the Mediterranean and itself engulfed in civil conflict, sexual violence becomes a routine hazard, prompting women to preinject contraceptives to prevent pregnancy.

Rape is endemic at the migrant camps around the Libyan port—sometimes in official facilities, other times just in repositories where smugglers hold human cargo before sending them off to sea. An Eritrean woman described to Amnesty International how rape was systematized at her camp in Libya: "The guards would drink and smoke hashish [cannabis] and then come in and choose which women they wanted and take them outside. The women tried to refuse but when you have a gun pointed at your head, you don't really have a choice if you want to survive. I was raped twice by three men . . . I didn't want to lose my life."

Vulnerability to sexual violence also hinges on other social hierarchies: wealthier refugees have the money and connections to purchase access to safer routes; black African migrants are often subjected to more abuse than lighter-skinned counterparts; labor and sexual exploitation blur into each other, generating subcategories of rape like "survival sex" or "protection sex."

In a study of African migration into Europe in recent years, researchers Sharon Pickering and Alison Gerard quote one migrant, Aziza, describing a climate of sexual coercion while held under armed guard in Libya: "The living situation is difficult because you are not free. There are people standing over you and you have to negotiate to leave. Some people pay money to leave, others provide sex or are raped."

In a UN-led study, "Oumo" recalled the banality of transactional sex, which she undertook twice to obtain a fake passport and then to get a spot on a smuggling boat from Turkey to Greece. "I had no choice. I fear that I will go crazy." The notion of freely offered consent becomes murky; the cost of returning home, rather than moving on, is too high.

Transactional sex can also serve as a legitimizing means of providing economic security. The devastating poverty facing Syrian refugee families in Jordan has led to an epidemic of child marriage, in a practical barter of youth and purity for marital "protection," often between young teens and much older men.

The sex work industry runs parallel to marriage, as another institution of survival sex. However, because prostitution is associated with poverty and social transgression, refugees who enter the sex trade—often because they cannot find other work—risk social stigma and imprisonment, in contrast to wives kept "secure" in subjugation.

The question of "choice" dissolves at these social peripheries. A woman's agency is mediated by basic needs, and sex becomes the last remaining vehicle for negotiating survival.

Whether it happens to Syrian refugees or to survivors of gang warfare in Honduras, sexual violation on the migrant trail is a cruel symbol of a community's dispossession and mass loss of dignity. Yet the institutionalization of sexual predation reveals a certain political economy of statelessness, in which rape serves as a currency of last resort for both sides of a social fissure. At the crossing, the migrant is never really charting her own path, but is being pushed by geopolitical currents.

In the Care of Strangers

Even in the supposedly more civilized "humanitarian" settings that Western countries offer migrants, rape culture is reproduced in binaries of security and deviance. Migritude extends relationships of colonial dominion.

At temporary shelters in the Global North, sexual exploitation and domestic abuse persist, often because they are normalized into a given camp's everyday functioning. Reported abuses have come from both migrants and security officers. Even in the better funded, more regulated detention centers in Europe, women face profound risks of sexual trauma along with social isolation and barriers to mental health services.

Refugees may soon be barred altogether from European territory; by the end of 2016, public backlash against migrants in the West prompted EU ministers to route thousands of Syrian refugees from Greece into even more precarious migrant camps in Turkey, effectively closing the border and, according to humanitarian groups, denying countless trauma survivors crucial relief.

In the US, Raquel, a former detainee from Central America, told aid lawyers about fleeing gang violence in her homeland to escape to what she thought would be a life of relative safety, only to wind up in federal detention and being sexually abused by an immigration officer: "I thought he was going to kill me. I thought I should have stayed in my home country if my life was going to end like this because at least I would have had more time with my children. He got in the cage with me and started unzipping his pants and pulling off my clothes. He exposed himself to me. He was angry that I would not take off my clothes."

Though she was eventually freed from detention and sought asylum, she remained traumatized by the abuse endured at the gates of refuge. "I left one problem in my home country and encountered another one here," she testified. "I felt afraid of everyone on the street, men and women, especially if they came near me or touched me . . . I cried at night and had a hard time falling asleep. Every time I closed my eyes, I saw him."

The "border management" regime in Australia, too, has given rise to a miniature colony in the isolated offshore detention site of Nauru, a tiny atoll where several hundred "boat people," including scores of children, have been dumped. The facility is largely kept out of public view, but thousands of recently leaked internal staff reports going back to 2013 include accounts of sexual assault and attacks on children and reveal layers of complicity threaded through the humanitarian bureaucracy.

According to a 2015 *Guardian* report, several detained children reported being molested by security guards. But their documented complaints were apparently quietly downgraded to less serious violations.

A young Iranian woman was found traumatized, bitten, and bruised outside the facility in May 2015. Then came two suicide attempts—first the victim, then her mother, who was isolated in detention while her daughter was hospitalized. A Somali detainee who reported she had become pregnant from rape sought an abortion but was initially blocked from traveling to Australia for the hospital procedure. Meanwhile, despite public outcry, officials have stalled on prosecuting abuse cases or reforming detention policy.

But the conservative Australian government's years of silence on Nauru don't just reflect embarrassment or incompetence. Systemic silence was what the government had budgeted for all along: from 2013 to 2016, it had reportedly sunk about $10 billion into its "border protection" system, just to keep the refugees offshore.

Imagining Migrants

In contrast to the wall of silence around rape in migration, rape culture has entered the mainstream Western political discourse on immigration policy, albeit at a distorted angle:

migrant (black, brown, or Muslim) men are stereotyped as rapists in Europe and the US, stoking fears they arrived eager to prey on the honor of "native-born" (white) women.

On New Year's Eve 2015, the festivities on the streets of the city of Cologne, Germany, were disrupted by a rash of reports of public sexual assaults against women. Police and media outlets quickly aired suspicions that Arab and North African refugee men were to blame. The allegations inflamed public fears that sexually deviant refugee youth posed a security threat in German cities. Signs scrawled with "rape-ugees" surfaced at protest rallies.

Ironically, conservative pundits who have often downplayed other issues of gender-based violence then zealously decried the "rape culture" supposedly inherent in Muslim societies. The media frenzy paralleled Donald Trump's scaremongering on the 2016 campaign trail about Mexican "rapists" streaming across the border. Some lambasted liberals for softening their vigilance toward migrants due to naive "political correctness."

In subsequent weeks, media analysis of the coverage of the sexual assault stories revealed not a systemic pattern of migrant attacks, but rather a preponderance of rumor-driven reports and hyperbole. The chivalric denouncement of migrant men, however, had less to do with the facts or protecting European women's dignity than with reinforcing the cultural patriarchy undergirding it.

The vilification of Muslim men, and criminalization of migration in general, in the Global North has proven profoundly destabilizing and alienating, resulting in, among other problems, a regressive gendering of resettlement and integration issues. The current policy discourse around migration policy tends to distinguish "women and children" as a separate category of victimhood (those deemed worthy of "rescue") from men and boys (who are seen as potential perverts or terrorists). European aid and asylum regulations, for example, have typically excluded male Syrian refugees, with the exception of children, seniors, and people with disabilities, on national security grounds. But advocates say this division leads to dehumanization of all migrants. When women and children are exclusively prioritized in humanitarian resettlement, the government might end up unraveling the very social bonds that are integral to rebuilding their lives.

Under conventional relocation programs, refugee populations are separated into one-dimensional portraits of public charges or criminals. Gender inequality is intensified, even for the "rescued" women and children, when host countries offer few opportunities for refugees to truly restore their social fabric as cohesive communities, with their own cultural and political integrity.

The structural violence besieging refugees echoes the legacy of imperialism in the Global South: on the landscape of systemic mass dispossession, rape culture is not "foreign," but rather, essential, to the Western worldview. Rape is integral to the cultures of war, colonization, and forced displacement that have turned gender oppression and sexual violence into a global currency of desperation.

Noting the structural deficits in humanitarian resources for treatment and monitoring of refugee rape survivors, psychologist Katie Thomas wrote, "government and non-state actor combatants usually share a low valuation of women. No other physical wound with injuries as severe as those perpetrated by sexual violence could be ignored or deprioritized without international outcry."

We speak of rape in migration as an "unimaginable" experience, a transgression relegated to the margins of civilization. But we can't make sense of rape culture more broadly, or the meaning of gender in migration, until we understand that both the social order within borders, and the chaos outside them, fold into a single binary that cannot hold.

Refugees' stories reflect the complexity of navigating the social vacuums between states. Yet the scourge of rape isn't rooted in the culture that crosses the border, but the culture of borders themselves. The line separating one society from another—and "us" from "them"—is what we make of it. The border crossers' never-ending quest for real security turns on the common ground we share—not the boundaries between us.

Wiping the Stain Clean

GABRIELLE UNION

TWENTY-FOUR YEARS AGO I WAS RAPED AT GUNPOINT IN the cold, dark back room of the Payless shoe store where I was then working. Two years ago I signed on to a brilliant script called *The Birth of a Nation*, to play a woman who was raped. One month ago I was sent a story about Nate Parker, the very talented writer, director, and star of this film. Seventeen years ago Nate Parker was accused and acquitted of sexual assault. Four years ago the woman who accused him committed suicide.

Different roads circling one brutal, permeating stain on our society. A stain that is finely etched into my own history. Rape is a wound that throbs long after it heals. And for some of us the throbbing gets too loud. Post-traumatic stress syndrome is very real and chips away at the soul and sanity of so many of us who have survived sexual violence.

Since Nate Parker's story was revealed to me, I have found myself in a state of stomach-churning confusion. I took this role because I related to the experience. I also wanted to give a voice to my character, who remains silent throughout the film. In her silence, she represents countless black women who have been and continue to be violated. Women without a voice, without power. Women in general. But black women in particular. I knew I could walk out of our movie and speak to the audience about what it feels like to be a survivor.

My compassion for victims of sexual violence is something that I cannot control. It spills out of me like an instinct rather than a choice. It pushes me to speak when I want to run away from the platform. When I am scared. Confused. Ashamed. I remember this part of myself and must reach out to anyone who will listen—other survivors, or even potential perpetrators.

As important and groundbreaking as this film is, I cannot take these allegations lightly. On that night, seventeen-odd years ago, did Nate have his date's consent? It's very possible he thought he did. Yet by his own admission he did not have verbal affirmation; and even if she never said no, silence certainly does not equal yes. Although it's often difficult to read and understand body language, the fact that some individuals interpret the absence of a no as a yes is problematic at least, criminal at worst. That's why education on this issue is so vital.

As a black woman raising brilliant, handsome, talented young black men, I am cognizant of my responsibility to them and their future. My husband and I stress the importance of their having to walk an even straighter line than their white counterparts. A lesson that is heartbreaking and infuriating, but mandatory in the world we live in. We have spent countless hours focused on manners, education, the perils of drugs. We teach them about stranger-danger and making good choices. But recently I've become aware that we must speak to our children about boundaries between the sexes. And what it means to not be a danger to someone else.

To that end, we are making an effort to teach our sons about affirmative consent. We explain that the onus is on them to explicitly ask if their partner consents. And we tell them that a shrug or a smile or a sigh won't suffice. They have to hear yes.

Regardless of what I *think* may have happened that night seventeen years ago, after reading all seven hundred pages of the trial transcript, I still don't actually *know*. Nor does anyone who was not in that room. But I believe that the film is an opportunity to inform and educate so that these situations cease to occur on college campuses, in dorm rooms, in fraternities, in apartments, or anywhere else young people get together to socialize.

I took this part in this film to talk about sexual violence. To talk about this stain that lives on in our psyches. I know these conversations are uncomfortable and difficult and painful. But they are necessary. Addressing misogyny, toxic masculinity, and rape culture is necessary. Addressing what should and should not be deemed consent is necessary.

Think of all the victims who, like my character, are silent. The girls sitting in their dorm rooms, scared to speak up. The wife who is abused by her husband. The woman attacked in an alley. The child molested. Countless souls broken from trans-violence attacks. It is for you that I am speaking. This is real. We are real. Sexual violence happens more often than anyone can imagine. And if the stories around this film do not prove and emphasize this, then I don't know what does.

It is my hope that we can use this as an opportunity to look within. To open up the conversation. To reach out to organizations which are working hard to prevent these kinds of crimes. And to support its victims. To donate time or money. To play an active role in creating a ripple that will change the ingrained misogyny that permeates our culture. And to eventually wipe the stain clean.

What We Didn't Say

LIZ ROSEMA

I Said Yes

ANTHONY FRAME

THE OPENING SEQUENCE OF OUR WEDDING VIDEO CON-
sists of a montage of photographs, first of me, then of
my wife, then of the two of us, tracking our lives from our
separate childhoods until we met and, a year later, were married. The first time we watched, my wife squeezed my arm
and giggled at the early snapshots of me, a couple photos
of a chunky toddler and then a few school pictures leading
toward junior high. In the first few, the boy, small and stout,
poses without embarrassment, pinching his own fat cheeks
and offering the camera a wide, worshipful smile. In the
sixth-grade picture, though, the boy has changed. A sudden growth spurt had lengthened and distorted my face to
something like a tree knot; a set of glasses the circumference
of softballs seemed to match the scruffled hair I had refused

to comb. And my baby smile had fallen, scrunched down into as close to a scowl as I, in my privileged private school uniform, could muster.

My wife paused the video and looked at me, her eyes darting as they scanned my face. "I know," I said. I'd heard this a hundred times from my mother over the years. "My smile's gone."

"No. It's not that." She kept looking at me, eye to eye, and held my hand. "It's your eyes. They're so . . . Was that the year it happened?"

I WAS ASLEEP IN MY FRIEND'S BED. THE NIGHT WAS COOLER than summer should have permitted but he decided to sleep in the hammock in his backyard anyway. I, on the other hand, needed blankets and walls to keep away potential wind and rain so, in a T-shirt and boxers, I stumbled sleepily inside and into his room, anticipating the holiday fireworks and grilled corn and classic rock blasting from his dad's stereo. The blankets may have been too much, so I was still in between sleep and wakefulness when his father came in the room, sometime after midnight. I heard the stutter-shuffle of his feet first, then the bottle slipping from his hand, bouncing off the hardwood floor, somehow managing not to shatter.

He coughed. He swore. I tried to keep my eyes shut, thinking he just wanted to see that I was sleeping safely, comfortably. But he groaned as I felt his weight fall at the foot of the bed, a sound like the wolves at the zoo, and I could feel him as his weight shifted, I could feel him as he leaned over me.

When I opened my eyes, his beard was inches from my face, damp with sweat and from the stale beer I could smell on his breath. His eyes were wide, so wide it was as if they couldn't blink, and they scanned my face, my hair, my ears, my mouth. His lips started off as a straight horizontal line, then curved to a crescent moon smile before becoming a small hole as he saw the worry on my face.

He brushed his fingers across my cheek, along my shoulder, and down my chest, pulling the blanket off as he went. I opened my mouth but he put a finger to his lips.

"Shh . . . it's okay. I'm gonna show you something."

With one hand over my mouth, he pulled the blanket off and slid his fingers in the flap of my boxers. I crunched my eyes shut.

"Don't worry. We're gonna make you a big boy."

At first, the way he stroked my penis was soft and quiet, using his filed fingernails until I had an erection. Then he grabbed and pumped, his calloused palms rubbing raw against me. I turned my head, breathing hard and fast at the moon through the window. Somewhere nearby, someone had started the holiday early and flashes of fireworks broke through the darkness. And he kept whispering wetly the whole time, beer-stained spittle dripping on my face, his grin growing, growing.

"That's good. Good. Good boy. Yes?"

It was the first time I'd ejaculated while awake. When it

was over, he took his hand from my mouth and smiled, wide, crooked. He sniffed my semen, stuck to his fingers.

"There. Good boy. Didn't that feel good?"

In my all-boys high school, the walls were white, the floor and ceiling were white, the school was scrubbed meticulously every evening. Cleanliness is next to godliness, we were told, and we were always to have our thoughts on the Lord. Sports were encouraged by the priests and principal because, as they explained, vigorous exercise is the best way to shunt aside sexual thoughts and urges. Neither worked.

I tried to hide in plain sight, my head low, my voice quiet, my every move completely average—even my grades—so as not to attract attention. I surrounded myself with loud friends around whom I could become invisible. Nondescript and forgettable. It was the most successful survival technique I'd found after I had been molested.

The only one of us who could have been called cool was Josh. Tall, leather jacket, hair dripping with grease, he was our grunge god. From him I learned to swear like a man, to drop the words *fuck, bitch,* and *pussy* in my sentences as smoothly and as frequently as the word *the*. He was a hard boy, even in his button-down shirts and clip-on ties. He smacked us on the backs and asses at every opportunity, then called out to passing math geeks, "Off to your formulas and butt sex, fags? Wanna take Skinny with you?" he'd say, pointing at me. "Fucking pussies."

"God, how old are the Olsen twins now?" he asked at lunch halfway through our freshman year, pushing his hair behind his ears. "I'm too ready to jerk off to them." I stared out the window and watched as the groundskeeper circled the lawn on his riding mower. Josh looked around the table at us while drumming his fingers on the table. "Come on, they're still jailbait, right? Don't tell me none of you haven't thought about it." Someone murmured that if it's in our heads, there can't be anything wrong and a debate over pubic hair quickly raged next to me.

Josh looked across the table at me: he couldn't have known that my stomach was tightening, that the night before I'd dreamed of razor blades and of a man masturbating me, or that whenever I touched myself I couldn't help but think about the moon and fireworks.

"Which one do you jerk off to, Skinny? And don't try saying they look the same or I'll know for sure you're a fag." I pushed my lunch across the table toward him. "Come on, we all know you're doing it."

Could I tell him? I'd had four years to figure out how to tell someone, anyone, what had happened to me, but Josh didn't give me the chance. "Yeah, I knew it," he said, without waiting for me to answer. He pointed and laughed, "You love to jerk off, don't you, you sick shit?"

IT'S HARD TO DESCRIBE WHAT WE DID AS HAZING, AT LEAST AT first. Two other sophomores were just messing around a little with Stephen, the smallest freshman on our cross-country team. Waiting for our parents outside the school building, we pushed him aside as he was changing from his cleats to his tennis shoes. Fred held him against the wall while I grabbed a shoe and tossed it to Matt. We played keep-away for a couple minutes, Stephen trying to catch the shoe as it floated above his head. He was laughing, enjoying the game, or at least enjoying being somehow included.

When we finally let Stephen catch his shoe, Matt nudged him on the shoulder and told him he was a good sport. Stephen, crouched on the ground and sliding his foot into his Nike, smiled up at us, his grin wide, his hair scattered across his head from all the jumping. I hated him, suddenly. I hated how small he was. I hated how willing he was to play along. I hated his weakness. Before I knew what I was doing, I shoved him hard against the concrete. I knelt on top of him, shouting, "Fucking pussy! Grow up, asshole!" I kept pushing him against the ground even as I heard him crying. I wanted to hear him squeal.

Matt and Fred pulled me off him, shouting at me. "What the hell's wrong with you, man?" they yelled as they threw me against the building. But I was gone, watching myself watch Stephen picking himself off the ground and wiping the tears from his eyes.

The assistant coach came outside, surveyed the situation and, after Matt and Fred told him what happened, dragged me into his office. As he screamed at me, I started sobbing. I couldn't explain myself because I didn't understand: I had never felt that kind of rage before, I had no idea where it came from, I couldn't comprehend what had happened. In between my tears I tried to apologize but it felt like my mouth was sewn shut. It felt like a hand was pressed over my lips; it felt like I couldn't breathe. I prayed the coach would see, prayed that he'd hear the fireworks in my head, prayed that he'd take me in his arms and tell me everything would finally be okay.

He looked at me and shook his head. "Pathetic," he said. "Tell me, do you feel like a big man, now?"

IN OUR JUNIOR YEAR, WE THREW A PARTY AT AARON'S HOUSE, just five of us with pizza and pay-per-view professional wrestling. We each brought a case of Natty Light and Josh brought his girlfriend, Kate. She stood two inches taller than him and wore a tight white tank top and jeans with ripped holes around the curves of her ass. As we drank and watched the steroids on display, he whispered in her ear and, when she laughed, he wrapped his arm around her waist and squeezed her breast, all while watching us watching him.

Halfway through the night, the rain came. I could hear the wind blowing against the aluminum siding, a whistle without a discernible tune. Josh nudged Kate and pointed at Aaron. She looked and nodded, then moved next to Aaron and started licking his ear. Josh told Aaron to stand up and, as he did, Kate grabbed his crotch and rubbed. Josh had his hand in one of the holes in her jeans. She smoothed out Aaron's khakis to show his erection, but she was watching me.

The beer in my hand had gone flat, it tasted rancid in my mouth. My stomach tightened and I could feel the night's pizza pushing its way up my throat. "You wanna go next, Skinny?" Kate asked, blowing me a kiss. I moved upstairs as fast as I could to the bathroom and heard Josh's howling laugh behind me. "Not him! Everyone knows Skinny's as queer as a unicorn."

I didn't throw up, but when I came out of the bathroom, Josh was waiting for me. "You all right?"

I nodded and apologized, said I was sorry for being a lightweight. We sat down at the top of the stairs and he took my hand. "Dude, you know I love you, right?" I just looked at him. I hadn't noticed before how blue his eyes were, hadn't known before that eyes could have freckles.

He took off my glasses and brushed his fingers along my eyebrows, then through my weak attempt at a goatee. "Jesus, you've got a lot of hair." He put my glasses back on and smiled. "I mean it, man. I love you, more than any of those other guys. More than her even and I fuck her. It doesn't matter that you're a fag. I mean, what do I care, right?" He took my hand again and I watched him rub the flap of skin between my thumb and index finger. I wanted to love him back but then a cut on his thumb scraped against my hand, just a slight tug, and I could feel those calloused hands pulling the blanket away, I could smell beery breath again.

Josh didn't notice any change in me or, if he did, he ignored it and kept talking. "I just want you to know, anyone gives you any shit, and I mean anyone, you let me know. Cuz I love you, bro." Downstairs, they were laughing and Kate hollered for us to hurry up. "You know, you could sleep with her, if you wanted," Josh went on. "She'd let you. I don't know but maybe that'd help or something." I shook my head and stood to leave but he kept talking. "Well, you wouldn't have to be alone. I could be there. It could be, like, the three of us. And if you're not into her, you know, you could be into me or something." I thought about Kate downstairs, tried to imagine her overhearing this conversation. I tried to think of her eyes but couldn't picture their color. I didn't even know if her hair color was natural but Josh was offering her to me like she was some toy we could share. Or maybe I was the toy. I thanked him, I even apologized to him, though I felt sick about the offer, about what Josh must think about Kate, what he must think about me.

I started walking down the steps but Josh didn't move. He just sat there, hands folded as if in prayer. He looked down at me. "Tony? You do love me, too, right?"

LATER, AFTER EVERYONE HAD PASSED OUT, I STRUGGLED TO sleep. The batting of the couch seemed to dig into my legs and bright spots danced in the darkness whenever I closed my eyes. The storm had passed, taking the wind and the front with it, and I missed the numbing noise. Upstairs, I could hear feet rustling in the hall, moving from room to bathroom and back, not bothering to try to walk lightly.

After a couple hours, Kate came downstairs. She was still

wearing the tank top but had left her jeans behind and her white panties clung tight to her hips. She started when she saw me sitting up, then said she needed a smoke and asked if I wanted to keep her company.

Outside the air had turned crisp. Most of the clouds had moved on and through the suburban trees we watched the stars fading in and out behind the city's atmosphere. Kate lit her cigarette, inhaled deeply, and blew a heavy column of smoke into the air. "I know you're not gay," she said, offering me a cigarette. I declined.

"Never said I was," I told her. "And I think Josh's the only one who actually thinks I am. Doesn't really make a difference. It's just easier not to say anything."

"Doesn't it bother you? When they call you a fag?"

I shrugged. "They're gonna call me that anyway." Sitting next to her, I could see her blond hair was a dye job, and not a very good one. Strands of brown hiding near her scalp tried to come out, creating a spiderweb effect along her head that could only be seen up close.

She dragged again and, as she blew the smoke out, said, "Insomnia's a bitch, huh?" She rubbed her arms, which were covered in goose bumps. I wished I had a jacket for her, wished for better arms, for hands that could hold her without grabbing at her body. She flicked her cigarette into the grass. "I blame my dad," she said suddenly. "I'm pretty sure he was the only one happier than me when I started growing these tits." She watched me out of the corner of her eye. "If you know what I mean."

She then looked at me, straight on, and I saw my face

reflected in the brown surface of her eyes. I wanted to tell her that Josh was using her, tell her about all the things he said when she wasn't around, how she was fun even if she is sloppy seconds, how he loves to screw her in the ass, how, when she went to the bathroom, he'd told Aaron he'd better have his ear checked for VD, tell her something. But I didn't have the heart, or the guts. I just sat there, looking back at her.

And she looked at me, carefully, and then drew a quick breath.

"Holy fuck. You really do know what I mean, don't you?"

My old roommate loved to masturbate. He did it at least once a day, often two or three times. Our two-bedroom apartment was small enough that I could hear every rattle of his bed, every shake of his wrist, every word. "Fuck!" he'd cry out at all hours of the night. Or, "Hell yeah." "That's right." "Now, bitch. Now." He quickly started taking advantage of my job at a local video store that carried a wide variety of porn. I soon learned to distinguish the sounds of his bed sliding under his weight from the sounds of the couch banging against the living room wall. And as loud as he turned up the TV, he made sure his narration was even louder. Often he would eat a bag of fast-food burgers, turn on his latest rental, and chug Bud Light after Bud Light, pointing his can at the girls' breasts and laughing, his mouth full of half-chewed meat.

One evening, I looked up from my American history notes

and saw him, beer on the TV tray, hamburger in one hand and the other hand in his pants. He ground the meat with his teeth, his eyes growing wider and wider. I moved toward my room and, as I passed the TV, he pulled his penis through his open zipper and continued stroking. He grinned at me.

"You like that, don't you?"

The yellow stubble above his lip was stained with ketchup and small bits of meat fell from his mouth onto his stomach as he talked. I kept walking to my room.

"Come on, don't you wanna watch?"

I slammed my door and heard him yelling.

"I want you to watch!"

That night, I woke just as my door swung open. He rushed in, his white T-shirt stained with beer. At first I didn't realize he was naked from the waist down. I leaned up in my bed and he shoved me down hard. I tried to get up again and, again, he shoved me down. He punched me, in the shoulder, then the leg, growling and spitting with each punch.

"This is my cock! Fucker! This is my cock!"

I'd stopped trying to get up but he kept shoving me, pushing my head against my pillow, pulling at my legs, screaming the whole time.

"This is my cock! Look at my cock, goddamnit!"

It hung there, erect, wiggling as he moved, bouncing up each time he flexed to shove me again. He grabbed me by the side and pushed me against the wall. The Led Zeppelin LP I'd nailed above the bed fell and shattered against my head.

"This is my cock and you are my pussy! You get it, fucker?

This is my cock and you're gonna look when I fucking tell you to look, pussy!"

After a few minutes, he left my room. But, later that night, I heard him slumped outside my door, banging his head against it. I heard the sounds of a beer can being thrown against a wall. And I heard him crying, sobbing, wailing.

"Don't leave me. Oh, fuck, please don't leave me. I love you, you can't leave me."

He banged his head harder and harder against the door.

"I swear, I'll fucking kill myself if you leave me."

The next day, he set his TV tray full of tacos aside, started a movie, and pulled down his pants. He grinned that wide grin of his.

"You ready to watch?"

I SAID YES. TO EVERYONE. EVERY TIME.

When my wife asked—just before we started dating—if I was straight, I said yes. When, a few weeks later, she asked if I was a virgin, I said yes.

I said yes when she asked if I was okay, first after we'd made love for the first time and again after I told her about the man and the blanket and the fireworks.

I said yes. It's always seemed easier. Because I'm not sure whether I'm gay or straight or bisexual or asexual or antisexual. Because I've only been in one relationship, an opposite-sex relationship with the woman I married. Because I can't understand a sexual identity that doesn't involve rage or terror or power. Because even when I'm attracted to men, male bodies—even my own—it turns my stomach. Especially my own.

Because I'm still that eleven-year-old boy and I love to smile, and I want to smile, but that hand is still covering my mouth.

So I said yes, I'm okay, even though to this day, for a moment, my mind leaves the room every time I undress in front of her. Even though I tighten every time she runs her fingers through my pubic hair. Because I love her and I love making love with her. Even though, after twelve years with her, I still find it hard to initiate sex. Even though, after twelve years, I want her more than ever but I don't know if I'll ever be able to differentiate that kind of longing from the male eyes I've seen up close. And what if that longing that makes me sick is what she sees in my eyes when I look at her?

And I said yes because I'm lucky. Not having a hymen, I've never had to have the difficult discussion about what it means to be a virgin. As a man, I've always been able to control exactly how and if and when my story is told. So I said yes, I'm okay, because I know the statistics, because it only happened once, and because I didn't die, by my own hand or anyone else's. Because, despite every razor blade I've held and then thrown in the garbage, one way or another, I survived.

I said yes because now the nightmares are rare, because I don't know how to tell the woman that I love that, when I dream, death is never the goal: it's just the obvious outcome of trying to carve my body into something less dangerous.

I said yes because I'm sick of using my past as a crutch to explain the present. Because everything feels like being trapped in a spider's web and at the center is a pair of softball-sized glasses and running cleats and ripped jeans. And I don't know if I'm strong enough to push through the web.

But I said yes because I have to hope, someday, I will be.

Knowing Better

SAMHITA MUKHOPADHYAY

BY THE TIME I TURNED THIRTY, I THOUGHT I HAD MY SHIT together: I had managed to turn a life of substitute teaching and hanging out at raves into a career in writing and a day job in media strategy, just from the exposure I was getting at a well-known feminist blog. I had just sent in my first print piece, for the anthology *Yes Means Yes!: Visions of Female Sexual Power and a World Without Rape* edited by Jessica Valenti and Jaclyn Friedman. I was in talks for my first book deal, I was finishing my MA at night, and I was booking my first set of speaking gigs, touring the country to lecture young women about the importance of telling their stories.

I had found my voice and it was resonating with people who didn't even know me. For someone who never thought she would ever have a real career doing anything she actually liked, the possibilities started to seem endless. For once, after decades of bad grades, aimless career ambitions, and rejection from jobs, schools, and boys alike, I felt worthy.

But I was also going through a nasty breakup from a toxic relationship fueled by the coke and Ecstasy we'd get nearly every weekend at raves, on top of drinking and experimenting with God knows what else. And after the breakup, I had started to spiral out: my friend Jessica called it my "trampage," and I spent it going to parties alone, staying out until 4 a.m. on weeknights, getting drunk, ending up in random beds and having lots of casual—often mediocre—sex.

I justified my lifestyle with my politics: I was independent, and independent women could fuck random men without remorse or judgment. I didn't get attached either because I was a "cool girl." *I am literally fighting heteronormativity*, I told my feminist self—my political identity carefully constructed around defying the norms of what was expected of a straightish single woman.

I knew better than to get myself raped. But it happened anyway.

I met him at a club, and we were dancing and kissing. His name started with a "K" but I can't really tell you what it was anymore; I definitely knew at the time.

He was tall and handsome. Really tall. And I remember telling him I didn't want to have sex.

"Should we go to your place?" he asked.

"Not tonight," I responded, tipsy.

We kept dancing. And kissing. It wasn't bad, but I was tired and I had an early morning.

"I just want to smoke a blunt and massage your feet," he

asked sweetly. I giggled, because I always fucking giggle when I get nervous.

"Sure." I conceded. At that point, I was pretty drunk.

We went back to my place, and we smoked weed; I was still drunk. Normally, I just get the spins; that time, I passed out.

I woke up to him penetrating me in my own bed, unclear how we had gotten to that point or when we had gone upstairs to my room. I passed out again. I was in and out of consciousness the rest of the night; in the morning, I fully woke up and he was trying again. I said no and forcefully pushed him off me. I looked away, trying not to cry, and noticed that the fucker had even been considerate enough to use condoms.

I asked him to leave; I said I had to go to work. I did have to go to work; I did go to work, somehow. Numb with something more than a hangover, I texted my best friend and said that I had an "intense night with some dude." She just said "Oh, girl," unsurprised to get another text like that from me.

I was a feminist activist and writer and thought leader. I knew better. That wasn't rape. That was just some shitty sex. I would shake it off.

I didn't talk about it again for a year.

A year later, I was thumbing through that anthology my first essay was in, *Yes Means Yes*, when I saw Latoya Peterson's essay "The Not Rape, Rape." But instead of being excited about being included in a special project, about having my first byline in a book, about being published alongside people I adored and admired, I got a terrible feeling in the pit of my stomach: that night, the year before, I had been raped.

I still didn't want to talk about it.

I got that book deal I'd been in talks for, to write *Outdated: Why Dating Is Ruining Your Love Life*. It was an honest look at how women incorporate their feminist ideals into their romantic lives, specifically geared toward strong, feminist women who also happen to have that one terrible flaw—we date men and have to navigate the ins and outs of patriarchy while doing so.

I wrote an entire book about love and dating and sex without mentioning having been raped—not to my editor or to most of my friends.

I did travel the country, speaking to college students about the importance of women being brave, speaking for themselves, and telling their own stories. I became a campus evangelist for feminist blogging: the revelatory, connected, speaking-truth-to-power kind. Women would come up to me after my talks to tell me about the things with which they were grappling: sexism at school, the sexualization of their bodies, the pressure to be feminine, the pressure to have it all, and, of course, rape culture on campus.

I helped women tell their stories about rape without talking about my own story of being raped.

I also stopped having sex, for a long time. The first time I did it again, I sobbed uncontrollably, trying to hide it from the overly eager man who I'd let inside me. It happened the next time I had sex, too.

I put on weight, digging myself deeper into overeating or drinking too much. I threw myself into my work, too; at least

I had my work. *I help women tell their stories*, I thought. *My story isn't as serious, it isn't as important. I am dealing with it. I am okay.*

The chasm between my vocation and my story kept growing, the more I worked. *If I had been raped, could I still be strong? Could I still teach other women how to escape the gripping, harsh reality of rape culture if I had succumbed to the forces that silence women about their own assaults?*

I kept silent.

I doubled down: instead of encouraging women to tell their stories, I started editing the stories of women who have been raped. I've had to rigorously analyze and fact-check their stories, knowing that they are probably true but having to navigate a professional system—journalism—inextricably tied to the legal one in which they won't be believed or in which their cases are hard to prove. Shaking, sometimes, but editing stories that are so close to mine: a girl unconscious raped in college, a girl raped by her boyfriend, a girl raped by someone she loves, a girl raped at a party, a girl raped by a friend. Women like me and yet, not me, because they were doing what I couldn't do: tell my story.

The constant drumbeat of stories of sexual assault—from R. Kelly to our own goddamn president—keep me in a constant state of postrape PTSD. Some days, I feel like I have to hold my breath just to read the news so I can get through it and on with my workday. I am two parts of this system: I am an editor, and I was victimized and survived the same thing I'm reading, writing, and editing.

People often get into this work to help survivors and to grapple with their own stories. I dug myself deeper into it to avoid grappling with mine.

Last year, I was invited to a retreat about storytelling to talk about how to bring your most authentic self into your professional life—how to live a life that is not manufactured for your career, but a reflection of who you deeply are.

It was on that retreat that my silence began to unravel, after listening to one of my best friends share something I already knew with a room full of near strangers: that she had been sexually assaulted. She had learned, somewhere in the interim, to do more than simply reveal what had happened to her; she had learned to tell the story of it so that it didn't become her only story. And as I listened to her, as I watched her be an encourager of other people's storytelling, an independent, smart woman and a survivor of sexual assault, I felt, finally, like maybe my story was worthy of telling, too. And maybe I was worth the telling of it.

And so I told it.

Not That Loud

Quiet Encounters with Rape Culture

Miriam Zoila Pérez

I KEEP A LIST OF EVERYONE I'VE EVER KISSED—TWENTY-FOUR people—in my journal. I started it sometime postcollege, when my romantic and sexual life picked up considerably after coming out as queer. The first name on the list is not even a name—"Boys @ spin the bottle party (age: 11)". There were three that night, I think; two of them were brothers.

About half the entries have asterisks next to their names—my own not-so-subtle way of indicating that we had sex. Since the vast majority of the people whom I've kissed (eighteen total) aren't cisgender men, the definition of what constitutes "sex" is a bit murky; it's hard, even for me, to shake the heteronormative definitions ingrained in me since childhood. I can't even tell you at this point what exactly I did with the woman who is tenth on the list that constituted sex: I remember a picnic dinner on her bedroom floor; I remember her wrought-iron headboard; I remember I got higher than I wanted to before we hooked up. But at the time that I documented our relationship on my strange, bordering-on-obsessive list, I'd felt like we'd had sex. So I scribbled a sloppy star next to her last name.

A few years ago, I noticed another pattern among my sexual partners, undocumented on my list: my lovers were, more often than not, survivors of sexual abuse. The fact of it had registered in my subconscious but it wasn't until last summer, when I was dating someone new and we both admitted that neither of us were survivors, that I realized just how unusual such a situation is in my sexual history.

The person I was dating shared a history so similar to my own, of partnering and sleeping with many survivors, and teared up as they talked about how unfair it was that so many of their lovers had been harmed in that way.

Sexual assault is no longer an undercurrent in political life: it shouts at us from news headlines, colors the electoral debates, shapes rally slogans and protest chants. But something doesn't have to be loud to be deafening, to suck up all the oxygen in the room, to shroud the windows and dim the lights.

In my personal life, sexual abuse has been a barely audible, inescapable presence when I have sex. It's a silent partner as I get to know a new lover, learn what they like and don't like in bed, how they want to be touched, what is off-limits. I rarely learn the details of my lover's experiences; sometimes they never even call themselves survivors. But I know those experiences are nonetheless there, in the shadows in the corner of bedrooms and living rooms and kitchens. They showed up in the whispers of one lover—"don't ever put your hands around my neck"—and in the tears of another every time she climaxed in the five years that we were together.

Being invited to engage with someone in an intimate way, to entwine your lips with theirs, to slip your tongue into their mouth, to put your hands on their body in ways that no one else does is a gift, an act of vulnerability and trust. So when that almost inevitable moment comes when I realize that, for a new lover, this act that we are undertaking together once began for them as a violation, my stomach faithfully drops. The best I can do, usually, is to try to stay present and loving, as an act of resistance and reclamation.

I'd like to think that the fact that so many of my partners are survivors is exceptional: maybe it's because I'm queer; maybe it's because I'm Latinx, a child of immigrants; maybe it's because many of my partners are people of color and immigrants too. I know the statistics—that one in four girls and one in six boys (based on how they were assigned at birth) are sexually abused as children; I know that for people of color, especially Black and Latinx folks, those rates are even higher.

In the grand scheme of things, even though the kiss list in my journal takes up a full page, my sample size is small. It's likely that many of my friends are survivors too—or that many of them find themselves having the same realization, over and over again, with new lovers as I do.

I know that my own trauma shapes all of my relationships and interactions: though I'm not a survivor and I wasn't sexually abused as a child, my early family dynamics have left me with all sorts of distorted ways of relating to others. I'm a caretaker and a caregiver; a top and *caballero* if I'm feeling romantic and want to reclaim my machista Cuban roots in my own queer feminist way. But the shadow side of it means that my default is to put other people's needs and desires before my own.

In some ways, my instinct to put myself last has served me well in my relationships, particularly with the partners who have experienced sexual abuse: being deferential, attentive, and accommodating has helped my lovers feel some sense of safety as they navigated their own complicated relationships with sex and boundaries as survivors.

But I was also forced to confront that, in other ways, my selflessness may be the result of my own coping mechanisms, and be reinforcing unhealthy approaches to sex. If I peruse my list of partners, there are probably only one or two people about whom I could say confidently that our relationship never involved any sex that I performed out of obligation, rather than actual desire.

Then, during sex with a relatively new partner recently, we agreed at the outset of one encounter that we would focus on my pleasure. A few minutes into it, I burst into sobs and cried for the better part of ten minutes.

I didn't know exactly why; I still don't. I know it has something to do with my high school boyfriend—it usually does, right? Well, "boyfriend" is probably a loose term: we'd met on a youth group ski trip during which I'd given him an unreciprocated hand job without as much as a kiss. The lack of reciprocation continued as our relationship evolved into a hookup game of "defend the goal"—his goal, my defense—including after junior prom, when I'd almost let him enter me in the parking lot of a shuttered CVS, but stopped short because I decided that losing my virginity on prom night—to someone I wasn't even technically dating—was too cliché.

Some of the details of the night a week later are crystal clear—we were in the backseat of my two-door Honda Civic, it was dark, we were in a parking lot, and Lauryn Hill's "To Zion" was playing on my car stereo. I wasn't really sure if I wanted to have sex with him, but the boundaries I put up were weak at best, and he dutifully approached them over and over until I conceded. It was painful and brief—I remember he didn't orgasm, which was unusual.

And though my life no longer involves being pressured into sex in a car with a boy that I didn't really want and never enjoyed, it's hard to escape wondering why it is that, in encounters I wanted and even initiated, it's rare that I seek the same pleasure I want to give to other people.

I know that there is a huge divide between feeling pressured into having sex too quickly by a high school boyfriend and being sexually abused, but some version of those violations and so many others have so thoroughly shaped all of my sexual and romantic relationships that I no longer really can imagine a world in which I could have sex that didn't resonate with some sort of trauma.

Rape interferes with how my partners and I can experience joy and connection even within incredibly loving, supportive, and nonnormative relationships. Rape culture means that even as someone who realized just how nonconsensual that high school relationship was just a few months after it ended, I still struggle with the repercussions of that experience and the many that followed it. Even though I had the strength to confront that boyfriend over AOL Instant Messenger to tell him just how I felt about our relationship (in the form of a badly written and very emo poem, of course), I kept doing sexual things that I didn't really want to do for years after.

When I interviewed activist and writer adrienne maree brown, we spoke about her work as a pleasure activist, and her perspective on sexual honesty stuck with me for days after our conversation. "What becomes possible when we're being real with each other?" she asked. "Maybe your feelings get hurt when I tell you I don't like the way you're touching me." *How many times have I hesitated to tell a partner what I liked or didn't like, for fear of hurting their feelings, for fear of having to care for their emotions in the aftermath of that disclosure?* I thought to myself as she talked.

"But what is possible after that?" she continued. "Learning new ways of touching. Once you've experienced that erotic awakening you cannot settle for suffering."

That's where I live now; I won't settle for suffering. I won't settle for small compromises of my own desires in service of others' needs, for ignoring my own truths, or for trying to take the easy route of not naming the elephant at the foot of the bed when I'm being sexual with lovers. We don't have any power over what we've experienced: we can't change our own, or undo the harm that was done to those around us.

But I—we—can make different choices. I can try with every kiss, every touch, every orgasm, with every new person who invites me to share in intimacy with them to believe that another world is possible, and that I am building it with every new name I add to the silly list in my journal.

Why I Stopped

ZOË MEDEIROS

W HEN I FIRST STARTED TO TELL PEOPLE WHAT HAP-
pened to me, I told anyone who showed the tiniest
bit of interest, and I told as much as they could bear to hear
(which was always a vanishingly small proportion of what actually happened, and it was never enough). I was young, and
it was new to me to talk about it, and for a moment I became
almost drunk with the power of speaking it aloud, deliriously
revealing the worst things to people with whom I wouldn't
trust my bus fare these days.

I don't tell anyone now—not the details, anyway, not
what actually happened. There is a woman who is one of my
best friends and dear to my heart: we walk our dogs together,
for hours, in all weather; we talk over everything; and if someone has been the tiniest bit mean to me she shouts, "We hate

them!" and plots their immediate downfall. There is a man with whom I work every day, who knows the intricacies of my family situation, who brings me coffee on the days when I'm falling asleep at my desk, who always does his best by me. I haven't told them. I'm not going to tell you.

It did not help me to tell. I felt a momentary burst of clarity, like walking out into a cold night and feeling that icy slab of air hit my face, and then I felt gutted, every single time.

Here is a list of things that have helped me, in no particular order.

The episode of *Criminal Minds* (Season 8, Episode 18) where Derek Morgan confronts his abuser in jail and then vomits, alone, in the bathroom.

The book in Jacqueline Carey's Kushiel's Legacy series where Phèdre and Joscelin rescue Imriel. What they go through to rescue him, and that it's worth it to go through that in order to bring him home.

Giving up Christmas. Giving up Thanksgiving.

Reading what other survivors have to say in our own words, and not literature by people writing about us, or mental health practitioners having opinions. Stories where survivors tell what happened, stories where they don't, stories where they explain why they can't sit with their back to the door in a restaurant, or why they can't use dressing rooms, or how running marathons or planting orchards or knitting helped them save themselves—all the weird life hacks and tricks they have to get through things.

The subcategory of romance manga in which the beloved
has survived abuse of some kind, and the lover never
once says the beloved is dirty or unlovable, never acts
that way—where it is just a solid wall of unstoppable
love. (Hopefully there is also revenge.)

Revenge stories, generally, like the scene where Inigo
Montoya kills the man who murdered his father,
only more so. The revenge does not have to be specifically related to abuse, although that helps.

Avoiding media about time travel. The melding of times,
flipping back and forth between months or years, is
too much like flashbacks. Remaining anchored in
this time line is hard enough for me without leaving
it for recreational reasons.

Cognitive behavioral therapy, for the anxiety attacks that
brought me to my knees. I chose a therapist who
laughed at my jokes and had an office by the sea, so
that it was really easy for me, after a session, to go
stare at something bigger than me, bigger than what
happened, bigger than anything and completely
uninterested in any of it, just busy being the sea. My
sister had to make me go to therapy, though, to talk
me into the office over the phone and convince me
to sit down in the waiting room, and then convince
me to stay there, because I can be both stubborn and
foolish, and she is my older sister and therefore occasionally the boss of me. If you have someone who is
sometimes the boss of you, it can help to give them
the job of making you go, at first.

Sometimes I imagine black wings. Specifically, I am lying on my bed at night, on my left side, and I imagine someone climbing in next to me and wrapping
long black wings over me.

It took a long time to learn that these things helped, and
talking about it did not. When I talked about it, people would
cry, or get disgusted, or horrified, or say they just didn't understand how anyone could do that, or they would have elaborate
thoughts about the failings of our justice system and how it
could be better in particular ways that might or might not
involve the death penalty.

Or they would wish out loud that they could kill my abusers, as though that was a thing they were actually going to do.

Frequently, the person I just told would need *me* to be
supportive while they went through a range of emotions and
feelings, sometimes very intensely, and then they would usually tell me nothing would change in how they felt about me.

And then things would change.

People you tell will make comparisons. They will compare
you to everyone else they have heard of who has experienced
something similar, and they will rate how you are doing according to that metric. *Are you more or less functional than
their college roommate? Are you more or less sexual than that one
woman at the office? Are you thinner or fatter than the other survivors they know, does it sound like something they heard about
on TV, did they read a book about it, can they tell their partner
about it over dinner that night as a sad story and shake their
head?* They will want details, as many details as you can give

them, until they suddenly don't want details anymore, and it's too much.

Then they will revise backward. They will take every opinion they've ever heard from you, every personality trait, every action, and recast them in light of what you told them. This will be particularly true of your sexual behavior and your appearance. *Probably this is why you are such a slut. Probably this is why you don't date at all. Probably this explains everything about you, really, why you fuck the people you fuck and love the people you love, or do neither, ever. Probably this is why you are such a mess and they are safe.*

Even many people who are mostly on your side will think that you must have done something. That it would not happen to them, or to the people they love, because their lives are organized better, they don't take chances, they don't know anyone who would do anything like that.

I have had people who are otherwise loving and kindhearted tell me that they just don't understand how people who go through this can get up in the morning. I have had people tell me that they would rather be dead than be what I am. I have heard people say that they just don't believe that it can be that bad, that PTSD doesn't exist, that families don't do things like that, that I'm just doing it for the attention. (I will tell you right now that if someone were to offer me one crisp dollar bill for every single bit of attention being a survivor has ever gotten me, I would take the dollar.)

Will everyone react that way? No. Of course not. And most people who do are not doing so out of malice; they just don't know any better. It still doesn't make it all right.

I never want to stop anyone else from telling. For many people, all of the terrible responses are even more of a reason to be open, to be radically honest, to reveal the places that they have been hurt the most deeply. It helps lots of survivors to talk about it, and I want us to talk about it whenever and however we want. I will always listen. I want us all to listen. The more of us who come out as survivors, the harder it gets to ignore that there is too much to have to survive, the harder it gets to pretend like this doesn't happen or it only happens to certain kinds of people.

But that doesn't mean you have to give your whole story to anyone who asks. Not telling my story doesn't mean it didn't happen. I don't have to be open about my experiences, about all of them or even any of them, to be a real survivor. I am a real survivor because I survived, even if some days it feels like I didn't survive at all.

Other people do not get to tell me what my experience means, or where they would like to place me in their pantheons of suffering. There is great danger in letting those around you determine what your experience means to you, and I have found that one of the best ways to combat that is to keep my story for myself.

You can keep it to yourself today and tell tomorrow, and you can tell everyone you know and then never talk about it again. You don't owe anything to anyone. Your story is not the currency you exchange for love, for understanding, for getting what you need. You are allowed to get what you need without justifying why you need it, regardless of what you choose to reveal and what you keep private. No one is entitled to that part of you and you have no responsibility—none—to make your experience easier or more palatable by constructing a narrative other people find acceptable.

I need the accommodation because I said I need it. I do not do that thing because I have said that I do not do it. No one gets to rake over the details of my life and determine if they think what happened to me was bad enough for me to have earned my scars, my limitations, my superpowers.

Broken people understand this better. One of my friends told me a few years ago that she didn't have anyone close to her that had a healthy, functional relationship with their parents, because she couldn't relate to people like that. It's not a deliberate exclusion. People with cracked foundations will understand better why sometimes you do crazy shit to shore up your own.

It's not that I don't want to love unharmed people; I just don't understand them. The scales are all off, the proportions are wrong for when we talk about how something hurts. This is not a bad day at the office, this is not a breakup, this is not that time that someone really hurt your feelings. It is more like carrying something really heavy, forever. You do not get to put it down: you have to carry it, and so you carry it the way you need to, however it fits best.

Once I was at a wedding, and a friend of my youth, a person I trust with my life to whom I have to tell things to make them real, wanted me to go dance with her. We were all superdrunk, and I didn't want to, so she grabbed my hair, in a totally playful way. We were drunk and she pulled my hair and the next thing I knew I had her up against a wall with my forearm across her throat.

She apologized. I apologized.

Drunk people are fairly floppy so nobody got hurt. But I have never forgotten that moment: one second I was fine, and the next there was nothing, and then I had one of the people I love most up against a wall.

I don't drink like that at parties anymore.

I am a happy person most of the time: not just content, not just getting by, but happy, and often so overflowing with joy that I look around myself and revel in my luck, in my work, in my love.

I also have a lot of bad days, and a powerful liking for bourbon, and an intimacy problem.

All of those things are true. This is what being a survivor looks like for me.

Sometimes I see ghosts. The worst ghosts for me are not usually the flashbacks, although those can be pretty bad, but the ones who show me what I might have been if it never happened. It's like suddenly feeling what it would be like to run on a leg that had never been broken, just for a second, and then it's gone and the old bone-deep pain is with me again.

I see phantoms in relationships sometimes; certain ways people are with each other that I can't be. I wonder if maybe I would have wanted kids, if none of this had happened. Maybe I wouldn't—maybe that part would have been the same and it would have just been clearly not for me. But I think I might have, and that life is a ghost for me, haunting, distant, just out of reach across the line of my life.

For me, it got better and worse and better again. I lost some of the most important people in my life because they could not stand by me while I was walking into darkness. Others said they would, and then did not, and that changes a person. I am less trusting now. When people say they'll be there, I think, *We'll see*.

But there are rarely days that lay me out, now. It's hard to knock me down for long.

This many years into living with these scars, into being a person who carries this thing with me, I am fairly adept at it. I can shift the weight of it around, I know what it looks like on different days, how it moves with me through the seasons, through the years.

I own my identity. I am a survivor, and I am out as a survivor, and I keep coming out as one over and over again. I am not shy about it, and I am not ashamed.

But if people want details, if they want the easily consumable tragedy so that they can file me away somewhere and not have to think about it again, they are not going to get it from me. This story is in the bedrock of me. It's in my bones, what happened, and I have grown around it and over it, and you can't have it. It's mine.

Picture Perfect

SHARISSE TRACEY

DADDY MOVED US OUT TO CALIFORNIA WHEN I WAS FIVE; Mommy didn't like it there. I hated being there as an only child mostly because, if I'd had a brother or sister, I would've had someone to play with. Daddy said that I was spoiled, but I worked more at thirteen than he did; like Cliff Huxtable, he was home a lot while Mommy worked at the phone company.

My dad was a freelance photographer who worked steady for a while until he got too sick with sickle cell. I never really saw him in a photo shoot with models (or women wanting to be models), but I sure saw the results in his albums. My mom didn't seem to mind about the pictures—or, if she did, I didn't know. I never heard them arguing about his photography or the women in the shots.

Despite moving around a lot, we always had a darkroom

where he developed his precious photos; he'd spend hours in there, but I had strict instructions never to enter. He smelled after being in there, a caustic cologne of chemicals and Benson & Hedges from which I was largely spared because he rarely ever even hugged me. The only time I was close to him was when I helped him do test shots.

"Stand there and look straight into the lens, Tracey," he'd say. "Don't move."

I would stare at the lens or the tip of his cigarette; I was just a prop, a way to test out new equipment and practice before the occasional big freelance gigs that helped camouflage the fact that he wasn't the primary breadwinner.

The year I was thirteen, my friends and I wanted model-like pictures of ourselves, the Glamour Shots kind that would eventually infiltrate every mid-American strip mall. Our pubescent hearts were set on mature photos—racy even—in our bathing suits, and we'd pinned our hopes for them on the one photographer who captured all the young girls in Pasadena—Tate. I'd already tagged along with another girl from school and witnessed her photo session. I knew the setup. Safety was not my concern.

"That old guy in the wheelchair?" said my mother when I asked. "Oh no, no no no. I don't trust him."

"But, Mom, he takes everyone's pictures in Pasadena!"

"Sharisse," she said, "you don't know what that man could do!"

At the time, I didn't get what she was implying, but, yes, he was pretty much Child Pornographer #1 from Central Casting, an aging hippie in a wheelchair, making a living taking pictures of young girls in a dark house. But I never had any problems with him; he'd never said or done anything to me that felt off.

"Why not let your daddy take your pictures?" she said. "He takes great photographs."

"Daddy?" I'd never thought of my father. Why would I? I knew he took great pictures but we were talking about Glamour Shots, in swimwear. . . . And he was my father.

It wasn't just modesty, though: my father and I didn't have a good relationship because I had stubbornly refused to be a son. I would have never thought to ask him for anything remotely supportive; I didn't ask him for anything.

But I took my mother's suggestion because I was thirteen and impatient: I wanted pictures that made me feel pretty and important (and maybe a little bit sexy), and nothing says lightning-fast delivery quite like a man with a camera and darkroom already in your home.

When I asked my father to do something for me for the first time ever, I was alone in the house. He said yes and decided to do it right away: my friends, who had always been more skeptical of my mother's suggestion than I was, ended up being busy that day, and so it was just me.

Daddy set up our dining room that day to look like a photography studio, putting up the blue backdrop screen that he used with his Real Models without talking much. He was always very serious when taking pictures. He told me to put on my bathing suit, but I didn't actually have one, despite my plans with my friends. My last known bathing suit had gotten lost in the six months we were homeless. According to the boys at school, only my legs, forehead, and smile were getting bigger, not my butt or breasts. As much as I loved the water, I hadn't had a reason to replace it. All I had was my new blue-and-white polka-dot bra and panty set that Mommy just bought me from JCPenney.

"It's no different than a bikini, Tracey," he said. "Real models wear much less than this."

But I wasn't a real model, and he was my daddy.

He sent me to get the baby oil from the bathroom, then flipped open the pink top, and poured the oil into his hands. He showed me how to apply it, the way his real models did. My father rubbed the oil on the uppermost part of my back and shoulders as if he were frosting one of the delicate cakes he baked. He wanted my body to glisten.

"Just relax, Tracey, you're doing fine, there is nothing to worry about."

I didn't feel fine, but I tried to reassure myself. *I know Daddy is a photographer*, I thought. *I know he takes good pictures. I know Mommy thought it was a good idea. She didn't want Old Man Tate to take my pictures. Maybe if Mommy was here I would be more comfortable. I should say something to Daddy, tell him I want to wait.*

I didn't. Instead, I kept telling myself, *If I'm ever going to be a Real Model, I have to get used to this.*

Finally the photo shoot ended, and I went to change clothes in my room when he called to me.

"Yes, Daddy?"

"I need you to come in here for a minute."

Daddy had an idea: he asked me to lie down on the bed for a few shots in my bra and panties. I was confused; all the other pictures were taken in the makeshift dining room studio.

"Everything will be okay, Tracey," he said. "Just relax."

He laid me down gently and, one hand holding his camera, the other moved the crotch of my brand-new blue-and-white polka-dot panties to one side.

For once, I was glad I didn't have a little sister.

I TOLD MOMMY A WEEK LATER.

She looked at me hard and then she hugged me even harder. She asked why I'd waited seven days to tell her, but I didn't have an answer. Mommy didn't say anything else; we just went and rode home from her job in silence.

Of course Daddy denied it; I expected that. I didn't expect Mommy to believe him, and she didn't.

So after Daddy finally confessed, I assumed Mommy would throw him out; all along, I had thought that Mommy stayed with Daddy because he was sick and she felt sorry for him.

But she didn't make him leave.

It was her house, she paid the bills, and she worked. He didn't. Why did she still care for him and let him stay, after what he'd done to their daughter? I was so filled with rage; I couldn't understand her pain and I didn't understand her choices. How could she, after all this, love us both equally, maybe even love him a little more than she did me? Even though he raped me, it was treated as something we were both guilty of; I just refused to wear my half of the shame.

My father attended our church sporadically. His health was always an excuse for absence while his photography afforded him plenty of opportunities to be seen at his best. Our pastor, reverends, and deacons all held him in high regard, so when my mother sought advice from our church, it was treated much in the way as the counselor had. No one could believe it. They left us to deal with the matter the best way we knew how, on our own.

A counselor coworker of Daddy's warned my mom that she should let him stay because if my father were forced to leave, the overall damage to our family could be irreversible. I thought it very ironic, given all the times my father was unemployed, that it was an associate of his who came to our aid. As a counselor, he volunteered his services to the family as a favor to my father. This doctor, like most of the people my father was in contact with, believed him to be a good and decent man.

"Your father told me what happened, Tracey," the counselor said as I sat on the edge of the chair in his hospital office two weeks later. "Do you think you can forgive him?" he asked.

My parents sat on the couch on the other side of the room, my mother on one side, gripping her purse, and my father quietly on the other, his head down and his eyes up. It was the second time in two weeks that I'd been asked to forgive something I was struggling to comprehend on the most basic level. (Daddy had also asked me for my forgiveness, after he stopped denying to my mother that he'd raped me.)

The psychiatrist paused expectantly, as though I'd missed my cue.

"I'll try," I said.

"Good, good, good, Tracey," he said.

"My name is Sharisse," I said. "Only Daddy calls me Tracey."

Daddy, and his whole family, had wanted me to be a boy, so they never used my first name: they all called me Tracey because it could conceivably be a boy's name.

"Okay, Tracey . . . sorry, Sharisse," the so-called counselor droned on. "I've had a long talk with your father. I know him quite well, you know. He's very sorry and I don't think he will ever do this again. This was just a onetime thing."

Daddy's friend was so glib about Daddy raping me, as if it was just a fluke, a regrettable blip on an otherwise unblemished record, like that one time you drove blackout drunk, or that one time you stole your grandmother's purse and did black tar heroin: that one time you raped your only child.

"Besides, you'll come back to see me. We'll talk about whatever's confusing you. You're a good girl, Tracey, right? Tell me, Tracey, where's your favorite place to go?"

"What do you mean?" I said, without correcting him about my name again.

"You know, your favorite place!" he said enthusiastically, as if it were a perfectly natural segue from talking about That One Time Your Father Raped You Which Will Totally Never Happen Again He Swears.

"I think the three of you should go someplace. As a family. You pick!"

"I don't know," I said.

"C'mon, Tracey," he wheedled. "Where's your favorite place to go? Where would you *really* like to go? Anyplace at all!"

"I just went to Magic Mountain with my eighth-grade class."

"That's it," he said, clapping his hands with a satisfied grin at my stricken parents. "Magic Mountain. There. Take her to Magic Mountain."

WHEN MY FATHER WAS INSIDE ME, THERE WAS A MOMENT that I didn't cry. The minute before I didn't cry, I tried to scream and realized that no sound was leaving my mouth.

So I lay there, eyes shut, and tried to distract myself with thoughts of something that felt good. I pictured the boy who was supposed to be my date for my eighth-grade graduation field trip to Magic Mountain. I was in love with that boy for the entire second semester and I'd felt so special until two days before the trip, when he dumped me.

"Does that feel good, baby?" said my daddy.

"Yes . . . NO!" I said, when I registered it was the voice of the man who'd raised me for thirteen years and not the boy I'd been trying to focus on.

I was feeling pain like I'd never experienced before, tearing, breaking, and throbbing in a place I didn't know could feel that. The weight on top of me and inside, combined with the heartache that my father was causing, was unbearable. No darkness or daydream could take that away.

"No," I said.

He continued.

"No!" I yelled.

He paused.

"No, no, no," I said as I held my hands fanned and spread out to try and cover as much of my body as possible. My eyes flew open and then he resumed thrusting to my cries, as if he were trying to silence me with his pounding, as if he were imagining my screams could be something other than pain and terror.

"How does that sound, Tracey?" the hazy blob calling me by my wrong name said, pulling me out of the memory of my rape. "Your parents have agreed to take you to Magic Mountain, all three of you. A family trip!"

"Fine." Tracey was fine with whatever they said. Sharisse was shattered, she wanted to yell and refuse to go and never forgive, but Tracey would say whatever the therapist wanted if they would all leave her and Sharisse alone.

"This is a good sign, Mom and Dad," he said to my parents, who were still rigid on the opposite couch, not touching, looking anywhere but at my face. "This will be good for all of you."

The doctor continued to speak to my parents and I tried

to tune him out but couldn't entirely. Divorce is hard on any family, he explained, but it would be a real tragedy for a Black Family to divorce. A broken home is the absolute worst thing that can happen to a child. (*Worse than getting raped by your father?* I thought to myself.)

"Are any of your friends' parents divorced, Tracey?"

"Uh-huh."

"You're very lucky to have two parents that love you," he said, as if parents who got divorced loved their children less. "What happened to you is a terrible thing but I don't think it will happen again. Go to Magic Mountain, Tracey. Have some fun and come back to tell me all about it."

The more he said it, the more it took on a mystical quality—Magic Mountain—like it was a bonus quest in *Lord of the Rings*. Magic Mountain would erase the trauma of my rape, would instill in me some trust in my father that I'd never had, and would restore our cohesion as a Black Family.

So we went. My father paid for my admission, he bought me a rainbow twirled lollipop from the souvenir shop at the entrance and even agreed to go on my favorite ride, a roller coaster, first, despite the long lines.

"Just father and daughter today," the attendant said cheerfully, when we were finally ushered in; my mother refused to get on a roller coaster.

My father smiled but showed no teeth. I just looked at the attendant as he assisted us with our red safety harness.

"Give it a tug, make sure she's safe and secure now," he said.

My father pulled on the harness.

"She's daddy's little girl," he said, "I'm sure you don't want anything to happen to her."

We took off.

"Tracey," I heard, just as my toe hit the hallway after a shower. It was as if he'd been listening, waiting for me.

"You'll have to wait," I told my father not looking in his direction. "I need to get dressed."

"No, you don't."

It was three years later; I was sixteen. My hand clutched the brown antique doorknob when I turned to look at him. "What!?"

"I just want to look at you. Just look." I stared in disbelief. "Let me look and you can practice your driving hours in my truck."

It wasn't going to stop. He was *never* going to stop. The therapist, my mother, they had been so wrong. I knew then that I wasn't safe—how could I ever be safe sleeping just one room away from my rapist?—and I ran to the kitchen to grab a knife.

My father was in the doorway of his bedroom when I returned, waiting. I brandished the knife, but my rage only seemed to amuse him. He raised his eyebrows and I lunged toward him. But my towel slipped off, landing at his feet on the midnight blue carpet and three years of running from him, avoiding him, carefully concealing myself, of constant vigilance was all undone. I was naked before him.

He'd gotten everything he wanted, and all he'd had to do was wait. I knew what was next on his wish list.

"You are a sick motherfucker," I yelled, running into my bedroom and pushing the heavy five-dresser bureau in front of my door. I wasn't sure if I was protecting myself from my father's advances or myself from a murder charge.

"Who do you think you're talking to, Tracey?" he admonished. He was deranged, I thought, thinking he could slip back into fatherly privilege just moments after he propositioned me, his daughter, like a five-dollar hooker.

"Come near me and I'll kill you," I yelled.

There was no safe place for me to go, no relatives nearby or close family friends that I could trust. I'd lost all my faith in adults, so I called my friend Robin to pick me up; she wasn't afraid of adults. I also called my mother.

"Your husband did it again," I spat in a mix of shouting, crying, screaming, and yelling. "He did it again."

"What are you talking about?" my mother asked as if she had no idea what "it" could possibly be.

"He did it again," I shouted toward the bottom receiver. And I hung up the phone.

The phone rang but my father answered it right away. I looked out the window, waiting for Robin to arrive before I moved the bureau. I would've gone out the window, but they were all nailed shut: shortly after he raped me, my father caught me with a boy and thought that not being able to open the windows would keep me inside. As far as I was concerned, the real danger was on *this* side of the glass.

A horn honked outside and I struggled to push the bureau away from the door and be quiet. But my footsteps were loud once they hit the hardwood floors in the living room. Then I heard the horn again, three times, more frantic. Time to go.

"Where do you think you're going, young lady?"

The sound of his voice right after the horn made me jump. I knew if I got the door open and Robin saw me that I'd be safe. I just needed the door open. I rushed to unlock both the dead bolt and bottom lock and flung it wide.

"You're not going anywhere," he said, as I stepped onto the porch. *Just keep walking* I said to myself. *Ignore him, Sharisse. Just keep moving.* But it's impossible.

"Leave me alone before I tell them what you just did," I said, turning back. His secret was my one available weapon, and being outside gave me more courage. Our neighbor across the street was standing in his driveway; our next-door neighbor, Andy, was smoking on his porch; and the Mexican family two doors down was in their yard.

"You better get your little butt back in this house."

Robin honked again. "Sharisse, c'mon," she called. "Just get in the car!"

"But he did it again." I started to cry. I wanted her to understand why, safely outdoors, I couldn't just walk away without him admitting it.

My father insisted that I come back in the house, infuriated at me and embarrassed in front of our neighbors.

"Tell them!" I shouted, suddenly brave with rage and a public audience. "Tell them how you tried to fuck me just now so I could drive your piece-of-shit truck!" He blinked in the sunlight, registering what I'd screamed in front of so many witnesses.

"Be quiet, little girl," he hissed.

"Let's go, Sharisse!"

In all the noise I didn't immediately hear my mother's heels on the sidewalk.

"What's going on here?" she asked, taking in the scene in our driveway. I was angry at my mother for the look of surprise on her face. What did she expect, after all? It's not like he changed the way he treated me after the incident. Nothing changed.

"Ask your husband," I said and got in the car.

I lived with Robin for a short time but, as much as I'd always wanted siblings, her house was too busy. Brothers and bullies from school had free rein at her house, and some of Robin's best friends were girls who had threatened to beat me up. I decided it was better to take my chances at home where I knew what to expect. Maybe my pulling a knife on my father showed him I wasn't the one to be fucked with.

After I moved back in, I wrote a series of letters to adults—family members, people from church, and good friends of my mother who also happened to be her coworkers—getting the addresses from my mother's telephone book and stealing stamps from her wallet.

In the letters, I wrote that my father had tried to rape me a second time and I had run away from home but couldn't stay where I'd been. I asked for each person to send me money because my part-time job after school wasn't enough to allow me to get a place on my own.

My mother's father in Philly got a letter, even though Grandpop and I weren't really close. A nice lady at church who was a friend of my mother's and she was always nice to my father got one: she was a woman and I thought she would help. My mother's coworker who had a daughter my age got one: she made me tacos when I was eight and I spent the night at her house, so I was sure she would help.

I'd expected return letters with checks within two weeks and, every day, I opened the black squeaky mailbox lid hoping for letters addressed to me. After a month passed, it was clear that no one was going to write me back.

A few months later, an uncle died in Philadelphia and my mom went out for the funeral. After she got back, she told me that my grandfather asked if things were okay because he'd received a letter from me with some "horrible lies" in it. She told me she cried when she read the letter he'd kept and told her father that it was true.

"Did he say why he didn't send me money?" I asked her.

"He said he assumed you were lying and making up stories for attention," my mother said.

"But once you told him it was true?"

"He didn't say anything."

I later learned that all of my letters reached their addressees. Every single one of the people I sent them to had a conversation with my mother about them. The general consensus boiled down to one dismissive phrase that unified them all: *That's y'all business.*

"Your daddy is dying," my mother said to me when nineteen-year-old me got home from my new full-time job as a receptionist. My husband of seven months and I had decided to live with her because my father had been sick and he'd been splitting his time between a psychiatric and medical hospital for most of that year. The stays were longer each time he'd go in, and the few times I'd seen him he looked more and more decrepit.

"I figured as much," didn't seem to be the response she was looking for; whenever my mother delivered any news about my father, she looked at me and waited, like I hadn't done enough for him, like today was the day my heart would thaw and have this outpouring of sympathy for him—sympathy that would absolve her for choosing her man over her child every time.

The look pissed me off. Had she forgotten that I'd been the one in the house with her these past years, with him? No daughter should have to help her rapist father get to the doctor because he's in pain. Did she not realize how hard it was for me to look past him and focus on her, just to get him to the help that he needed?

"He needs your forgiveness, Sharisse," she said. "I think he's holding on for it."

But we'd played that game years ago with the therapist: he'd been sorry, "Tracey" said she forgave him, and he tried to rape me again anyway three years later. Now that he was dying, the only difference was that we were 99.9 percent sure he wouldn't have the strength to rape me.

I told my mother no.

She stared at me through her glasses: I'd disappointed her. The feeling was mutual.

Later that evening, my husband, Bryant, and I spoke about my decision to not visit my father; he wanted me to go, "just go so he can die in peace." Bryant was a good person, and I wanted to be a good person for him—but it bothered me that it was more important that my dad found peace than that I did. Bryant knew what my father had done, but they had somehow still bonded. Everyone who came in contact with my father liked him.

It made me sick whenever I saw them together laughing, joking, and exchanging small talk in our living room. It was bad enough that they had my body in common; I hated that they'd found more than that.

We made plans to go see my father the next day.

It was difficult to go to work with the weight of forgiveness on my shoulders; after, my husband met me at the hospital. As we turned the corner and reached the nurses' station, I recognized people and heard voices: friends of the family, church members, coworkers of my mother, all there for my father. People parted to let me by and whispered, shaking their heads in disapproval. Somehow the shame was still on me, the victim; my father was to be absolved in death as he had been in life.

My husband gripped my hand. "Do you want me to go with you?" he asked.

"No," I said.

My mother offered as well, but I didn't want either of them in the room with me. I figured that I might as well finish with my father as I had started with him: alone.

The room smelled like I imagined death would—flannel

blankets and Clorox, camouflaged in a potpourri of church-lady powder and perfumes. My father had tubes coming out of every opening that I'd allow myself to look at. His chapped lips parted but no audible words came out.

He motioned with the hand nearest me to sit. His eyes were dull and quiet but they followed my every move.

"Do you want more light?" I asked. He motioned me again to sit in the chair next to his bed.

A large clear tear ran down his cheek. My father turned his hand over to the backside so the tube hit the bed and raised it up and down; he wanted my hand. I hesitated, and he did it again. Another tear.

I put my hand on top of his and turned my head toward the door, unable to watch his final act of touching me. He curled his fingers toward the center. I didn't move. The sound of him trying to find his voice scared me.

"You don't have to talk," I said.

"I'm sorry," he said in a small voice.

More tears fell, disappeared under the tube, and re-emerged.

"I know," I said, "I forgive you, Daddy."

I was lying, but I knew he would believe me because he wanted to. He'd waited for it; everyone in the hall had been waiting for the lie, so they could feel better about them-selves. I sat for as long as I could stand to have my hand in his.

I leaned over and brushed his paper-thin cheek with my lips. "Good-bye."

———————

THAT GOOD-BYE WASN'T THE END, OF COURSE. I STILL CARRY
the weight of being a rape survivor, and of the demand that
I forgive and forget to uphold the myth of the perfect Black
Family. I carry the weight handed to me by the Black moral
majority, who ignored my father's crimes and who knows how
many other men's, who tried to buy off a terrified thirteen-
year-old with a one-day trip to an amusement park. They were
so desperate to project the image of the respectable, righteous,
picture-perfect Black Family to the world that they were willing to let the women and girls in those pictures suffer.

I never asked to be a model minority. I just wanted, for a
few minutes, to believe I could be a model.

To Get Out from Under It

STACEY MAY FOWLES

I SAID THE WORD NO SIXTEEN TIMES.
I don't know that I truly remember exactly how many times I said no, especially given the circumstances—the passage of time blots out any kind of vivid, detailed memory, and the world fills you with doubt over the legitimacy of your own story.

But for whatever reason, that's the number that I repeat in my head. It's the number that I used when I finally started talking about what happened to me. It's the number that I told counselors and psychiatrists, and whispered to close friends in quiet, covert moments.

Sixteen.

It's almost sad that my fragile memory picked out that number to use every time I tell the story, as if saying no sixteen times is so many more than one that it makes my claim of violation more valid.

I said no more than a dozen times.

Does that sound better than saying it once?

Exactly how many times did I need to say no to make what happened to me wrong and worthy of care?

ON A COLD AFTERNOON IN MAY, I ARRIVE FOR MY APPOINT-ment at the Domestic Violence and Sexual Assault Care Centre to find that someone had given its clients a package of brightly colored chalk. With it, the clients had written all over the institutional-beige waiting room walls.

I sit down and wait for my counselor to collect me, absently scanning the multicolored aftermath. I assume the graffiti was allowed because today is the last day that the center will be open, that the scrawl is appropriate only because the aging building is closing, its contents and staff moving to their bright and shiny brand-new home.

The new crisis center, I'm told, will be more accommodating, more hopeful, more comfortable. It will have tighter security and a greater sense of anonymity. It will be better able to protect its most vulnerable clients, the women who live in fear of their abusers and are worried that they'll be found. The future waiting room will be less claustrophobic, its furnishings better than a worn, salmon-pink velour living room set inherited from a generous staff member.

Of course I know it will be better, that everyone who works here, I'm told, has been looking forward to the move for months, but I still feel a pang, a sense of loss at the building's closure. I've spent a great deal of time here over the past few years. It is the humble, private place where I've finally stared at so many things head-on, a secret refuge that became safe and predictable while everything else seemed untethered.

The outdated furnishings and faded paint job belie the medical environment in which they are housed and, though designed to make me better, this place never made me feel that I was broken.

A client who sat in this room before me added a quote by feminist writer Nawal El Saadawi in bright red. "I speak the truth and the truth is savage and dangerous," it reads.

To my right, another survivor has scrawled "silence will not be my enemy" in blue chalk, above what I assume is her full name, the date of her rape, and the name of her rapist.

Everyone here wants to say a terrible thing out loud; so many are stifled by lives that keep them silent. This is the place in which we are all finally safe to speak about the awful, secret things that have happened to us, and unveil the disturbing thoughts that have plagued us for hours, days, months, and years as a result.

Here at the crisis center no one will tell on us, yet I still struggle with speaking the truth. In the safety of these tiny clinic rooms, when I hear my voice articulate what I've been through and how it's made me feel over so many years, I often feel like it can't be real. I recount, and recount again, as if to remind myself that, yes, something terrible happened to me. Yes, that's the reason I turned out this way.

I doubt I'll ever really be sure how I ended up in this place, how my life brought me here, despite the fact that I've gone over it again and again in my mind.

The brightly colored box of chalk is still open, its contents splayed out on the heavy wood coffee table. But today I have nothing to write.

WHAT I REMEMBER: I WAS FACEDOWN WHEN HE PINNED down my wrists, one at each side of my body. His hands were strong and large and rough, but they were, before the moment that he held me down, hands that I had wanted to touch me.

I struggled against him when, for a brief moment, he finally loosened his grip, and I saw a possible window of escape. I made a futile effort to cover myself with my hands and push him off me with my body while still under his weight. While I did that, I chanted that word *no*, until it became like the call of a struggling animal trying to free itself from a trap, haplessly trying to wriggle free from a predator.

I started to panic. He was too heavy, having at least fifty pounds on me. I couldn't breathe.

No became a meaningless word while I was under him. It evolved into a plea or prayer instead of an instruction as intended. And then, in all the futility, it was nothing but a cry, a feral squeal with no one to witness it.

In the dark, there was no one to call out to, no one to help me, but I cried out the word nonetheless, just as I had been taught to do.

I'M ALONE IN THE WAITING ROOM TODAY, AS I AM FOR MOST of these monthly sessions. I leave my full-time job early to get to them, telling my manager only that I have "an appointment"—something that thankfully no one questions. The appointments are always at the same day and time, Mondays at 5 p.m., because they are hard to rebook, both due to high demand and the challenge of anonymity. In the interest of client safety, calls from the clinic always come from a mysterious blocked number, which always triggers a deep anxiety in me.

Most things, to be honest, trigger a deep anxiety in me.

A counselor always struggles through coded conversations on the phone, so as not to betray the secrets so many victims keep from their loved ones and coworkers.

"I can't really say right now. I'm at work," I will tell her.

It's hard to live fully and authentically when you're keeping secrets like this. It's hard even to feel alive when there's so many things you can't say. So few people even know that I come here—just a handful whom I deem safe to tell: my husband, my closest friends, that one sympathetic guy at the office who in an exchange of confidences relays to me his own mental health struggles and covers for me when I need a break. I have a strict inner circle that I feel comfortable sharing my recovery with, as if I am doing something dirty and wrong that I should be ashamed of.

I know that if I was "sick" in the traditional sense that would not be the case. People would rally around me and bake me casseroles. They would send cards and flowers and hope for my speedy recovery. They would take to social media and wish me well. Instead when I walk into the hospital that houses the clinic, I am equipped with acceptable reasons for being there that most survivors have practiced, excuses at the ready on the off chance I will run into someone I know.

I have a routine medical test. I am picking up a prescription. I am visiting a friend's relative.

It's nothing serious, nothing to worry about, I will say, hoping that it's true.

From my seat in the waiting room, I nervously fumble with my phone, check baseball scores and television recaps, return messages, and try to ignore the muffled voice of an assessment nurse on the phone in the office behind me. She is likely the same nurse who asked me to tell her my story the very first time I came here.

THE REFERRAL CAME FROM A STRANGER—A DOCTOR WHO was filling in for my regular provider when she was on vacation. At the urging of close friends who were concerned about my behavior, I made a same-day appointment and, when I was ushered into the replacement doctor's office, I told her I thought I might be depressed, that I was drinking a lot, that I had trouble sleeping and eating.

"I was sitting in the shower. I was crying. And the idea flashed in my head. I thought how I could make it end," I said.

It was a moment that had been a long time coming: I spent most of my life to that point only barely coping, grappling with various incarnations of clinical anxiety—hypochondria, agoraphobia, claustrophobia, and panic attacks. I had had an irrational, desperate, terrifying fear of disaster and dying, an ongoing flight impulse, and a penchant for panic at the most inopportune times. I found being alone in the world difficult, yet I also found being surrounded by people difficult. But the severe depression was a new development, one that had whittled away at my constant, debilitating fear of death and suddenly made it an ugly option for escape.

At the point of my same-day appointment, I hadn't slept properly in weeks, and my mind was caving in on itself via a particular brand of sleep-deprived psychosis. A well-intentioned friend had slipped me a generous supply of heavy-duty prescription sleeping pills she had taken from her boyfriend, handing them to me in a Ziploc bag in the hope of relieving my pervasive exhaustion. Sometimes I counted out the pills on the coffee table and wondered how many it would take.

Sometimes I eyed the contents of the cutlery drawer, studying the knives and pondering their effectiveness. Friends would come to visit and bring me food in Styrofoam takeout containers, watching me slowly eat with barely concealed worry. I was in such a constant state of desperation, exacerbated by sleeplessness, that I cried hysterically in front of a complete stranger, this medical professional, while begging for help.

The doctor, whose name I don't even remember, calmly took me through a depression assessment questionnaire and generously prescribed me Ativan. She encouraged me to consider antidepressants. She wanted me to get in touch with my family practitioner immediately for a battery of tests.

When I finally managed to splutter out, "something bad happened to me," she just knew.

Without saying a word, she slipped a small square of yellow paper across the desk toward me. It was printed with information about the rape-counseling clinic.

I was struck by the ease with which she provided me with the contact, as if she'd done it hundreds of times before.

THE FIRST TIME I WENT TO THE CRISIS CENTER, I SAT WITH the intake nurse and together we googled the man who had assaulted me, if only so I could have the satisfaction of a single other person knowing his name, knowing what he looked like, and where he is now. She slowly keyed his name in the image search as I spelled it out for her, and there among the photos was his smiling, unassuming face.

A man, not a monster.

I slowly raised a finger to indicate to her which one of the many men he was in the collection of images on-screen. I had done this search by myself so many times, an obsessive action with the intent of self-protection, a rather futile way to ensure he was always far enough away from me, so that I could feel safe.

I remember, with that photograph of him on her computer screen, she told me that she actually knew the names and faces of so many rapists—businessmen and journalists, professional athletes and real estate agents, husbands and fathers.

That nurse, who books STD tests, helps clients through reporting to the police, and sets them up with mental health care, is also the keeper of so many women's fiercely guarded secrets. She is an initial repository for their frantic fear and shame and is so often the only other person who will ever know what happened to them.

She stayed with me in her tiny office until 10 p.m., long past when she was due to go home, to make sure that I was no threat to myself. I remember apologizing to her when I realized how late I had kept her there, and she laughed kindly.

"There's no better place for me to be than here with you," she actually said.

I REMEMBER THAT I SAID NO SIXTEEN TIMES AND I REMEMBER that he accused me of being *fucking dramatic*. They always do that. They do that before, when you refuse, and they do that during, when you protest, and they do that after, when you cry.

I remember he told me not to be so emotional, told me to relax. Maybe he didn't actually say the word *fucking* but my mind remembers it that way, as if the aggression of his profanity too makes my claim of violation more valid. As if swearing at me makes him a monster and not just a man. (We always need them to be monsters.) As if his profanity reinvents him for listeners as someone to be afraid of, just as he was reinvented for me in that moment.

Just as I was reinvented.

THERE IS THIS IMPOSSIBLE PARADOX WHEN YOU ARE VICTIM-ized by sexual assault. You want to—you have to—convince yourself that it wasn't "that bad" in order to have any hope of healing. If it really is as bad as you feel like it is, how will you ever get out from under it? How will you ever get "better"?

On the other hand, you need to convince others it was "bad enough" to get the help and support you need to do that healing. To get out from under it. To get an appointment at the clinic. To get friends to come over with Styrofoam food containers when you can't feed yourself.

You tell yourself how bad it is and then you numb yourself to how bad it is. You repeat as needed, for so many years.

Does saying no sixteen times make me worthy of pity? Does it make me worthy of help?

UNLIKE MOST HEALTH PROFESSIONALS, MY RAPE COUNSELOR always arrives on time to collect me from the waiting room. She also always seems genuinely happy to see me. And today, like she always does, she politely asks if I'm ready, or if I need a few more minutes.

There is something about her predictable question that buoys me, feels empowering, as if she is affirming that it is my choice to be there to tell my story every time I arrive. I look up from my phone and smile at her, tell her yes, I'm ready as I slip it into my bag, and we leave the waiting room, engaging in small talk and pleasantries before we go into her office and do the necessary work.

The smallest gestures make this therapeutic process different from what I've experienced before; a previous series of strictly scheduled $175-an-hour cognitive behavioral therapy appointments, or a desperate fifteen-minute window with a doctor to refill a much-needed Ativan prescription. None of my previous therapy has actually stuck, and my hope is that this difference will bring some sort of finality.

The promise of an end to the way I feel is the only reason for momentum.

My rape counselor seems noticeably younger than me—her hair shaved to the skin on one side of her head, her clothes fashionable in a youthful way that I am increasingly confused by as I grow older. I will discover later that we're actually very close in age—early thirties—but anxiety and depression both have a nasty habit of aging you, or at least the way you perceive yourself. She seems full of an optimism and energy, with a love of life that I have long since lost.

It would be easy to resent her if she hadn't done so much work to help me.

I've seen so many counselors, therapists, psychologists, and psychiatrists since I was sexually assaulted for the first time: a hapless guidance counselor at school who dragged me in for "a talk" after an English teacher flagged some dark poetry I was writing; a series of mental health professionals at the university clinic, all of whom seemed completely unequipped for me, primarily charged with doling out condoms and spotting eating disorders; and later, an ever-changing roster of costly psychologists with varying sensitivities to the issues around and reactions to sexual assault.

A cognitive behavioral therapist once admitted that she

felt helpless to treat my rape trauma, that it wasn't her area of expertise, and that I should seek help elsewhere. It was an admission that scared me, made me feel like I was too far gone to be fixed.

Yet the day I met this particular counselor, she immediately seemed to be the most noticeably prepared and understanding of all the therapists I've had, constantly reaffirming herself as open to any strange thought, impulse, feeling, or action of mine.

In some ways, my rape counseling has felt entirely divorced from the traditional therapeutic model. It's permissive in comparison, focused on harm reduction and careful reassurances. It seems that, if something makes you feel better, it is a healthy option. Want to sleep all day? That's okay. Drink too much? That can be a valid coping choice. Isolating yourself via a fear of the outside world? Self-preservation is important.

To me, all of this is revolutionary, and it means that I can finally be honest with someone about my behavior without the fear of their disappointment.

I usually walk into rape counseling assuming I am totally failing and floundering, that the people in my life deem me helpless, and she confidentially assures me I am making real, solid progress where I see absolutely none. My sessions with her are a short period of time where the expectations to be "better" are radically shifted from those of the world outside.

In her office, I discover that the tiniest of steps I am taking to be emotionally free of my attacker are actually monumental for someone who suffers this hypervigilance and fear that can follow in the years after sexual assault.

I feel lucky to have her, but alongside this is the knowledge that I wasn't assaulted in a particularly violent way. I sometimes feel like maybe some more worthy victim's space is being taken up by my twenty-year-old troubles, that I should be able to manage this by myself rather than gobbling up much-needed and sparse resources because of my inability to move on.

When I raised this in counseling, she told me: "The survivor who was raped at knifepoint feels guilty she has taken up the space of a survivor who was raped at gunpoint. Everyone believes there is suffering worse than her own, that they should be strong enough to cope without me."

WHEN YOU START ANY FORM OF THERAPY, YOU'RE USUALLY informed that everything you say is confidential—barring a threat to harm yourself or someone else. But I was told in my first session at the clinic that, although that still held true, my counselor understood the validity of the fantasy to harm your attacker as part of healing, and that the thought does not equal intent.

"Sometimes I think about him getting hit by a bus," I admitted to her in one of those first sessions. She wasn't in any way rattled.

"Why a bus?" she asked, genuinely interested.

"Because then it's nobody's fault. It's an accident. Quick and clean," I said.

"Do you want him to suffer?"

"No. I don't want that kind of revenge. I just want him gone. I just never want to be afraid of running into him again."

My counselor has told me of countless women talking in detail about castrating their rapists. They've explained visions of him dying in a fire, of him being beaten to death with a baseball bat, of him being attacked by wild animals. My lack of need for gratuitous suffering doesn't make me better or worse than any other survivor. In this space, I never feel like I'm disappointing anyone with what I'm thinking, or how I am reacting or coping.

In the context of rape therapy, our terrifying feelings are normalized as part of the process—as is the insidious fantasy of self-harm. With rape recovery, it's just as normal an impulse to want revenge as it is to want to disappear, to want to die.

My counselor has a specialized understanding of the kinds of "inappropriate" things women say in these private, fluorescent-lit offices, the secret language in which they speak to her and to each other. She's heard all the gallows humor, the obscene jokes, and the offhand remarks women need to make life tolerable, the darkness that they employ when facing the unimaginable task of simply living after being violated.

Did you know him? Did you invite him in? Did you go willingly? Did he hurt you? Did he have a weapon? Did he force you? Did you wear something that provoked him? Did you want to have sex with him? Did you cook him dinner beforehand? Did you put on makeup? Did you tell him you liked him? Did you tell him you loved him? Do you regret anything you did that night?

How bad was it, really?

I ONCE ASKED MY COUNSELOR WHY SHE DOES THIS JOB, HOW she could stomach it every day, confronting all this female suffering at the hands of men.

"I feel blessed to be able to see so many women being so strong and seeking help," she responded without hesitation.

This answer seems both rehearsed and impossible to me, but I believed her nonetheless. She offers the perfect balance of concern and reassurance, creating a space that smells like lemon verbena and that has ample art supplies I'll never use, and books I'll never read, so that we can have conversations no one else will ever have with me. I trust her, and that is a monumental thing when you've learned—been conditioned—to trust absolutely no one.

This has become the safe space where I can finally say the thing I've needed to say for so many years.

"I THINK I MAY HAVE RAPE-RELATED POST-TRAUMATIC STRESS disorder," I blurt out.

I've used the internet to catalogue my symptoms with the growing fear that something is wrong with me. I've long denied the possibility and yet I come back to it again and again. I've weighed the stigma of being sick against the hope of finding reprieve. I've gone back and forth again and again for years and I am finally given the room to say it out loud.

"I think you might be right," she replies, as if she has been waiting all this time for me to say it.

She hands me a sheet of paper. Printed on it is a simple questionnaire that will be the first step on the road to a PTSD diagnosis.

It is a step I'd been waiting decades to take.

SEXUAL ASSAULT MUST SIMULTANEOUSLY BE TERRIBLE AND BE something you're able to accept—which is an impossibly hard thing to negotiate. Inevitability must also be a key factor, because God forbid if there was something you could have done to stop it.

How many times did you say no?

I have realized that maybe I no longer need anyone to think it was "bad enough." I don't need to prove that I am worthy of pity or help. I don't need you to feel sorry for me. What I need is what most women need when they talk about the sexual violence they have endured. I need someone to listen. I need someone to believe me.

Whenever I tell the story I say "sixteen," even though now I know once was enough.

Reaping What Rape Culture Sows

Live from the Killing Fields of Growing Up Female in America

Elisabeth Fairfield Stokes

IF NOT FOR THE FATHER WHO FIRST TOLD ME THAT RAPE WAS wrong and a gentle, patient husband, I think I could have easily gone through the rest of my life without ever having sex again. I wanted to deny that my body is part of who I am, because it had been used against me.

In 1981, I was ten years old. I was watching an episode of *Little House on the Prairie* with my family when my little sister asked, "What's rape, Daddy?" He answered, "It's when a man puts his penis in a woman's vagina when she doesn't want him to," in the same tone of voice he used when he explained other hard-to-understand facts about the world, like the threat of nuclear proliferation. My sister nodded and turned back to the television.

That episode (it was actually two episodes, "Sylvia: Part One" and "Sylvia: Part Two"), ended up giving me nightmares for years, made me hate my breasts, when I got them, and hate *Little House.* In it, a girl, Sylvia Webb, developed breasts ahead of other girls in her class, attracting attention from the boys in Walnut Grove. Her father blamed her, first for the unwanted attention, and then when she was raped by a man in a clown mask.

My father's explanation of rape affected me the same way his explanation of the Cold War had: it was abstract and theoretical and terrifying. It didn't jibe with the chubby, happy-looking man and woman lying in bed with hearts all around them in Peter Mayle's 1977 children's book about sex, *Where Did I Come From?*, which explains that "the man wants to get as close to the woman as he can, because he's feeling very loving to her. And to get really close the best thing he can do is lie on top of her and put his penis inside her, into her vagina."

The act was clearly the same, but the idea that a man would do that when the woman didn't want him to was alarming, to say the least. But adults have no way of knowing what children do with the information they are given, a fact of which I am now aware because I have two daughters.

If, however, my dad's explanation was straight lecture, that *Little House* episode was an object lesson: rape was a man in a clown mask watching you from the bushes while you picked flowers, then grabbing you when you're distracted by a flock of birds, throwing you on the ground and apparently putting his penis in your vagina. And it was your fault, because you had breasts.

Sylvia, if you never watched, didn't survive her experience: she died after a dream sequence in which she was wearing a yellow dress and marrying a boy who loved her (notice that her wedding dress wasn't white).

It's hard to overemphasize the impact that show had on my sense of my body and my sexuality in general. When I learned ten years later that Michael Landon had died, my first thought was of the boy in my eighth-grade gym class who jeered at my chest, pointing and laughing at how my breasts flopped around when I ran. Sylvia's father had made her bind her breasts flat so they wouldn't show, and I longed to do that somehow, sure in the logical way adolescent brains work that, now that I had breasts, a stranger in the bushes wasn't far behind. I refused to walk anywhere alone.

The world in which we lived reinforced the sense that I had no say in the matter of how men treated my body. Boys could laugh at our breasts in gym class and not get in trouble for it. Every day in high school our bras were snapped, our skirts flipped up, our butts lightly spanked as we walked to class. If our nipples showed through our shirts, some asshole would inevitably say, "Cuttin' any diamonds lately?" On the rare occasion that any one of us girls complained to a school official about the catcalling and unwanted touching, it was met with, "it just means they like you," and of course, "boys will be boys."

The clown-mask rape was the real worst-case scenario, though. That was "real" rape; anything less than that seemed like it was supposed to be tolerable. Anything "less" than that, well, at least you could say it wasn't as bad as what happened to Sylvia. Date rape was a risk you took because you were a girl and you'd agreed to go on a date. The line between just being a girl on a date and being a "tease" never even existed. The prevailing message from the unchecked harassment we experienced at school was that if you did anything even remotely sexual—a kiss, or holding a hand—you were leading that boy on and you were responsible for anything, and everything, that happened.

When I was fifteen, two years before I was "really" raped, I found myself alone in a car with a football player I'd had a crush on for a while. He kissed me; I was thrilled. He started unbuttoning my shirt; I wasn't thrilled. He was strong and he held me down but he didn't have time to force himself inside me because he was a teenage boy and had no sexual stamina: he sprayed my jeans, his arm across my throat, smashing my head against the car window as he humped my leg. I twisted away from him as far as I could get, my feet braced against the steering wheel, but he pinned my arms so I couldn't open the door. "We'd be hot at the prom," he said as he stuffed himself back into his underwear.

You can cry quietly, or you can howl. You can scream softly, or you can pierce the air like a missile. But silence is just silence. It doesn't sound any different no matter how deep it is. It doesn't look like anything you or anyone else can see, especially when you don't look in mirrors anymore. If I didn't look at myself, I could pretend that nothing had changed.

But silence smells: his sour, astringent acne cream biting the cold air, hot salty semen and rank sweat like burning rubber. Silence feels, too, like you've swallowed rocks, especially when your throat is bruised from where his elbow crushed it even though it didn't leave a mark, and it feels like his sticky mouth all over your face, his tongue like thick meat, slimy and choking, his spit dried rough on your cheeks.

That wasn't rape, though, as I understood it then: he hadn't put his penis in my vagina when I didn't want him to. I don't think I had ever even heard the term "sexual assault," but I know now that's what it was. At the time it was just me making a bad choice by getting into his car in the first place. As Sylvia Webb's father told her after she was raped by the clown, "you reap what you sow." Same letters, different order: reap, rape.

When I was raped, two years later, actually penis-in-my-vagina raped, it wasn't a stranger in a clown mask. It wasn't a stranger at all. It was someone who took what he wanted, because the world taught him that when it came to women's bodies, he could do just that.

Senior year of high school: I had been drinking and I was semiconscious on a bed at a friend's house, my leg in a knee brace after a skiing accident. A guy I knew came into the room. I opened my eyes slowly. He was putting a condom on with one hand and reaching for my underwear with the other. I tried to push him off, saying, "No, no, please no," but there was nothing I could do: I couldn't walk without crutches, I had been drinking, I wasn't strong enough, I couldn't get away. Hot pain flashed through my whole body. I felt a burning surge in my face, my fingers, my toes. After he was done, I turned on my side, crying, drawing the leg that would bend up into my chest, seeing with half-closed eyes the bloody condom coming off, milky liquid dripping onto the floor. He looked at me and grinned. "What are you cryin' for? You said 'please.' You were fuckin' beggin' for it!"

I told no one. It wasn't a stranger in a clown mask, but I knew that time that it was rape, and that it was my fault, for drinking, for hurting my leg, for being a girl. Reap, rape.

I'm far from the only child of the '80s whose understanding of sexual violence was impacted by that particular *Little House* episode. It's inspired fan pages and strange obsessions, things like Sylvia's dying dream sequence set to "Hallelujah," for example. I couldn't bring myself to watch it, or any of the scenes from the original episodes.

My avoidance probably just makes the anxiety I feel about clowns, *Little House*, and Michael Landon (he wrote and directed both "Sylvia" episodes) worse, but I'll take the walls I've constructed over the panic that those scenes might induce. I see no benefit in desensitizing myself to that particular trauma. Despite the lingering damage it did to some of us, the show is a minor skirmish on the killing fields of growing up female in America.

Looking back, I can almost rationalize those episodes as an attempt at social commentary on rape culture. Perhaps Landon was trying to portray Sylvia's plight as a microcosm for the very real situations girls and women face and was trying to call attention to it, rather than just calling it entertainment. But really, I don't buy it: his portrayal of the way a girl's body and the community betray her as she goes through puberty never felt like a full-throated critique even before Mrs. Oleson's character reinforced everything I would later internalize about the unwanted attention girls got from boys at school. She insisted that Sylvia was leading the boys on, that she should be blamed for attracting their attention and that, by extension, she should be blamed for the rape. Mrs. Oleson was the stereotypical small-minded gossip. Even though the episode contains a scene with the school council siding against Mrs. Oleson on the matter of whether or not Sylvia was encouraging the boys' attention, that message was not nearly as strong or as clear as it needed to be.

I didn't even recall that the council sided with Sylvia until I recently read a synopsis of the episode. When I was ten, I couldn't get past the fact that there was even a school council meeting held to discuss whose fault it was that boys were sneaking up on a girl's house to peek in at her getting undressed. All these years, I only remembered that Sylvia had to get up and defend herself. If this was social commentary, an attempt to decry the hostility women regularly face on all fronts, it failed miserably.

I knew women like Mrs. Oleson when I was in high school; they were the conservative "Christian" mothers of people I was friends with, and the mothers of a lot of the boys who snapped bras and flipped up skirts. These women loudly proclaimed their views about how boys and girls were supposed to behave.

One of them found my friend Jamie making out with her son; she blamed Jamie, saying, "I won't tell your mother about this, if you promise it won't happen again. Boys will be boys and there are other girls they can go to for that." The twisted view of the two things women are supposedly for—either marriage or sex but not both—still makes me shudder. I saw the sexism and the hypocrisy in it, but the Mrs. Olesons of the world wielded too much power then. I couldn't outshout them.

It was hard enough being sexually assaulted at fifteen and raped at seventeen; compounding it was the mind-fuck perpetrated by people like these mothers who promoted the biblical view of women as tempters, of boys and men helpless against their lusty instincts at the sight of a woman, dividing women into Eves and Marys, whores and virgins. I felt betrayed by my gender; not only were men not to be trusted, but neither were women, apparently.

There were, at least fictionally, the "Ellen Jamesians," the women in John Irving's *The World According to Garp* who cut out their tongues in solidarity with a woman whose tongue was cut out so she couldn't identify her attackers after she was gang-raped. They were separatists. They wanted nothing to do with men; when Garp's mother died, they wouldn't even let him attend the memorial service held at the center she founded for troubled and abused women. These women, I thought, had each other's backs.

I encountered real separatists when I went to college, at Smith, but the jokes about two dead men at the bottom of the ocean being "a start" didn't seem funny to me. There was, after all, still the saying "Smith to bed, Holyoke to wed"—

more of the whore-or-virgin dichotomy. My first weekend as a college first-year (we were *not* "freshmen"), in a study carrel at the library, I saw that someone had drawn a picture of an erect penis, complete with balls and pubic hair, and written, "What could be more fun than a long hard one?" Someone else had scrawled underneath: "Cutting it off!"

I could identify with neither sentiment: there was no pleasure in sex for me, nor did I hate men. I didn't quite yet understand my collegiate landscape; it seemed to be an improvement over the misogyny I had left behind, but this men-for-sex-or-not-at-all worldview was not particularly uplifting either.

While I appreciated calling out half the population for creating a situation in which many women rarely feel safe, and I understood how tempting it was to pin it all on men, I didn't have the energy to be angry all the time. I also wasn't gay, despite how easy it seemed to be gay at Smith—especially after what I'd been through, after what a lot of women go through. Trying to be gay, though, seemed like a way, perhaps, to be protected from violence, from abuse, from my own distorted view of my body and my sexuality. And I thought women wouldn't hurt me.

But it wasn't true, and there was neither comfort nor safety in pretending to be something I was not. Women are just people, for better, for worse, as the Mrs. Olesons had shown. Evil is evil wherever you go, and I encountered a lot of it at Smith, too. Men weren't the problem.

For a while when I was in my twenties, I faked orgasms with men, just wanting the sex (on the rare occasions I had it) to be over. I wanted to be loved but not touched. I *wanted* to want sex, and I settled for the small comfort being close to someone brought me, but the assault, the rape, and the silences around them had created an almost total disconnect between my mind and my body. It wasn't until the guy I eventually married made it clear that he knew I was faking, and wanted me to stop, that I started to care if I was enjoying sex or not. I knew only that my body was useful for other people's desires, not my own. There had been moments here and there when I sensed something like physical attraction or sexual arousal, glimpses or sips of something delicious but elusive. It wasn't enough, though, for me to believe that anything good could come of trusting those feelings or even exploring them, of willingly surrendering my body to someone else. There was pleasure in being wanted; that, I could control. There was no pleasure in wanting. I was too afraid.

A clown had gotten into my head and a man had put his penis in my vagina when I didn't want him to, and the world, I had learned, was a place that didn't condemn sexual violence; it accepted and excused it. I had wanted to believe that each day without sex would get me farther and farther away from the man in the clown mask, the football player in the car, the bloody condom. I wanted those things to fade into such distant memory as to dissolve permanently.

But I have had to take it all with me, because it is part of my story. I grieved for many years the woman I would have been if I had not seen that episode of *Little House on the Prairie*, if I had not had a crush on that football player, if I had never been raped. She never got the chance to live.

This is rape's legacy, the countless deaths women die just trying to keep existing in the world as it is.

I have daughters now. I cannot protect them. I cannot get inside their heads and make them unafraid, or know what they are thinking; I know that their minds are as inaccessible to me as mine was to my father. But I can try to equip them. I can help them believe that there is something in them that is unquenchable, something that is impossible to kill. I will myself to believe that they can believe all of that about themselves, even on the days that I struggle with the memories of what happened to me.

They've never asked me or their father what rape is; we've already told them. We've talked about why it's wrong that the entertainment industry is obsessed with violence, particularly violence against women. We've talked about what it means that women are largely portrayed in pop culture as either victims, sluts, virgins, or gossips, and why that's not okay. We tell them that they can choose to live their lives in a way that is not defined by anything that happens to them, something that I have not yet been able to do.

They listen. They nod. They dismiss what insults their souls. They are stronger than I am.

This is what they reap; this is what I sow.

Invisible Light Waves

MEREDITH TALUSAN

BETWEEN TRANSITIONS WHILE I LIVED WITH FIVE OTHER recent nomads in Harlem, I met Paul in our kitchen one night. He'd worked with one of my housemates during a humanitarian service trip in China and was visiting her. He was fluent in Mandarin and majored in linguistics at Yale before enlisting in the navy, where he did intelligence work in Washington, DC. Maybe it was those experiences that gave him that efficient air I associated both with linguists and men in the military. I wanted him from the moment I met him, the way I wanted men I wasn't used to having: one of the strong, handsome white men on television I coveted when I was growing up in the Philippines.

But I also knew there was something wrong about me wanting him, so my eyes cast themselves down when he said hello, and I tried to keep out of his orbit while he stayed at our apartment for a week.

Then he came along when we went out dancing at an underground party in Brooklyn on his last night in town. I wore tight jeans and a black Lycra tank top to show off arms I'd toned from many hours at the gym, the shirt's low scoop making my breasts look bigger than they were. I'm usually too self-conscious about turning red from Asian glow to have any alcohol, but shortly after I drank the one vodka cranberry he offered me, I felt more free to hug him and smell his sweat.

By the end of the night we hadn't talked much, but he'd lifted me up onto a counter so I could rest my legs, which I wrapped around his hips from behind while he stood, while my lips couldn't help but touch his neck. Though I sobered up as we rode an hour in a taxi with my roommates to get back to our apartment, where I managed to leave him in the hallway and close the door to my room, alone.

He was waiting for me when I opened that door again, late enough the next morning that the summer sun was too bright behind me and his presence came as a surprise. So did his kiss, and the probe of his warm tongue.

"I'm leaving in an hour," he said.

He probably suspected that he just needed to have his lips on my mouth and I would crumple with want. I confirmed that suspicion—but my desire came with the need to get him over with so that my life could keep moving. It was easier to accept our attraction rather than listen to the part of me that knew it would be a mistake, to give in to the fun instead of saying the no I wanted to say.

I was almost thirty but hadn't been in a situation before where I felt so conflicted about someone I was so physically attracted to. Maybe it was just prejudice, I told myself, how him being in the military colored my feeling that he wanted me but didn't respect me, how it wasn't right for us to be together. I compromised, told myself I only needed to make him come, that he would go away once he was satisfied and that I didn't need anything else. I refused to let him undress me after he let himself into my room. He lay down on the futon mattress on my parquet floor and I focused on my mouth's task, the act that once gave me pleasure and did then, too, despite whatever else I felt. I marveled at the thick, almost egg-white quality of his ejaculate that tasted oddly pleasant, before my mind returned to things other than sex, how I'd promised myself not to get involved with men for a while—least of all him—because I'd grown to rely on them to feel as though I wouldn't break apart.

Yet he knew how to soften my barriers and so there we were, me not having said no, part of me wanting it and so we did it.

He left town and I became preoccupied—maybe even obsessed, as I had predicted I might—ignoring the signs, and seeing only how good he was on paper, the Yale graduate who spoke several languages and looked amazing in uniform, the kind of man I'd been taught I could never have. As we began to correspond, he told me over email that he'd just broken up with a Chinese girlfriend before coming back to America, and that he liked Asian girls in general.

I flirted in my messages, almost like I was preprogrammed;

I indulged in the game of prospective girlfriend, even though the part of my brain still engaged in self-preservation knew that he only wanted to fuck me because he hadn't gotten to. Maybe I wanted to believe that if I let him fuck me, then it wouldn't be true that he didn't respect me. I was too weak to say no anyway, and no objective court would consider me raped just because I'd wanted to say no, nor would I want one to hold him to account—even if there were moments when I asked myself if it was okay to feel raped even if I wasn't.

Instead of giving in to that thought, I volunteered to visit Paul in DC and we planned out dates and touristy things to do, like going to the White House and the Lincoln monument. But after I arrived, he made a move to fuck me every time we were about to go out.

Sunday morning, I was in his bedroom facing his bed, looking out the floor-to-ceiling windows onto his balcony, knowing I had to be at work the next morning but determined to visit a museum with Paul, to be part of a couple and not a dirty fling. We hadn't left his apartment in days, and his white sheets were a moist amalgam of our sweat and fluids. I willed my mind to be pleased with itself, to enjoy feeling naughty as I put on earrings to finish my outfit—a black silk blouse, a long deep violet skirt with hundreds of tiny pleats by a well-known designer, which I sold to a consignment shop after the trip even though it was my favorite.

We had agreed not to shower so we could smell the sex in our skin, and he told me not to put on underwear. I was too absorbed in finding the hole in my ear to notice that he had reentered the bedroom, and I didn't feel him raise my skirt.

He was inside me before I could even think to protest, and didn't protest because I wanted it, or willed myself to want it, or my body wanted it because for so long I didn't think that I deserved to be with men like him, even when the most important part of me wanted him to stop precisely because I wanted to feel like I deserve to be with any man, before I let someone inside me again. But how could I say no to desire? How could I say no to being fun, like those normal Asian girls he liked?

For years I've told that story and said, "It would have been rape if it weren't so hot," and then wondered to myself whether it could be rape, even if it was so hot.

I left a fool's poem on his pillow before I got on the train, and he thanked me over email only after I asked him if he got it. I didn't hear from him again until one night, seven years later, when one of my housemates from that period—the one who kept in touch with everyone—had a housewarming party and I identified his charming sycophant's voice before I remembered his face. I felt the too-close way he hugged me— like he had fucked me more than once—and only then did I know for sure that it was something I hadn't wanted, would never have wanted if it had only been up to me, in the way that my body tried to forget our contact even as our torsos touched.

"I'm here with my boyfriend," I said after hello.

"It's great that you're happy," he replied, like he knew or could presume to know.

I stayed to prove that he could not affect me, mingled and revolved amid the successful crowd in orbits that sometimes led to him. As I felt his presence in those rooms like invisible light waves, I came to understand that I may never rid myself of the feeling that I am grateful to him for fucking me, for making me feel like I could be fucked so much, that I could extract desire from a man so handsome and strong and smart. I came to understand that I have to live with being the type of woman who might—or probably always will—be grateful to the man she did not want to fuck, but who probably did not rape her.

I also have to live with being the type of woman who might—or probably always will—feel guilty that she never told this man she's trans.

Getting Home

Nicole Boyce

Two Days After

I taped a towel over the window in my front door. I had never really thought about it before, that window. It was small and decorative. Who put it there? Maybe it was supposed to be charming, a decorative quirk of our postundergrad rental home. Maybe it was functional, somehow—a way to watch squirrels or make eye contact with my letter carrier.

I had never thought much about this window before but, two days earlier, a man had masturbated at me at a nearby train station. Now, that window just seemed like what it was: a hole in the wall. I ripped masking tape into long strips with my teeth. I had already closed all the blinds, locked all the doors. My roommates weren't around, so I'd spent the last two nights at my boyfriend's house, delaying this homecoming.

The encounter at the train station—I'd convinced myself of this over the previous forty-eight hours—had been targeted. It had not been a man masturbating near a train platform, but a man masturbating at me, two minutes away from my house, wedged into the familiar banalities that made up my daily routine: the smell of the nearby barbecue joint, the automated transit announcements, the bushes I stood near each morning on my way to work.

He had masturbated at me near the city's third-best corn-bread.

He had masturbated at me at a train platform where I'd once been kissed in high school.

He had masturbated at me.

He had masturbated at me.

So I taped a towel over the window. It looked silly. It kept drooping, then falling down. I watched *Everwood* in my bedroom, going back to check on the towel every hour, feeling foolish. But I was very alone in the house that night, and the window seemed like the house's one remaining vulnerability: the perfect spot for a man to stand, eye to glass, and continue the looking he had started two nights earlier.

WHEN YOU DON'T WALK ALONE AT NIGHT, YOU ARE ROBBED OF the world's quiet. The world is, you hear, very peaceful after 2 a.m. You've been told it's pink-lit—awash in a stillness usually only achieved by plugging one's ears. You imagine other people enjoying these pockets of quiet. You imagine them strolling the empty streets, feeling safe and solitary, having late-night insights. They must encounter raccoons, stray cats—creatures made bold by sundown. You have little experience with these creatures. Encountering these creatures is not your priority.

Two Minutes After

I was on the phone. It was my first 911 call and it felt transgressive: Was this really an emergency? My classmates and I had been told as children that the police would fine you for unwarranted calls. *Don't call 911 because your sister cut your bangs too short.* But there was this masturbating man: the outline of his body in the bushes, the movement of his hand. So I was on the phone, my blood scraping through me like sheets of tin. Police? Fire? Ambulance? Dispatch seemed to operate too slowly. What is your emergency?

I told the operator how he'd held his hoodie shut with one hand, the other hand on his penis. I told her how he ran when I pulled out my phone . . . which way did he go? Toward the mall, I guess—he went in the direction of the mall. I told her his approximate height and weight, and how he'd yanked up his sweatpants before taking off.

Then the call was over. The first call, and then a follow-up call with the police. (*This happens often, unfortunately. We'll send a car to the area.*) Then I was boarding my train, still thinking about the man's sturdy legs. Had they been hairy? Should I have told the police about that? Already, I doubted what I'd seen.

If you'd asked me, a few weeks later, whether the man's knees were plump or knobby, I would not have been able to tell you. He was, already, a shape fading into the landscape, absorbed and dispersed through my neighborhood. It was the most vivid experience I'd ever had in which my brain couldn't supply all the details.

Some details I did hold on to, if not the relevant ones: I was listening to Bonnie "Prince" Billy when I noticed him; the T-shirt I was wearing—low-cut and black—showed what little cleavage my A-cups could muster.

Afterward I went to a music show and drank two Steam Whistle beers and stayed up until 3 a.m. I laughed with my coworkers and talked about work, and I didn't bring up the encounter because masturbators aren't small talk.

WHEN YOU DON'T WALK ALONE AT NIGHT, YOU SAVE $20 monthly on drunken burger purchases. But you take cabs home from the bar, so you bypass that caloric gauntlet of delicious fast-food outlets and spend the money anyway. People tell you about a late-night poutinerie that recently opened near your apartment, and how they spoon tiny pierogi onto the french fries. That poutinerie may as well be Willy Wonka's Chocolate Factory, for all the good it does you. You do not eat poutine alone at 3 a.m. Safety is your comfort food.

Three Years After

My university—in a different province—was on high alert. There had been six sexual assaults over the last seven months, escalating in their frequency. A man had been following women, groping them, trying to drag them to the ground. The women had fought him off. Sketches of the suspect were posted around campus. In the picture, the suspect wore a hoodie. He had sculpted cheekbones and a square forehead.

The campus—where I lived, worked, and studied for my graduate degree—was as tense as a stretched-out elastic band. People whispered outside classrooms; instructors broached the subject gently (*Stay safe*). Already that semester, the university had been steeped in controversy after students at a freshman week welcome event had been reported chanting: "We like 'em young! Y is for your sister, O is for oh so tight, U is for underage, N is for no consent, G is for go to jail."

As the assaults occurred, my residence put bowls of pink safety whistles in the common areas. I was sitting in there one day when a fellow student—who'd recently moved to Canada from the States—picked up one of the dinky plastic whistles. She scoffed, then said (to paraphrase): "This is ridiculous. Canadians have no idea what danger is. If you understood half the shit that happened in the States, you wouldn't be sounding the alarms over a bunch of 'attempted' rapes."

That student continued to walk to the library late at night. Meanwhile, I—along with many others—endured the lengthening waits for Safewalk. Students in our residence organized a volunteer team of walking escorts, on call to meet people at the bus stop. Over nightly meals in the dining hall, people spoke of potential encounters with the attacker with the self-doubting air of someone telling ghost stories.

"I think I saw him near the bus loop. He was just standing

there and then he ran—I think he was trying to cut me off. I speed-walked all the way home."

And then, in a broadcast email, the university finally stated outright what we'd been covertly hearing all semester: *Don't walk alone at night.*

I read that statement and I thought, *This is the wrong message. This is a misdirected, victim-blaming message.*

I read that and I thought, *What bullshit.*

But I also read that and thought, *I don't.*

And in a quiet, complicated place within me—where logic gets bullied by fear, and fear masquerades as protection—thinking those words, *I don't*, made me feel safe.

WHEN YOU DON'T WALK ALONE AT NIGHT—ESPECIALLY WHEN you also don't own a car—you are a pain in the ass to your friends. They get sick of escorting you home. Some of them are real champs—they'll walk you to your door even when it's frigidly cold out. Others will sigh and say, "Can't you just walk, just this once?"

The most frustrating friends are the ones who are gambles. When you dine with them, you spend the entire evening working up the nerve to ask whether they'll walk you home. Sometimes it's yes; sometimes it's no. You never know which it will be, so you're distracted while they chatter over nachos; you hear only the ticking of an internal timer, counting the minutes until you must leave the restaurant. It reverberates in your chest. Maybe your friend will escort you home one time, but the next time you make late dinner plans, that timer will wind up again. You will feel its tension in your palms as you eat ceviche. The timer exists for that final moment: the moment you reach your door safely. At that moment: ping! You feel a calm so thick that it startles you.

Two Weeks After

I wrote about the masturbator. I wrote about him because jokes are antidotes—they suck the power out of memories, right? So I posted a Facebook note. I wrote that masturbation, in my world, was only supposed to happen in *American Pie*, or behind the twin veils of locked doors and Catholic guilt. I joked about my clammy 911 call. I joked about the hoodie, the sweatpants, the sturdy legs.

Then I waited for closure. For praise. For high fives and quick relief. For a certificate to arrive in my mailbox that said, "You Are Tough and Self-Aware."

No certificate arrived. Instead, concern. Other women messaged me. They asked if I was okay. I told them yes but meant no. Some were women I knew well; others were women I barely knew at all. "It happened to me too," some of these women said. A man looking through a bedroom window. A stranger masturbating on the train in London. "He was right there, on the seat across from me," that woman said. "I was terrified. I just moved to a different seat and waited until the next stop."

One story. Two stories. Three. Women in my life lit up like coordinates on a secret map.

There was an unrequested camaraderie in it: a sense of uneasy companionship. We had all been touched without being touched. We shared something we'd never asked for. Part of the terror of my encounter, I realized, was this: it was unexceptional. In a way, I even felt lucky. I did not like feeling lucky. But there was sinister comfort in the sentiment: "It could have been worse."

WHEN YOU DON'T WALK ALONE AT NIGHT, YOU WISH THAT you did. You remember the times when you used to—before you made that decision (sudden or gradual, conscious or not) to stop. You used to walk the short distance home from the bus stop—never comfortably, but regularly—holding your keys as spikes between your fingers. You used to stride down the center of the street, your cell phone at the ready, then speed-walk diagonally across your back lawn. You pine for these memories. They're a bleak thing to pine for, but you can't help but miss those moments, fearful as they were. They seem—compared to the current situation—like a kind of un-appreciated freedom.

Fifteen Years Before/Two Years After/Ongoing

The news had advice for me: put a pair of men's shoes outside your front door. Don't wear a ponytail—too easy to grab. Get a sign that says BEWARE OF DOG, even if there's no dog. Carry pepper spray. Wear complicated pants.

Instructions came from the *Oprah Winfrey Show, Reader's Digest, Cosmo*: Pee on your attacker. Submission is sometimes a strategy for survival. Kick out the taillights if you're locked in a trunk. Wave your hands to get other drivers' attention.

My mother told me about a story she'd heard on the radio—a woman who'd covertly dialed 911 and narrated her surroundings as her kidnapper drove. "Where are you taking me? Why are we driving past the McDonald's on First Street?" I imagined myself as a forced tour guide, pointing out the local library.

The stories kept coming: tragic or heroic or both. Real or fictional. Survival is resourceful and marketable—on a winter weekend I read *Room* and found myself thinking through theoretical escape plans, remembering how I used to carry cups of scalding water when I walked home from my old job at a coffee shop, ready to throw them at the slightest sound.

Any and all media told these stories. Stories upon stories upon stories. The stories were not my experience, but they were a cousin to my experience. A violent cousin. And I thought about them every time I was afraid, every time my breath caught in my throat. I slipped into their plots like rotten pieces of clothing.

WHEN YOU DON'T WALK ALONE AT NIGHT, YOU'RE A COWARD. You don't talk candidly with other women, who disembark from the bus at stops that look like sunless galaxies. With grace and confidence, they put one foot in front of the other, moving fluidly into the pitch-black night. They wave back at you as the bus drives off, until the only thing visible is the reflective strips on their backpacks. You envy these women. You wonder, *How?*

You imagine that they must be unafraid, or oblivious, but you know that isn't true. No one is oblivious. Some of those women have been assaulted. Some of them have told you their stories, and others have stories they haven't told. Still, they walk home, out of necessity or private conviction or whatever else it is that makes people do what they do despite reasons to be afraid.

Knowing that, you feel like an imposter. Some of these women are survivors of something you've only glimpsed. At parties, braver women show off the special jabbing sticks they ordered off the internet. "I'll fuck him up," they say. And even though you too once bought mace from a sleazy spy store, and made a place for it in your purse, and rehearsed pushing the trigger, you can't bear to walk home through dark neighborhoods—you are untrained in navigating sunless spaces. So, after outings with those braver women, you pretend to start walking home, then turn behind a Starbucks and call frantically for a cab. Climbing into it, you feel ashamed of yourself. It is 10 p.m. You did not earn your fear.

Five Years After

Last May, I went to a barbecue at a friend's house, and I took the bus home. I was buzzed off red wine. It had been a perfect evening, but I was racing against time. It was 9:00 p.m. and verging on summer—the season of extended curfew. Still, it was not quite summer, and dusk was ticking through the sky. By the time the pink sunset started turning gray, I was six bus stops away from home. I counted the stops. My heart pounded. I felt like I was racing against something as light-sensitive as vampires, like Lestat would be waiting for me if I arrived after 9:30. I heard once that vampires are metaphors for sexual violence: they too are coming for your bare neck. *Why didn't I plan ahead?*

I arrived home safe that night. I speed-walked to my door as the last streaks of light left the sky, and I felt like I had cheated fate, like my life was *Final Destination.*

Looking back on it, now, I just wonder: *Why do I do this to myself?*

Is there some inherent flaw in me, that's made me react this way? There's such a drastic quality to my fear: letting one encounter affect thousands of evenings afterward. There's something so naive about insisting that daylight makes a difference. Why do I imagine that violence wears a wristwatch?

A friend of mine recently described being followed home by a strange van. The van sped off when a police car passed by. "It was scary, but I'm all right," she insisted. "I still think this is a safe city, and I'm not about to need someone to walk me home now." She sounded determined, if somewhat unconvinced. She sounded angry and steadfast.

I am not steadfast. Why? Is it because my mother keeps a bread knife in her sock drawer? Is it because, when my father's out of town, my lovely, paranoid mother locks all the windows in the house shut with climbing carabiners? I come from a family that believes in booby traps; we MacGyver against the bogeyman.

Maybe terror is passed down in the genes: I've always been anxious. I've been hooked to anxiety with one of my mother's carabiners.

Is that funny? I want my fear to be funny. Listen, it's funny that I've contemplated using Static Guard as a weapon. But if there's comedy here, it's grim comedy. I am embarrassed of it. I am embarrassed of the way I've let my fear change me.

There was another encounter, four years after the first masturbator. It was at a nude beach. I'd just been swimming—my first time going for an evening dip with fellow students from my university residence. My friend and I were climbing out of the water when we spotted a man masturbating nearby. A few of our friends were still swimming. The man was sitting on a rock. He looked so casual, half bored with his movements, as if stirring risotto. He was pretending to read a magazine—it looked like *The Walrus*. Who violates women while reading *The Walrus*? Maybe, I thought, he didn't even know he was masturbating. Maybe he had a neurological condition and believed he was gently scratching an arm.

But he did know. He must have, because he wore a smug half smile, a barely visible curl in his cheek. I watched it, as if in scientific study. I forced myself to stare at his crinkled balls. I decided that I would let a number of variables for the situation determine my reaction. If he was masturbating at the general idea of a nude beach, rather than at my friends and me specifically, I did not need to be scared. If he was masturbating at me and all my friends (i.e., not just me), I did not need to be scared. Even if he was masturbating at me, as long as we didn't make eye contact, I did not need to be scared. These phony variables empowered me. I toweled off and pulled on my shorts. "Gross," my friend said. "Let's get out of here." Our other friends were still bobbing in the water, framed by the perfect sunset like some cheesy oil painting. I was on one of the most beautiful campuses in the world, and there was a man jerking off six feet to my left. And I was displeased, but I was not scared.

What can account for the discrepancy between the first masturbator and the second? Someone explain the math to me. Why do some encounters change a person, when others do not? Why do some encounters change one person but not another? I imagine a quiz:

HIERARCHY OF TRAUMA, PUBLIC MASTURBATION EDITION
Were you alone when you saw the man?
Did the man masturbate or just expose himself?
If he masturbated, did you see cum?
Did he say something cryptic while he masturbated?
Did he say something benign?
Was the incident in your neighborhood?
Have you previously been described as "unflappable"?
Have you previously been described as "chickenshit"?

WHEN YOU DON'T WALK ALONE AT NIGHT, YOU ARE SAFE. YOU are safe, you are safe, you are safe. You are safe from men in sweatpants, each with one hand around his penis. You are safe from that other man who once trailed you home, forcing you to run fast and slam your apartment door behind you. You are safe from the ponytailed gawker who—just a week ago—rode past you on a bike and yelled, "I'd have that for lunch!" You are also safe from the man who ordered a "pussy burger" from you at your high school job (Why do you still remember how his tongue pointed when he stuck it out?). You are safe from any man who's ever thought you were food. From anyone who ever thought you were a resource, less than human, available for theft.

And because you believe you are safe, you must admit complicity to a faulty logic: *When you don't walk alone at night, you don't get raped.* You hate this logic. This logic skews blame and ignores reality. And yet you must believe it, because this logic accounts for your caution. This logic has shaped your behavior. This logic is part of the problem, but you wear it as protection. It is a dangerous kind of double thinking, a face-off between understanding and fear.

When you don't walk alone at night, you think a lot about contradictions.

Still Five Years After, and Counting

I'm living back in my hometown again, in a new neighborhood now. Recently, I took the train to visit my parents, and I rode past that old platform. And, like I do every time I pass it, I looked at the bushes, half expecting to see someone standing there. I waited for the flash of skin between leaves, for the re-alization of a body where a body shouldn't be. The station has lost any sense of familiarity it once held for me: it is someone I once knew, who has since grown cold to me.

There have been thousands of nights since that night. Some of them, I've been at home. Others, I've been out and about, awaiting the moment when I'll have to leave. When I'll be, once again, caught in the space between two perceived safeties. Not home, then home. Not safe, then safe.

I think about that imagined in-between because I don't know how to stop thinking about it. It's a lie I can't talk my-self out of. That night on the train platform remains unflinch-ingly recent: it is of the past, but immune to nostalgia.

Where does it end? I'm not sure. I'm not sure whether there's a breaking point, and after that, a seeking of counsel, and finally a healthier way of coping. I don't know at what point habit becomes unsustainable. I just know it's been five years now, and I still don't listen to that Bonnie "Prince" Billy album. I got rid of that black T-shirt, and I never wait for a train without remembering.

Why I Didn't Say No

ELISSA BASSIST

BECAUSE I THOUGHT LOVE AND SEX WERE SUPPOSED TO hurt.

Because my favorite author in high school was Ayn Rand.

Because women have been going through the wringer for True Love and Hot Sex stretching back to cuneiform. Because of how attractive the straight white knights in fairy tales come off, the ones who exalt and heal distressed damsels—after degrading and breaking them—and of how relatable the degraded-exalted, broken-healed women are once they've submitted themselves, body and brain, to Great Men.

Because I was watching my back for *real rape* and avoided fraternity-sponsored spring break booze cruises and walking alone while scantily clad at sinister times of night in foreign neighborhoods' back alleys.

Because we met-cute à la rom-com: a striking antihero

and a double-decade virgin cross paths in the backyard of a house party, and later on—through the unnatural and unexplainable—fall in love, a love demonstrated by grand gestures, plagued with conflict, marked by sexual difference, and reinforced by moments of choice.

Because that fall Friday evening junior year of college I saw him balanced on top of a concrete cylindrical pipe, and when he jumped down he stood next to me and watched as other partygoers tried to do the same but couldn't, and I near sprained myself from yearning. His epic act, my tortoiseshell glasses. "You must skate or surf," I said, to impress him, but he ignored my seduction. Because I was ready to crucify myself over this boy for whom I would wait, forever and ever, for an answer, for a glance, for a scrap, for him to rescue or destroy or define me. Because after a delay he said, "Both." How charming! Because I couldn't tear myself away, though he had left.

Because we re-met-cute the next spring, when a friend and I went to the playground near the freshman dorms and notorious stoners who ran the university radio station were also there. Because I sat on a swing and was in the air when he, the skater/surfer who could have been a model/actor in a toothpaste/vodka commercial, approached my swing and said "Hey." Like a touch from God.

Because I was breathless. Because he was breathtaking.

Because soon I figured out his schedule, learned his routine by heart, and knew where he'd be and when he'd be there so that I could be there too, dressed sacrificially. Because the next time I saw him—at another party, this time encircled by a blond-girl halo—I sauntered over to him and delivered the line I'd rehearsed. *Remember me? From the swings.*

Because he remembered.

Because when we first kissed, we kissed until sunrise, until there was steam on our clothes.

Because he and I made out again, and then again, also again, additionally again, until one morning, recovering from gymnastic dry humping, I realized, á la romantic-comedian Emma Bovary: *I have a lover! A lover!! And he's a slutty DJ with a longboard and a six-pack, of both beer and stomach-muscle.*

Because I wanted to be his girlfriend; and because I would've settled for being his waitress.

Because when our senior year was under way he told me that he didn't want to have uncommitted, unspecific-someone, brainless-slut sex anymore, that he'd gotten it out of his system, that he'd spurn all other girls for me.

Because I was terrifically excited to notch my spotless bedpost, to be Intimate with him. Because in the sexual debut of my mind's eye, I'd concurrently discover and execute the maneuvers of a soft-core seduction that prefaced what would resemble a physical struggle—a catalogue of spiritual sexual practices (some standing); a parade of romantic lechery—we'd give everything of ourselves and take everything of each other, we'd get lost unto it, searching each other's bodies in a carnal interrogation that would most likely ignite a blind fury—fervid, raw, athletic, durational, demonic, transformational, professional—he'd possess me, and I'd surrender out of strength, as my gift, and yield to him as he bore through my flesh, passion all unbridled, until at some point

I begged for mercy, seared to the bones, ravaged, and I'd collapse next to him on the (God-willing unbroken) bed, our designed-for-each-other limbs entwined in damp sheets, and trembling, we'd lie together postcoitally for hours, emptied, undone, our unquenchable hunger quenched.

Because in a nutshell I figured I was in store for some crazy fucking.

Because I'd anticipated some initial agony but thought it would, over time, be rewarded with tons of ecstasy, like the first sex scene in *The Fountainhead* that I'd read at eighteen, when I registered a heartbeat south of my heart as Howard Roark took Dominique Francon by force.

Because I was well-rounded and also read *Cosmopolitan*. Because I could flip to any page in the aughts and find tips and tricks that promised we can all be beautiful if only we learn to give a better blow job. Because of more advice to surrender sexually and to accept the double standard that a man's pleasure is fundamental to his well-being and hers optional or nonapplicable. Because almost always the *number one goal* was to nimbly accommodate and *sa-tis-fy your man* by indulging his *uncontrollable primal biological urges*.

Because women like me get guidance up the wazoo re: what men want and how women can give it to them. Because the self-not-helping formula of media aimed at women sells sex as the end-all be-all, empowerment through disempowerment, and self-improvement via self-destruction.

Because I wanted to have, or to be perceived as having, a bomb-ass pussy.

Because growing up, beyond Rand and *Cosmo*, I was exposed almost exclusively to male narrators and protagonists and found myself inside the male mind, championing his desires, aligning with his frustrations. Because I'd think *Give the man sex*, my thoughts indistinguishable from his; *He needs to have sex!* I'd tell myself, merging obsessions, and assuming, as many do, that hot, hard-core, superlative sex was his God-given right. Because I was indoctrinated to the point that I demonized my own resistance for getting in between what he needed and how he wanted it. Because anyone who gets in between is, by default, wrong, withholding, and un-fun.

Because what was important to him became the only important thing.

Because most of what I knew about myself, about history, the future, Earth, came from his POV. Because I hadn't yet read film theorist Laura Mulvey, who called out traditional storytelling in cinema, marked by a certain split: men are the subject while women are the spectacle, a sight to be seen and not heard—and so without a voice and without a story, and defined in terms of her relationships with men, and so without independence or agency, which—without even green-screen technology—dehumanizes her.

Because real-life women internalize all this from the moment we first turn on a TV and learn how to read, then we make it our filter, our mythology and philosophy and religion, our every other thought and basis for interaction.

Because we're porous, susceptible to anything.

Because we are surrounded with 24/7 access to text, images, and audio that inflate and distort what we think of as love, sex, and gender with the histrionic and pathological, the inexplicable and unattainable, the misogynistic and incomplete. Because first our thoughts reshape, next our emotions, then our behaviors, finally our identities and view of life itself.

Because my boyfriend and I were born; we grew up; we'd been appropriated into the milieu; and because as special as my parents told me I was, no one deftly eludes media's teeth. As Rebecca Solnit put it, "the elephant in the room is the room itself."

Because of the trap that one is inevitably in: a man pulls a woman's hair—likely he once saw an actor pull an actress's hair and the actress gasped in pleasure—so he pulls and she gasps; maybe she gasps in pleasure, or in pain, or because she's seen something, too, or has had a legacy shoved down her throat before she could learn what she desires, or because she wants to be "normal"; but a gasp is a gasp is a gasp, and maybe he thinks it's kosher to then choke her, so he pulls or chokes and she gasps, in an attempt to experience sexuality and to fulfill the expectation, regardless of if she's enjoying herself as long as she's performing enjoyability. Because maybe, eventually, she pulls her own hair, to please him.

Because audiences assimilate these oft-interchangeable cinematic and societal scripts, the principles that represent and reflect the ruling ideology, and then echo them, in united agreement, without asking why.

Because media have colonized everything from social dynamics to intimate moments.

Because media often present intercourse violently and violation as fundamental to its eroticism.

Because of our appetite for drama and our desensitization to damage.

Because we learn how to have sex from someplace. Because even personal, singular desire is a product of environment. Because my behavior and word choice were a convergence of marketed clichés of how women are supposed to act and sound in sexual scenarios. Because I knew how to say "Yes! Harder!" in a thousand languages, how to moan in eight octaves, how to bend over backward, how to ask for it, how to beg God for it, but not how to say, "No. Stop." Because instead I told him—using adjectives like *slow* and *soft*—what I wanted, what I'd learned in Women and Gender Studies courses works for women, which in practice wasn't a preternatural frenzy but to be kissed and licked crazily, him down on his knees for me and his mouth on my thighs, his hands going all in and around me.

Because he could be tender. Because I could be seduced and secure. Because everything could be soft and steamy, and he could get me all the way off with devoted fingers.

Because everything I'd learned in Advanced Contemporary Female Sexualities—like that when a woman is turned on, her brain sends messages to the back of the vagina to expand and loosen, and to the cervix and uterus to pull back and lift to high heaven to allow room for the penis (or dildo or whatever your pleasure) readying her for sex, and that this arousal is what hunger is to eating—seemed as out of reach for real-life application as Chaucer or differential geometry. Because in class I could rattle off the seven erogenous zones at breakneck speed (inner thighs, nipples, nape of the neck, lips, ears, butt, clit), but it was the classic I-can-talk-the-talk-but-not-fuck-the-fuck dilemma. Because I couldn't talk the talk either.

Because even if I *knew* better, even I didn't know better. Because intellect can miss the gospel of intuition. Because it's one of the more minor human tragedies: to know better and still. Because although I studied gender and sexuality as part of my degree, culture had called dibs on our psyches and souls.

Because despite my entreaties, and my liberal arts education, and his short-lived tenderness, he'd work into his factory-setting rhythm, fast and hard and every which way that stylized women scream they want it, and I'd be beneath him, pinned down, hurting, but hoping, but cringing, but hoping, while he'd pound and grind against me, and I couldn't say anything. Because all I could do was hold on, stare at him, and focus on the bond between me and some guy no longer aware of me.

Because when I cried, sometimes he'd say, "Should I keep going?" and in my head, I screamed, *No! Stop!* but it came out quiet and ragged, as if ripped out, and like this: "Keep going," so he did. Because when a question seems to have a single answer, then you supply that answer, even if you don't mean it.

Because, after, we spooned on warm sheets and said, "I love you," and meant it.

Because you know how you think of what to say once you've walked away? Because you know how the words they want to hear can be the only words we know how to say? Because at times it seemed the only word I knew was his name.

Because telepathy might be a thing.

Because I wanted him to want to stop without me having to ask, to know without being told, to take crying as a sign, to be a hero and come to my rescue. Because I settled for him to keep going, to show his love for me like this.

Because when he said he loved me the first time, facing me under what was most likely pale moonlight, somewhere trumpets blared, confetti exploded, doves cried; above us a chorus of angels sang *Hallelujah*, and my heart ejaculated.

Because love had an analgesic effect, and my empathy reached a pitch where if sex felt good to him, then it felt good to me, although at times it really felt like I wouldn't survive it.

Because love's a temple, a higher law, a psychosis, an addiction, a supernatural and socially constructed biological necessity and eternal torture. Because you always hurt the one you love. Because I was supposed to love the way it hurt. Because "The cult of love in the West is an aspect of the cult of suffering," Susan Sontag wrote. Because in *The Fountainhead*, I'd underlined this: Dominique "found a dark satisfaction in pain—because that pain came from him."

Because in *Atlas Shrugged*, alpha male Francisco d'Anconia tells railroad company VP Dagny Taggart that she sounds happy in her new relationship: " 'But, you see, the measure of the hell you're able to endure is the measure of your love.' "

Because I believed I would've died for him, so I would've done a lot less than that for him, too. Because there wasn't anything I wouldn't do for love!

Because, in our no-pain-no-gain dogma, the cost of something is often mistaken for its value.

Because I'd decided that what I felt was probably whatever love is.

Because I couldn't let that love die.

Because love rewards the optimistic and punishes those who vocalize their fury.

At first we had sex despite my pain; months later, we still did—because women are bred for pain, for giving birth when birth splits us open. Because we learn to live with it; because we learn to live for it. Sontag again: "It is not love which we overvalue, but suffering." Because rom-coms train us that if we suffer enough, then everything works out.

Because I wanted to be a good sport and not make a big deal. Because I sucked it up and powered through.

Because when he'd complain his hand hurt doing what I'd wanted him to do, I was busy saying, "Don't worry about it," and he didn't.

Because I didn't want to ruin his experience of me.

Because bad sex was on me. Because sex that feels out of one's control is called "bad sex," "disappointing sex," "regrettable sex," phrases that take on a myriad of meaning that pervert meaning.

Because I knew I was being ranked on how good I gave it and how well I took it.

Because when I went to a gynecologist, she brought out a medical device that she called a vaginal dilator, and when she lubed it up and inserted the stiff, opaque medical-grade silicone, I went momentarily blind, but I took the smallest one home with me anyway and let the cloudy white thinger lifelessly dangle in me nightly for ten to fifteen minutes while

I watched *Family Guy* or played soft instrumental folk CDs. Because whatever was wrong could be solved, possibly, by starting my last semester in college with a prescription ghost dick.

Because the next gynecologist recommended more sex. Because my boyfriend agreed, using the practice-makes-perfect line of this-isn't-my-problem thinking.

Because it seemed, as liberated, educated, nonreligious women, we're encouraged to have lots of sex—great sex!, whatever sex!, sex like a straight guy!—but not no-sex. Because it's now more of a public disgrace and bodily phenomenon to be prude than promiscuous. Because I wanted to be a whore for him.

Because unless women become better in bed, we implode.

Because I'd remind myself that he was *My Boyfriend, my Boyfriend, My boyfriend*.

Because I questioned myself and my sanity and what I was doing wrong in this situation. Because of course I feared that I might be overreacting, overemotional, oversensitive, weak, playing victim, crying wolf, blowing things out of proportion, making things up. Because generations of women have heard that they're irrational, melodramatic, neurotic, hysterical, hormonal, psycho, fragile, and bossy.

Because girls are coached out of the womb to be nonconfrontational, agreeable, solicitous, deferential, demure, nurturing, to be tuned in to others, and to shrink and shut up.

Because speaking up for myself was not how I learned English. Because I'm fluent in Apology, in Question Mark, in Giggle, in Bowing Down, in Self-Sacrifice.

Because slightly more than half of the population is regularly told that what happens doesn't or that it isn't the big deal we're making it into.

Because your mothers, sisters, and daughters are routinely second-guessed, blown off, discredited, denigrated, besmirched, belittled, patronized, mocked, shamed, gaslit, insulted, bullied, harassed, threatened, punished, propositioned, and groped, and challenged on what they say.

Because when a woman challenges a man, then the facts are automatically in dispute, as is the speaker, and the speaker's license to speak.

Because as women we are told to view and value ourselves in terms of how men view and value us, which is to say, for our sexuality and agreeability.

Because it was drilled in until it turned subconscious and became unbearable need: don't make it about you; put yourself second or last; disregard your feelings but not another's; disbelieve your perceptions whenever the opportunity presents itself; run and rerun everything by yourself before verbalizing it—put it in perspective, interrogate it: *Do you sound nuts? Does this make you look bad? Are you holding his interest? Are you being considerate? Fair? Sweet?*

Because stifling trauma is just good manners.

Because when others serially talk down to you, assume authority over you, try to talk you out of your own feelings and tell you who you are; when you're not taken seriously or listened to in countless daily interactions—then you may learn to accept it, to expect it, to agree with the critics and the haters and the beloveds, and to sign off on it with total silence.

Because they're coming from a good place.

Because everywhere from late-night TV talk shows to thought-leading periodicals to Hollywood to Silicon Valley to Wall Street to Congress and the current administration, women are drastically underrepresented or absent, missing from the popular imagination and public heart.

Because although I questioned myself, I didn't question who controls the narrative, the show, the engineering, or the fantasy, nor to whom it's catered.

Because to mention certain things, like "patriarchy," is to be dubbed a "feminazi," which discourages its mention, and whatever goes unmentioned gets a pass, a pass that condones what it isn't nice to mention, lest we come off as reactionary or shrill.

Because he'd make me grilled cheese at 3 a.m., and I'd get him five tacos on Taco Tuesdays, and once, when I was sick, he delivered a single white rose, a plain buttered bagel (my favorite), and a card with a bulldog wearing an ice pack, where inside he wrote that I was his favorite.

Because when I said I didn't want to have sex, he didn't talk to me for the rest of the night. Because when I would plead, he would plead (my panic, his smile). Because I preferred not to fight or appear culpable. Because I'd lie: "It's fine," I'd say, desperate, like I could discover another sensation, dispel the anxiety through a sleight of psyche, and keep on loving him. Because lying is just performing, and perform is what we're encouraged to do. Because besides, even if I'd said, *No, Stop*, there are those who'd think I'd meant *Yes, Please*, anyway.

Because I was at a loss for even the wrong words; because words escape us, they fail us, they miss.

Because I woke up one night to him hard and upon me from behind, jabbing me—my vagina, my heart, my threshold—and I said, "What the—?" semiasleep, "WHAT THE—?" and he said, "Don't be mad" as warm semen trickled down my inner thighs, coating and staining them. Because I didn't know what to call *that*.

Still, I slept beside him almost every night until graduation, willingly, just because.

Because! Grilled cheeses at 3 a.m.! Taco Tuesdays! Bulldogs wearing ice packs!

Because I remember leaving Student Health Services and passing black-and-white posters of a group of resolved faces underneath a statistic in large bold red font—"one in four college women experiences sexual violence"—and thinking *What a god-awful statistic that has nothing at all to do with me, a woman in love.*

Because I'd told my friends, on the rare occasion I saw them, "We're violently in love."

Because what you call art or "art" or superficial distraction or clickbait is alive and haunted and an ideological weapon of mass self-destruction.

Because I didn't inquire, *What power structures are operating here?*, and opted to believe that consent is an individual, uncomplicated *yes/no* articulation and action.

Because even after I'd read preeminent scholar-activist-feminists, if my boyfriend said he loved me while hurting me, then I'd consent to be hurt.

Because beggars can't be choosers.

Because you could say it was a choice, one muddled by inculcation, mood, altruistic deceit, fear, insecurity, risk, cornering, the chaos of the heart, and free will.

Because I didn't want to entertain the idea that there was anything going on that should have to be contested and stopped.

Because though it takes a while to nail those sex tips worth trying, it takes longer to figure out what's not okay.

Because who fantasizes about *ethical sex*, about *moral principles that govern a group's behavior*?

Because instead, at times, I wished he'd hit me so I'd have an ironclad justification to find a curb and kick him to it, to say it.

Because there are some things I have to say only to know I don't mean them.

Because I could still get weak-kneed around him.

Because I was more afraid to go untouched.

Because "Girls are cruelest to themselves," writes Anne Carson in "The Glass Essay."

Because I didn't, and so he didn't.

Because he didn't want to hear it.

Because then we'd have to discuss it, and if we discussed it, then we'd have to discuss everything else—rape culture, masculinity, gender inequality, femininity, patriarchy, complicity—and who wants to get into that?

Because women who get hurt or humiliated on a smaller scale in broad daylight, persistently, is non-news, or non-newsworthy.

Because amid pandemic, most are voiceless.

Because sidelining women's stories/voices/visages, and also glorifying—thus neutralizing—their suffering, are not only prerequisites to sexual violence against women, but also ensure that sexual violence isn't seen as sexual violence but as totally normal, sanctioned behavior.

Because saying it out loud wasn't even The Solution.

Because we didn't even say, *It's over.* We allowed postgraduation distance to do its work, or I should say he emailed me confessing that he'd cheated five times with four different women while we were together and I'd worried I might've had syphilis. Because life can be this way, unexplained by sad songs.

Because his now-wife would say he's a Good Guy, with a human heart, who doesn't even watch rom-coms or read about libertarianism.

Because when a third gynecologist asked me when I'd given birth, and when I went pale and told her no, stop, truly, I'd never been pregnant, and when she said that my cervix was shredded and looked like I had—even then, when the pain was not just inexperience or theatrics; when acknowledgment imposed proof of force (and proof was somehow necessary), even after *Fucking eureka,* even with the truth inflicted, what was there to say? Because the doctor said to herself, "Wow," and didn't offer much beyond the explanation that the tear he tore continued to rip the more he had sex with me, and as she finished the exam, she said, "You'll feel some more pressure," but I didn't feel anything, not for two years.

Because I wasn't sure when I went from thinking *I was having sex* to thinking *I was being had sex with*.

Because love and sex left me as my entertainment said and I'd hoped it would: passion shattered.

Because worst-case scenario is murder.

Oh, because it wasn't *that* bad.

CONTRIBUTORS

Roxane Gay (Editor) is the author of the *New York Times* bestsellers *Bad Feminist* and *Hunger*, which has been nominated for the National Book Critics Circle Award and received the NBCC Members' Choice Award; the novel *An Untamed State*, a finalist for the Dayton Peace Prize; and the short story collections *Difficult Women* and *Ayiti*. A contributing opinion writer to the *New York Times*, she has also written for *Time*, the *Virginia Quarterly Review*, the *Los Angeles Times*, *The Nation*, *The Rumpus*, and *Salon*, among others. She is the author of *World of Wakanda* for Marvel. She lives in Los Angeles.

Elissa Bassist edits the "Funny Women" column on *The Rumpus* and teaches humor writing at the New School and Catapult. Visit elissabassist.com for more literary, feminist, media, and personal criticism.

Nicole Boyce's writing has appeared in the *Awl*, *Joyland*, *McSweeney's Internet Tendency*, *Big Truths*, and more, and has been short-listed for the *New Quarterly's* Peter Hinchcliffe Fiction Award. She's an MFA student at the University of British Columbia, where she's working on a collection of personal essays about nostalgia.

Amy Jo Burns is the author of *Cinderland*, and her writing has appeared in *DAME*, *Good Housekeeping*, *Jezebel*, *The Rumpus*, and *Salon*. She currently writes for *Ploughshares* and is at work on a novel.

Michelle Chen is a contributing writer at *The Nation* and contributing editor at *In These Times* and *Dissent* magazines.

Jill Christman is the author of *Darkroom: A Family Exposure* (AWP Award Series in Creative Nonfiction winner), *Borrowed Babies: Apprenticing for Motherhood* (Shebooks 2014), and essays in magazines and journals such as *Brevity*, *Fourth Genre*, *Iron Horse Literary Review*, *Literary Mama*, *Oprah* magazine, *River Teeth*, and *Brain, Child*. She serves on the board of the Association of Writers and Writing Programs (AWP) and teaches creative nonfiction writing in Ashland University's low-residency MFA program and at Ball State University in Muncie, Indiana, where she lives with her husband, writer Mark Neely, and their two children. Visit her at www .jillchristman.com.

Elisabeth Fairfield Stokes is from Alaska. Her writing has appeared in numerous national and international publications, including the *New York Times*, *Pacific Standard*, *Salon*, *Reader's Digest*, and *Time*. She teaches at Colby College in Waterville, Maine.

Stacey May Fowles is an award-winning novelist, journalist, and essayist. She is a columnist at the *Globe and Mail*, coeditor of *Best Canadian Sports Writing*, and author of the essay collection *Perfect Game*. Her work has appeared in such publications as the *National Post, Elle Canada, Deadspin, Jezebel, Rookie, Hazlitt, Vice Sports,* and *Toronto Life.* She lives in Toronto, where she is writing a memoir to be published by McClelland & Stewart.

Anthony Frame is an exterminator from Toledo, Ohio, where he lives with his wife. He is the author of *A Generation of Insomniacs* (Main Street Rag, 2015) and four chapbooks, including *To Gain the Day* (Red Bird Chapbooks, 2015) and *Where Wind Meets Wing* (forthcoming from Sibling Rivalry Press). He is the editor/publisher of Glass Poetry Press, which publishes the Glass Chapbook Series and *Glass: A Journal of Poetry.* His poetry has appeared in *Third Coast, Harpur Palate, Boxcar Poetry Review, Muzzle* magazine, *The Shallow Ends,* and *Verse Daily,* among others. He has twice been awarded Individual Excellence Grants from the Ohio Arts Council.

Aubrey Hirsch is the author of a collection of short stories, *Why We Never Talk About Sugar,* and a chapbook, *This Will Be His Legacy.* Her stories and essays have appeared in *Third Coast, The Rumpus, American Short Fiction, Hobart,* and the *New York Times,* among others. She currently teaches in the Creative Writing program at Oberlin College.

Lyz Lenz's writing has appeared in the *Washington Post,* the *New York Times, Marie Claire, Pacific Standard, BuzzFeed,* and the *LA Review of Books.* She has her MFA from Lesley University and lives in Iowa. You can find her on Twitter @lyzl.

Vanessa Mártir is a NYC-based writer, educator, and mama. She is completing her memoir, *A Dim Capacity for Wings,* and chronicles her journey on her blog: vanessamartir .blog. Vanessa is a five-time VONA/Voices and two-time

Tin House fellow; and the creator of the Writing Our Lives Workshop, through which she helps writers pen memoirs and personal essays. Vanessa's writing has appeared in the *Butter*, *SmokeLong Quarterly*, *Poets & Writers* magazine, *Kweli Journal*, *As/Us Journal*, and the VONA/Voices anthology, *Dismantle*, among others.

So Mayer is a poet and film critic. Her most recent books are the poetry collections *(O)* and *kaolin, or How Does a Girl Like You Get to Be a Girl Like You?*, and *Political Animals: The New Feminist Cinema*. She is a contributor to *Sight & Sound*, *The F-Word* (UK), *Women & Hollywood*, *VIDA*, and *Literal* magazine, and a member of feminist film collectives Club des Femmes and Raising Films. "floccinaucinihilipilification" is part of a longer project on language, identity, and memory, *Disturbing Words*, available at tinyletter.com/sophiemayer.

AJ McKenna's work has appeared in *Bustle*, *Vada*, *Gadgette*, *Clarissa Explains Fuck All*, and *So So Gay*, of which she was deputy editor. As a spoken-word artist she has performed throughout the UK; her one-woman show *Howl of the Bantee* was described as "powerful and important" by Stand Up Tragedy. Her poetry film, *Letter to a Minnesota Prison*, was shown at the Southbank Centre in 2014 and has been screened internationally.

Lisa Mecham writes a little bit of everything and her work has appeared in Amazon's *Day One*, *Mid-American Review*, and *BOAAT*, among other publications. A Midwesterner at heart, Lisa lives in Los Angeles with her two daughters, where she's finishing a book about mental illness in the suburbs.

Zoë Medeiros graduated from Bennington College with a BA in literature and writing. She's lived in nine states and has worked in education, insurance, tools, and fish. Zoë currently lives in northwest Washington with her brown dog and is working on a young adult novel.

Lynn Melnick is the author of the poetry collection *If I Should Say I Have Hope* (YesYes Books, 2012) and coeditor of the anthology *Please Excuse This Poem: 100 New Poets for the Next Generation* (Viking, 2015). She teaches poetry at the 92nd Street Y in New York City and serves on the Executive Board of VIDA: Women in Literary Arts.

Samhita Mukhopadhyay is a writer, editor, and speaker. She is the senior editorial director of culture and identities at Mic and former executive editor of award-winning blog Feministing.com. She is the author of *Outdated: Why Dating Is Ruining Your Love Life* and coeditor of the anthology *Nasty Women: Feminism, Resistance, and Revolution in Trump's America*. Her work has appeared in *Al Jazeera*, the *Guardian*, *NY Magazine*, *Medium*, *Talking Points Memo*, and *Jezebel*.

Miriam Zoila Pérez is a queer Cuban American writer based in Washington, DC. Pérez's work ranges from reporting about race, health, and gender for outlets like *Colorlines*, *Talking Points Memo*, *Rewire*, and *Fusion*, to personal essays for anthologies like *Persistence: All Ways Butch and Femme*, *Click: When We Knew We Were Feminists*, and *Yes Means Yes: Visions of Female Sexual Power and a World Without Rape*. In 2012, Pérez self-published *The Radical Doula Guide*, a political primer that has sold more than twenty-five hundred copies. In 2016, Pérez gave a TED talk about the impact of racism on maternal health, which has been viewed by more than seven hundred thousand people.

Liz Rosema wrote the cartoon series *Butch Stories for the Toast*. You can find her on Twitter where she will mostly talk about LEGOs.

Nora Salem is a writing and ESOL teacher in Brooklyn, New York.

Claire Schwartz is a PhD candidate in African American Studies, American Studies, and Women's, Gender & Sexuality Studies at Yale University. Her poetry has appeared in *Apogee*, *Cream City Review*, *PMS: poemmemoirstory*, and *Prairie Schooner*, and her essays, reviews, and interviews in *Electric Literature*, the *Georgia Review*, the *Virginia Quarterly Review*, and elsewhere.

V. L. Seek is a lawyer and playwright whose work focuses on traditionally dispossessed peoples and violence against women. She was a 2012 recipient of the Maryland State Arts Council's Individual Artist Grant for Playwriting. She strives to dismantle the patriarchy, colonialism, and other oppressive forces through prose and legal briefs. She currently resides in Boulder, Colorado.

Ally Sheedy is an actor, author, director, and teacher. She has appeared in more than sixty films and TV projects including *War Games*, *The Breakfast Club*, *St. Elmo's Fire*, *Short Circuit*, *High Art*, and the recurring role of Yang on the series *Psych*. Her indie film *Little Sister* was released on Netflix in 2017. She adapted the book *Turning 15 on the Road to Freedom* by Lynda Blackmon Lowery for the stage and a national tour in 2017–2018. Ally has published two books and several essays, is artist in residence at a New York high school, and has taught theater at Bard College.

Emma Smith-Stevens is the author of a novel, *The Australian* (Dzanc Books). Her short stories and essays have appeared in *Subtropics*, *Conjunctions*, *Wigleaf*, *Joyland*, and elsewhere. She is currently at work on a memoir.

Meredith Talusan is an author and journalist whose work has appeared in the *Guardian*, *The Atlantic*, *The Nation*, *WIRED*, *VICE*, *BuzzFeed*, *Mic*, *The New Inquiry*, and other publications. She has received awards from GLAAD and the Society for Professional Journalists and is a contributor to several edited volumes, including *Nasty Women: Feminism, Resistance, and Revolution in Trump's America*. She lives in New York.

Brandon Taylor is the associate editor of Electric Literature's *Recommended Reading* and a staff writer at *Literary Hub*. He has received fellowships from Lambda Literary, Kimbilio Fiction, and the Tin House Summer Writers' Workshop. His stories and essays have appeared in *Gulf Coast*, *Joyland*, *Necessary Fiction*, *Little Fiction*, *Catapult*, and elsewhere. He is currently a student at the Iowa Writers' Workshop, and his debut novel is forthcoming from Riverhead Books.

Sharisse Tracey's work has appeared in the *Los Angeles Review* and online at the *New York Times*, *Ebony*, *Babble*, *Essence*, *Yahoo*, *Salon*, *DAME*, *Elle*, and the *Washington Post*. She's an army wife, mother of four, educator, and writer. Sharisse's family is currently stationed in New York, where she's working on her memoir.

Gabrielle Union stars in the BET series *Being Mary Jane* and received a 2014 NAACP Image Award for "Outstanding

Actress in a Television Movie, Mini-Series or Dramatic Special" for her role. She has appeared in many films, including *Top Five*, *Sleepless*, *Almost Christmas*, *Bad Boys II*, *Deliver Us From Eva*, *Bring It On*, *Two Can Play That Game*, *Love & Basketball*, *Cradle to the Grave*, *Ten Things I Hate About You*, and *She's All That*. She is the author of *We're Going to Need More Wine: Stories That Are Funny, Complicated, and True*. A native of Nebraska, Union currently splits her time between Miami and Chicago with her family.

xTx is a writer living in Southern California. Her work has been published in places like the *Collagist*, *PANK*, *Hobart*, *The Rumpus*, the *Chicago Review*, *SmokeLong Quarterly*, and *Wigleaf*. *Normally Special*, a collection of stories, is available from Tiny Hardcore Press. Her story collection, *Today I Am a Book*, is now available from Civil Coping Mechanisms (http://copingmechanisms.net/today-i-am-a-book-by-xtx/). She says nothing at www.notimetosayit.blogspot.com.

ACKNOWLEDGMENTS

"Only the Lonely" by Lisa Mecham originally appeared in *Big Truths*.

"Spectator" by Brandon Taylor originally appeared in *Catapult*.

"Wiping the Stain Clean" by Gabrielle Union originally appeared in the *Los Angeles Times*.

Excerpt from "Photography from September 11" from *Monologue of a Dog: New Poems* by Wislawa Szymborska, translated from the Polish by Stanislaw Baranczak and Clare Cavanagh. Copyright © 2002 by Wislawa Szymborska. English translation copyright © 2006 by Houghton Mifflin Harcourt Publishing Company. Reprinted by permission of Houghton Mifflin Harcourt Publishing Company. All rights reserved.

THANK YOU FIRST AND FOREMOST, TO THE THIRTY PEOPLE who contributed work to this anthology. It is a privilege to share their work with the world. I will always admire their eloquence and courage in offering readers a part of themselves as they talk about what it means to live in a world shamefully warped by rape culture.

This anthology would not have come together without the editorial support of Megan Carpentier. She brought brilliant insight and empathy to these essays and was invaluable in helping me assemble this collection.

I also want to thank my assistant, Melissa Moorer, for helping me wrangle the hundreds of submissions received for this anthology and otherwise providing invaluable support. She has an eagle eye and a beautiful heart. Thanks also to my agent, Maria Massie, my editor, Emily Griffin, and Maya Ziv who originally bought this book. The usual suspects I am always grateful for know who they are. Last but never least, I want to thank Tracy Gonzalez, my best friend who always encourages me to take on new challenges and supports me no matter how they turn out and is the funniest, smartest person I know.

ALSO BY ROXANE GAY

BAD FEMINIST
Essays
Available in Paperback, eBook, and Digital Audio

"Roxane Gay is the brilliant girl-next-door: your best friend and your sharpest critic. . . . She is by turns provocative, chilling, hilarious; she is also required reading." —*People*

HUNGER
A Memoir of (My) Body
Available in Paperback, eBook, and Digital Audio

"Her spare prose, written with a raw grace, heightens the emotional resonance of her story, making each observation sharper, each revelation more riveting. . . . It is a thing of raw beauty." —*USA Today*

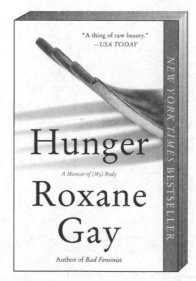